MARKED

MARKED

Race, Crime, and Finding Work in an Era of Mass Incarceration

DEVAH PAGER

The University of Chicago Press :: Chicago and London

The University of Chicago Press, Chicago 60637
The University of Chicago Press, Ltd., London
© 2007 by The University of Chicago
All rights reserved. Published 2007
Paperback edition 2009
Printed in the United States of America

18 17 16 15 14 13 12 11   3 4 5 6

ISBN-13: 978-0-226-64483-7   (cloth)
ISBN-13: 978-0-226-64484-4   (paper)
ISBN-10: 0-226-64483-9   (cloth)
ISBN-10: 0-226-64484-7   (paper)

Library of Congress Cataloging-in-Publication Data

Pager, Devah.
    Marked : race, crime, and finding work in an era of mass incarceration / Devah Pager.
        p.   cm.
    Includes bibliographical references and index.
    ISBN-13: 978-0-226-64483-7 (cloth : alk. paper)
    ISBN-10: 0-226-64483-9 (cloth : alk. paper)   1. Ex-convicts—Employment.
2. African Americans—Employment.   I. Title.
    HV9304.P23   2007
    331.5′108996073—dc22

                                                              2007003733

Contents

Preface

It was late in the day when Darrell finally made it back home, tired, hot, and utterly worn out. It had been over 90 degrees and humid all week, making it unpleasant just to be outside. But Darrell had woken up early each morning, put on a freshly ironed shirt, collected a set of résumés in his file folder, and set off to find a job. He had visited about three or four employers each day that week, driving up and down the highways of Milwaukee to track down the latest job opening. When he arrived at businesses, he was usually greeted with a flat stare, handed an application form, and told to wait for a callback. Darrell had yet to receive calls from any of the employers he had visited that week. Over fifteen applications submitted, and not one single shot at a job.

That day Darrell had had a particularly unpleasant experience. He had visited a local supermarket to apply for a job as a cashier. Darrell was caught off guard when the manager asked bluntly, "Do you have any convictions on your record?" Darrell wasn't expecting the question up-front like that. He was dressed neatly and presented himself well, but he hadn't had the chance to say more than a few words before the manager's question forced him to admit that, yes, he did have a criminal background. He had recently served time for a felony drug possession charge. The manager grudgingly allowed him to leave his résumé, but Darrell could tell that he had no chance of getting the job.

Darrell could have been any one of the hundreds of thousands of young black men released from prison each year, facing bleak employment prospects as a result of their race and criminal record. In this case, however, Darrell happened to be working for me. He was one of four college students I had hired as "testers" for a study of the barriers to employment facing ex-offenders. An articulate, attractive, and hard-working young man, Darrell was assigned to apply for entry-level job openings throughout the Milwaukee metropolitan area, presenting a fictitious profile designed to represent a realistic ex-offender. Comparing Darrell's outcomes to those of three other black and white testers presenting identical qualifications with and without criminal records gives us a direct measure of the impact of a criminal record and race in shaping employment opportunities.

I was drawn into this project first through my experiences with men very much like Darrell whom I encountered while working as a volunteer at the Transitional Housing Authority in Madison, Wisconsin. The housing authority provided services for homeless and jobless men, and I spent a good deal of time listening to their stories and learning about their experiences. One man in particular stands out in my memory. Greg was a black man in his early forties who had been looking for work for several months. He was of slight build and full of energy, and he talked at a rapid clip and with fluent prose. It surprised me that someone so charismatic and intelligent would have trouble finding a job, even at a time when the city's unemployment rate was very low. As I got to know Greg better, he explained to me what he saw as his primary obstacle: Nearly twenty years earlier, he had fallen in with the wrong crowd and had gotten into some big trouble, winding up with a serious felony conviction on his record. According to Greg, even though this record was nearly two decades old, it showed up on criminal background checks and was the reason no employer was willing to take him on. I wondered, could a single conviction from so far back make such a big difference? Or was this just an excuse for his poor performance? Was there something I wasn't seeing about Greg—about his level of effort, or about his personality—that was the real cause of his employment problems?

Greg's experience, and those of other young men I got to know at the Transitional Housing Authority, led me to think more about the possible consequences of criminal sanctions. Incarceration was becoming an increasingly common experience in the lives of young disadvantaged men. America's prison system has undergone a sevenfold increase in just thirty years. In addition to the more than 2 million individuals currently incarcerated, there are 4.9 million individuals under the supervision of probation or parole, and three times as many with records of felony convictions.[1] Perhaps Greg's story was not so atypical. And yet, despite striking evidence of a rapidly growing offender population, I found remarkably little evidence of planning for, or evaluation of, what happens to those inmates once they are released from prison. The scholarly literature in criminology indicates that ex-offenders who are unable to find legal work face increasing incentives to return to crime. And yet, as Greg's experience suggests, a criminal record may itself reduce opportunities for finding legitimate work. Understanding the barriers to employment facing ex-offenders, then, has become a pressing matter of public safety and social policy.

This book examines the impact of the rise of mass incarceration in the United States on its ever growing population of ex-offenders. In telling this story, I grapple with the complicated web of concerns that characterize contemporary discussions of crime and social policy: What happens to the hundreds of thousands of young men leaving prison each year? Does a prison record substantially diminish their employment prospects? How does race factor into the story? These questions prompt us to closely examine the living legacy of America's crime policies. Over the past three decades incarceration has been the centerpiece of the "tough on crime" approach. Now the time has come to ask what comes next.

Acknowledgments

This book would not have been possible without the enduring support of many friends and colleagues. My mentors at the University of Wisconsin guided me skillfully through my initial efforts on this project. I am deeply grateful to Robert M. Hauser and Erik Olin Wright, for their support, wisdom, and friendship. Numerous other Madison faculty and friends also contributed insights and encouragement; I especially thank Lincoln Quillian, Gerald Marwell, Franklin Wilson, Jeremy Freese, Tess Hauser, and Bobbie Marwell. Influential early guidance from outside Madison came from David Grusky, Marc Bendick Jr., and Harry Holzer. Bruce Western and Mitchell Duneier each deserve their own place in the readers' hall of fame, for careful readings, tough comments, and extraordinary advice that extend well beyond the pages of this book.

I had the good fortune to receive the generous support of several foundations and government agencies, as well as many organizations and individuals in the Milwaukee community. Funding from the National Science Foundation, the National Institute of Justice, the Open Society Institute, and the Joyce Foundation made it possible to mount a study of this scope, and I am grateful that these organizations were willing to take a chance on a young researcher. I am indebted to the Benedict Center for providing valuable office space during the course of my project; the Sociology Department at the University of Wisconsin-Milwaukee also provided space and critical logistical support in the initial phases of this project. Finally,

I thank the testers who participated in this study, whose hours of driving, applying for jobs, and filling out paperwork represented the backbone of this research. Without their dedication and conscientiousness, this project would not have been possible.

Over the duration of this project, I have been affiliated with a number of wonderful institutions and organizations that have provided both a physical and intellectual home for me and for this project. These include the Departments of Sociology at the University of Wisconsin–Madison, Northwestern University, and Princeton University, as well as the Centre de Recherches Sociologiques sur le Droit et les Institutions Penales, the Center for Demography and Ecology at Madison, the Institute for Policy Research at Northwestern, and the Office of Population Research at Princeton. In particular, I owe a special debt to the Princeton community, including a wide range of extraordinary colleagues and a superb administrative and library staff, who have provided exceptional support since I joined the faculty in the fall of 2003. Special thanks to Kristen Turner, Nancy Cannuli, and Barbara Sutton. The final version of this manuscript benefited from the skilled editorial advice of Madeleine Adams, Lauren Osborne, and Michael Koplow; and a light not just at the end of the tunnel, the ever-compassionate and charismatic Doug Mitchell.

In the preparation of the final version of the book, a number of colleagues have sharpened my thinking; I am grateful to Susan Fiske, Sara McLanahan, Paul DiMaggio, Martin Gilens, Doug Massey, Katherine Newman, Paul Starr, Debbie Mukamal, Chris Uggen, Michael Stoll, Steven Raphael, Becky Pettit, Shawn Bushway, Bruce Carruthers, Fay Lomax Cook, Larry Bobo, and Rob Sampson. For friendship, inspiration, and many other kinds of support along the way, I thank Kelly Musick, Eric Grodsky, Carolyn Chen, Shana Bernstein, Marcy Carlson, Shelley Correll, Ellie Buckley, Mario Small, Anne-Marie Mukhalu, Emily Pronin, Eric Klinenberg, Caitlin Zaloom, Glenn Martin, Kristen Carey, Anne Escaron, Nisha Ganatra, Julie Gedden, Thomas Leith, Emilio Castilla, Eli Finkel, Peter Condon, Rodger Roundy, Jolanda Sallman, Chad Kautzer, Mike Spittel, Mary Beth Spittel, Rob Warren, Carolyn Liebler, Amy Godecker, David Silver, Aaron Sachs, Christine Evans, Risa Goluboff, Sarah Carlson, Liana Bond, Marina Fineman, Tim Johnson, Clark Hoover, David Silver, Angela Williams, Joshua Newman, Ellen Pechman, Rene Levy, Renee Zauberman, Laurent Mucchielli, and Audrey Smolkin. And of course, special thanks and love to my family, who were there for me from the *very* beginning: Sylvia, David, Chet, Sean, Sheryl, and Sophie.

Above all, I want to thank Jeff Manza: who read and commented on the manuscript at every stage, always with smart, thoughtful suggestions; and who always called me his "hero," even when just the reverse was true.

Devah Pager
New York City
January 2007

Introduction

At the start of the 1970s, incarceration appeared to be a practice in decline. Criticized for its overuse and detrimental effects, practitioners and reformers looked to community-based alternatives as a more promising strategy for managing criminal offenders. A 1967 report published by the President's Commission on Law Enforcement and Administration of Justice concluded: "Life in many institutions is at best barren and futile, at worst unspeakably brutal and degrading.... The conditions in which [prisoners] live are the poorest possible preparation for their successful reentry into society, and often merely reinforces in them a pattern of manipulation or destructiveness." The commission's primary recommendation involved developing "more extensive community programs providing special, intensive treatment as an alternative to institutionalization for both juvenile and adult offenders."[1] Echoing this sentiment, a 1973 report by the National Advisory Commission on Criminal Justice Standards and Goals took a strong stand against the use of incarceration. "The prison, the reformatory, and the jail have achieved only a shocking record of failure. There is overwhelming evidence that these institutions create crime rather than prevent it." The commission firmly recommended that "no new institutions for adults should be built and existing institutions for juveniles should be closed."[2] Following what appeared to be the current of the time, historian David Rothman in 1971 confidently proclaimed, "We have been gradually escaping from institutional responses and one

1

can foresee the period when incarceration will be used still more rarely than it is today."[3]

Quite opposite to the predictions of the time, incarceration began a steady ascent, with prison populations expanding sevenfold over the next three decades.[4] Today the United States boasts the highest rate of incarceration in the world, with more than two million individuals currently behind bars. Characterized by a rejection of the ideals of rehabilitation and an emphasis on "tough on crime" policies, the practice of punishment over the past thirty years has taken a radically different turn from earlier periods in history. Reflecting the stark shift in orientation, the U.S. Department of Justice released a report in 1992 stating "there is no better way to reduce crime than to identify, target, and incapacitate those hardened criminals who commit staggering numbers of violent crimes whenever they are on the streets."[5] Far removed from earlier calls for decarceration and community supervision, recent crime policy has emphasized containment and harsh punishment as a primary strategy of crime control.

The Revolving Door

Since the wave of tough on crime rhetoric spread throughout the nation in the early 1970s, the dominant concern of crime policy has been getting criminals off the streets. Surprisingly little thought, however, has gone into developing a longer-term strategy for coping with criminal offenders. With more than 95 percent of those incarcerated eventually released, the problems of offender management do not end at the prison walls. According to one estimate, there are currently more than twelve million ex-felons in the United States, representing roughly 9 percent of the male working-age population.[6] The yearly influx of returning inmates is double the current number of legal immigrants entering the United States from Mexico, Central America, and South America combined.[7]

Despite the vast numbers of inmates leaving prison each year, little provision has been made for their release; as a result, many do not remain out for long. Of those recently released, nearly two-thirds will be charged with new crimes, and more than 40 percent will return to prison within three years.[8] In fact, the revolving door of the prison has now become its own source of growth, with the faces of former inmates increasingly represented among annual admissions to prison. By the end of the 1990s, more than a third of those entering state prison had been there before.[9]

The revolving door of the prison is fueled, in part, by the social contexts in which crime flourishes. Poor neighborhoods, limited opportunities, broken families, and overburdened schools each contribute to the onset of criminal activity among youth and its persistence into early adulthood.[10] But even beyond these contributing factors, evidence suggests that experience with the criminal justice system in itself has adverse consequences for long-term outcomes. In particular, incarceration is associated with limited future employment opportunities and earnings potential, which themselves are among the strongest predictors of desistance from crime.[11] Given the immense barriers to successful reentry, it is little wonder that such a high proportion of those released from prison quickly make their way back through the prison's revolving door.

The Criminalization of Young Black Men

As the cycle of incarceration and release continues, an ever greater number of young men face prison as an expected marker of adulthood. But the expansive reach of the criminal justice system has not affected all groups equally. More than any other group, African Americans have felt the impact of the prison boom, comprising more than 40 percent of the current prison population while making up just 12 percent of the U.S. population. At any given time, roughly 12 percent of all young black men between the ages of twenty-five and twenty-nine are behind bars, compared to less than 2 percent of white men in the same age group; roughly a third are under criminal justice supervision.[12] Over the course of a lifetime, nearly one in three young black men—and well over half of young black high school dropouts—will spend some time in prison. According to these estimates, young black men are more likely to go to prison than to attend college, serve in the military, or, in the case of high school dropouts, be in the labor market.[13] Prison is no longer a rare or extreme event among our nation's most marginalized groups. Rather it has now become a normal and anticipated marker in the transition to adulthood.

There is reason to believe that the consequences of these trends extend well beyond the prison walls, with widespread assumptions about the criminal tendencies among blacks affecting far more than those actually engaged in crime. Blacks in this country have long been regarded with suspicion and fear; but unlike progressive trends in other racial attitudes, associations between race and crime have changed little in recent years. Survey respondents consistently rate blacks as more prone to violence than any other American racial or ethnic group, with the stereotype of aggressiveness and violence most frequently endorsed in ratings of African Americans.[14] The stereotype of blacks as criminals is deeply embedded in the collective consciousness of white Americans, irrespective of the perceiver's level of prejudice or personal beliefs.[15]

While it would be impossible to trace the source of contemporary racial stereotypes to any one factor, the disproportionate growth of the criminal justice system in the lives of young black men—and the corresponding media coverage of this phenomenon, which presents an even more skewed representation—has likely played an important role. Experimental research shows that exposure to news coverage of a violent incident committed by a black perpetrator not only increases punitive attitudes about crime but further increases negative attitudes about blacks generally.[16] The more exposure we have to images of blacks in custody or behind bars, the stronger our expectations become regarding the race of assailants or the criminal tendencies of black strangers.

The consequences of mass incarceration then may extend far beyond the costs to the individual bodies behind bars, and to the families that are disrupted or the communities whose residents cycle in and out. The criminal justice system may itself legitimate and reinforce deeply embedded racial stereotypes, contributing to the persistent chasm in this society between black and white.[17]

The Credentialing of Stigma

The phenomenon of mass incarceration has filtered into the public consciousness through cycles of media coverage and political debates. But a more lasting source of information detailing the scope and reach of the criminal justice system is generated internally by state courts and departments of corrections. For each individual processed through the criminal justice system, police records, court documents, and corrections databases detail dates of arrest, charges, conviction, and terms of incarceration. Most states make these records publicly available, often through on-line repositories, accessible to employers, landlords, creditors, and other interested parties.[18] With increasing numbers of occupations, public services, and other social goods becoming off-limits to ex-offenders, these records can be used as the official basis for eligibility determination or exclusion. The state in this way serves as a credentialing institution, providing official and public certification of those among us who have been convicted of wrongdoing. The "credential" of a criminal record, like educational or professional credentials, constitutes a formal and enduring classification of social status, which can be used to regulate access and opportunity across numerous social, economic, and political domains.

Within the employment domain, the criminal credential has indeed become a salient marker for employers, with increasing numbers using background checks to screen out undesirable applicants. The majority of employers claim that they would not knowingly hire an applicant with a criminal background. These employers appear less concerned about specific information conveyed by a criminal conviction and its bearing on a particular job, but rather view this credential as an indicator of general employability or trustworthiness.[19] Well beyond the single incident at its origin, the credential comes to stand for a broader internal disposition.

The power of the credential lies in its recognition as an official and legitimate means of evaluating and classifying individuals.[20] The negative credential of a criminal record represents one such tool, offering formal certification of the offenders among us and official notice of those demographic groups most commonly implicated. To understand fully the impact of this negative credential, however, we must rely on more than speculation as to when and how these official labels are invoked as the basis for enabling or denying opportunity. Because credentials are often highly correlated with other indicators of social status or stigma (e.g., race, gender, class), we must examine their direct and independent impact. In addition, credentials may affect certain groups differently than others, with the official marker of criminality carrying more or less stigma depending on the race of its bearer. As increasing numbers of young men are marked by their contact with the criminal justice system, it becomes a critical priority to understand the costs and consequences of this now prevalent form of negative credential.

What Do We Know about the Consequences of Incarceration?

Despite the vast political and financial resources that have been mobilized toward prison expansion, very little systematic attention has been focused on the potential problems posed by the large and increasing number of inmates being released each year. A snapshot of ex-offenders one year after release reveals a rocky path of reintegration, with rates of joblessness in excess of 75 percent and rates of rearrest close to 45 percent. But one simple question remains unanswered: Are the employment problems of ex-offenders *caused* by their offender status, or does this population simply comprise a group of individuals who were never very successful at mainstream involvement in the first place? This question is important, for its answer points to one of two very different sets of policy recommendations. To the extent that the problems of prisoner reentry reflect the challenges of a population poorly equipped for conventional society, our policies would be best targeted toward some combination of treatment, training, and, at the extreme, containment. If, on the other hand, the problems of prisoner reentry are to some degree caused by contact with the criminal justice system itself, then a closer examination of the (unintended) consequences of America's war on crime may be warranted. Establishing the nature of the relationship between incarceration and subsequent outcomes, then, is critical to developing strategies best suited to address this rapidly expanding ex-offender population.

In an attempt to resolve the substantive and methodological questions surrounding the consequences of incarceration, this book provides both an experimental and an observational approach to studying the barriers to employment for individuals with criminal records. The first stage observes the experiences of black and white job seekers with criminal records in comparison to equally qualified nonoffenders. In the second stage, I turn to the perspectives of employers in order to better understand the concerns that underlie their hiring decisions. Overall, this study represents an accounting of trends that have gone largely unnoticed or underappreciated by academics, policy makers, and the general public. After thirty years of prison expansion, only recently has broad attention turned to the problems of prisoner reentry in an era of mass incarceration.[21] By studying the ways in which the mark of a criminal record shapes and constrains subsequent employment opportunities, this book sheds light on a powerful, emergent mechanism of labor market stratification. Further, this analysis recognizes that an investigation of incarceration in the contemporary United States would be inadequate without careful attention to the dynamics of race. As described earlier, there is a strong link between race and crime, both real and perceived, and yet the implications of this relationship remain poorly understood. This study takes a hard look at the labor market experiences of young black men, both with and without criminal pasts. In doing so, we gain a close-up view of the powerful role race continues to play in shaping the labor market opportunities available to young men. The United States remains sharply divided along color lines. Understanding the mechanisms that perpetuate these divisions represents a crucial step toward their resolution.

: :

The organization of this book follows a straightforward logic, beginning with a historical perspective on the rise of incarceration in the United States (chapter 1) and then moving to an investigation of its consequences.

Chapter 2 considers the range of economic effects associated with prison growth, examining the various mechanisms through which incarceration contributes to negative employment outcomes, with an emphasis on the stigma of the criminal credential, as well as the multiple and overlapping influences of racial and criminal status.

An important contribution of this manuscript is its attention to issues of measurement. Chapter 3 presents an overview of the dominant methodologies used to measure the economic impact of incarceration, followed by a detailed introduction to the experimental audit methodology and an extensive discussion of existing methodological critiques.

Building from the social and historical trends outlined in the first two chapters, the remainder of this book sets out to examine the implications of these trends for the allocation of labor market opportunities. Chapters 4 to 6 present the results of a large-scale experimental audit of employers in Milwaukee. In this study, matched pairs of young black and white men applied to real entry-level jobs using fictitious résumés and assumed criminal records. The vast differences in outcomes experienced among job applicants—on the basis of race, criminal background, and the interaction of the two—provides a clear picture of the barriers to employment facing minority and ex-offender job seekers.

The audit design provides a unique window into the hiring process from a job seeker's perspective. Recognizing that the matching of workers to jobs is a two-sided process, a final empirical chapter (chapter 7) shifts the focus from the experiences of job seekers to a consideration of employers' perspectives. Based on interviews with the same sample of employers, the findings reported here provide deeper insight into employers' considerations and concerns in evaluating ex-offender applicants. The book concludes with a discussion of the possible alternatives to our current system of offender management, focusing both on prison policy as well as policies dealing with the problems of prisoner reentry.

In this book, I grapple with the consequences of mass incarceration for the emergence of new forms of social inequality. As prison increasingly serves as a temporary home to young disadvantaged men, it becomes critical to assess the implications of these trends for individual and societal well-being. In the short run, incarceration may help to reduce crime, but in the long run it produces a growing population of individuals marked by a criminal record who are left with few opportunities for legitimate work. Moreover, there is evidence to suggest that the consequences of our crime policies reach far beyond the specific individuals convicted of wrongdoing. The growing numbers of black men behind bars may help to reinforce deep-seated stereotypes about race and criminality, with implications for persisting racial discrimination. In studying the consequences of incarceration, we can consider the extent to which our crime policies themselves may be a source of growing social and economic inequality.

1 Mass Incarceration and the Problems of Prisoner Reentry

In the fall of 1970, during his annual State of the Union address, President Richard Nixon boldly declared a new kind of war:

> We have heard a great deal of overblown rhetoric during the sixties in which the word "war" has perhaps too often been used–the war on poverty, the war on misery, the war on disease, the war on hunger. But if there is one area where the word "war" is appropriate it is in the fight against crime. We must declare and win the war against the criminal elements which increasingly threaten our cities, our homes, and our lives.

Prior to this period, crime and criminal justice policy had largely been regarded as a state and local problem, appropriately managed through decentralized police units, courts, and local governments.[1] Nixon's "war on crime" rhetorically elevated crime policy to the level of national concern, calling for a coordinated effort to combat the problems of crime and social decay.[2]

Nixon's stated policy emphasis on law and order appealed to vast numbers of Americans worried about rising crime and the perceived social disorder associated with protest movements of the previous decade.[3] This marked the beginning of an era of widening politicization of criminal justice and the steady growth of ever more punitive approaches to crime control. "Tough on crime" policies grew increasingly popular thereafter, resulting in an explosion in the size and reach of the criminal justice system. Recent trends in crime policy have led to the imposition of harsher sentences for a broader range of offenses, thus casting an ever-widening net of penal intervention.

The tough on crime movement shows little sign of abatement, with incarceration rates continuing to increase in the first decade of the twenty-first century. But alongside this sustained enthusiasm for "law and order" politics, a new set of policy concerns has made its debut on the national political scene. As states and cities struggle to accommodate the now large and growing influx of ex-offenders returning from prison, the problems of prisoner reentry have also now become a matter of national concern. With a small paragraph near the end of his 2004 State of the Union address, George W. Bush became the first president ever to acknowledge the vast social problem associated with America's policies of mass incarceration.

> Tonight I ask you to consider another group of Americans in need of help. This year, some 600,000 inmates will be released from prison back into society. We know from long experience that if they can't find work, or a home, or help, they are much more likely to commit crime and return to prison.

From Nixon's war on crime to Bush's proposal to aid ex-prisoners, what had changed? Surely it was not a softening on crime. During his tenure as governor of Texas, Bush oversaw a stiffening of the state's criminal laws and presided over more executions than any other governor in U.S. history. By all accounts, George W. Bush is an avid supporter of prison expansion and a strong advocate of a tough on crime approach. What had changed, rather, is a slow and somber recognition of the social costs associated with those crime polices. While Bush's nod to the problem was modest and his proposed commitment of resources trivial, for a conservative Republican leader to propose new domestic spending programs to address this problem is a sure sign of its troubling significance. Indeed, grappling with the problems of prisoner reentry is likely to help define social policy through the coming three decades, as prison expansion has helped to define the three just past.

This chapter situates the turn to prisoner reentry within the context of crime policy over the past thirty years. The realities of mass incarceration are by now well known. The dilemmas of prisoner reentry, by contrast, remain a significant challenge for research and policy evaluation. Through a careful accounting of recent trends in crime and punishment, we can begin to understand the specific conditions and constraints under which the problems of prisoner reentry have emerged. In particular, a shifting orientation toward punishment—marked by extensive changes in sentencing laws and increasing penalties for low-level offenders—has had profound implications for the scale at which incarceration is practiced. Simultaneously, reformulations of the purpose of punishment have altered the prevailing conditions of incarceration and release, with the retreat from efforts at rehabilitation leaving the process of ex-offender reintegration to largely unregulated market forces. By tracing the origins of mass incarceration and changes in the context of inmate release, we can begin to understand the constellation of factors that gave rise to the contemporary dilemmas of prisoner reentry.

The Prison Boom

The massive expansion of the inmate population in the United States is a relatively recent phenomenon. For most of the twentieth century, the size of the state and federal prison population remained fairly constant, a little over 100 inmates per 100,000 residents.[4] In the early 1970s, however, these numbers changed dramatically, doubling between 1972 and 1984, and again between 1984 and 1994. The rate of increase slowed somewhat after 1994, but continued to climb steadily to a rate of 486 per 100,000 by the year 2004 (see figure 1.1). By the end of the century, the absolute number of inmates (including those in jails and local detention centers) had reached an unprecedented level of more than 2 million individuals. In addition to those incarcerated, 4.9 million individuals were under criminal justice supervision through probation or parole, bringing the total population under criminal justice supervision to over 7 million individuals.[5]

Few social policies have met with such sustained support as America's tough on crime policies. In 1992, with a prison population already more than quadruple the size of two decades before, the U.S. Department of Justice released a report titled The Case for More Incarceration, arguing for longer and stricter sentences and more prison construction. The introduction of the report states: "Ask many politicians, newspaper editors, or criminal justice 'experts' about our prisons, and you will hear that our problem is that we put too many people in prison. The truth, however, is to the contrary; we are incarcerating too few criminals, and the public is suffering as a result."[6]

During this time, media accounts suggested that a menacing surge in crime was the source of rising incarceration. A study of network news coverage from 1990 to 1996, for example, found that crime stories were

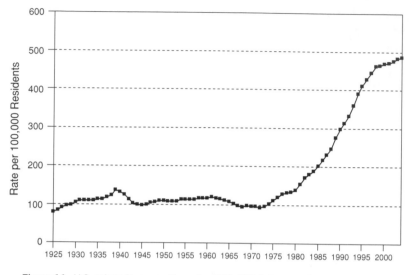

Figure 1.1 U.S. prison incarceration rate, 1925–2004. Source: Bureau of Justice Statistics, *Sourcebook of criminal justice statistics* (Washington DC: U.S. Department of Justice, 2003).

featured more often than any other topic, including the economy and health care.[7] And yet, over much of this period, official crime and victimization rates remained stable or declined even as the number of inmates continued to rise (see figure 1.2).[8] In 1973, there were twenty-three state and federal prisoners in custody for every thousand index crimes reported; by 1998, this ratio had grown more than fourfold. The growth in incarceration far outpaced any corresponding growth in crime.

The disparate trends in crime and incarceration are indeed provocative, and they have been the source of heated debate among researchers and policy makers.[9] To some, the trends provide clear evidence for the effectiveness of incarceration: as dangerous criminals are removed from the streets, the level of crime falls proportionally.[10] In addition to the straightforward benefits of incapacitation—preventing further offending for the duration of the prison term—incarceration may likewise provide a much needed "time-out" during the particularly turbulent and crime-prone years in offenders' lives.[11] The vast majority of crime occurs during adolescence and young adulthood, after which crime rates reliably and steadily decrease.[12] Given this strong age-crime relationship, holding offenders in prison during their years of most active offending may in fact provide lasting benefits after their release. If older, more mature ex-offenders are less likely to reoffend than their younger counterparts, the increasing length of sentencing associated with mass incarceration may

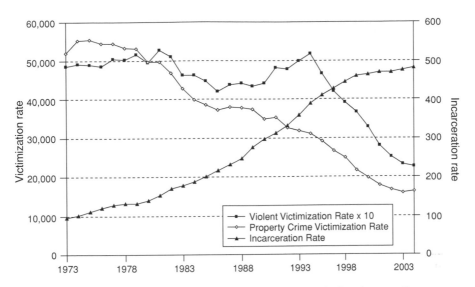

Figure 1.2 Rates of violent and property victimization and prison incarceration, 1973–2003. Violent victimization rate: per 100,000 persons age 12 or older (×10). Property crime victimization rate: per 100,000 households. Incarceration rate: per 100,000 persons. Sources: National Crime Victimization Survey, Bureau of Justice Statistics 2003.

contribute to the short- and long-term benefits of incapacitation and reduced recidivism (return to criminal behavior). Steeply falling crime rates through the 1990s (following two decades of steady prison expansion) are consistent with this perspective.

Critics of the prison boom, by contrast, argue that increases in incarceration since 1975 can account for only a small fraction of crime reduction over this period, with the crime drop better explained by other social trends, such as changes in the economy, demographic shifts, new policing tactics, and declining drug markets.[13] Further, these critics contend that, although low levels of incarceration may be effective in detaining the most serious and chronic offenders, increasing incarceration has diminishing returns. As the rate of incarceration increases and a wider range of offenders are included, the potential impact of each additional inmate is reduced, with vast expenditures on prison construction and maintenance resulting in very small gains in public safety.[14] Finally, counteracting the benefits of aging offenders, weakened ties to family and work associated with long spells of incarceration may themselves stimulate continued offending.[15]

Incarceration has undoubtedly played some role in reducing crime, but the magnitude of this effect, and its cost-effectiveness compared to other possible interventions, remains widely contested. This book does not try to resolve long-standing debates about the effectiveness of incarceration relative to other crime-reduction strategies. Rather than revisiting these discussions, this study takes as its starting point the reality of mass incarceration for an examination of its longer-term consequences. Cost-benefit analyses of the crime-incarceration relationship rarely consider effects that extend beyond the prison term. With the size of the ex-offender community now six times that of the inmate population, this group is arguably equally relevant to discussions of public safety and to assessments of the full range of outcomes associated with large-scale incarceration.

Just as the effects of incarceration on crime remain widely contested, the effects of crime on incarceration likewise present some curious puzzles. Though we often think of incarceration as a *response* to crime, trends in incarceration appear to have had an irregular relationship with corresponding rates of crime. During the 1970s, incarceration rates rose at a pace comparable to increases in crime; during the 1980s, official crime rates remained steady while incarceration rates doubled; during the 1990s, official crime rates fell by 30 percent, while incarceration rates rose by 60 percent.[16] Where crime rates have fluctuated over the past three decades, incarceration rates have followed a steady upward trajectory. In fact, criminologists Alfred Blumstein and Allen Beck estimate that, between 1980 and 1996, only 12 percent of the increase in incarceration can be accounted for by increases in crime (nearly all of which represents increasing arrests for drug crimes). What then accounts for the steady growth in incarceration? According to Blumstein and Beck, the vast majority of rising incarceration rates (88 percent) can be attributed to changes in crime control policies, including a 51 percent increase in the likelihood of incarceration following arrest and a 37 percent increase in the average length of sentences.[17] More recently, rising imprisonment rates have also been influenced by the growing number of individuals sent back to prison for violations of parole. Between 1990 and 1998, the number of new court commitments to prison increased by only 7 percent while the number of return parole violators increased by 54 percent. Of parole violators sent back to prison, roughly half had been convicted of new crimes, while the remainder were returned to prison for technical violations of the conditions of parole.[18] Changes in the handling of criminal offenders, more than increases in crime, have thus been primarily responsible for the growth in incarceration since 1980.

To some, these trends demonstrate the increasing effectiveness of the criminal justice system in holding offenders accountable for their actions. Replacing lenient sanctions with prison time makes punishment more effective and helps to prevent the escalation of crime. To others, rising incarceration in the absence of rising crime signals a troubling disconnect between crime policy and the actual crime problem. According to sociologist David Garland, "It is not 'crime' or even criminological knowledge about crime which most affects policy decisions, but rather the ways in which 'the crime problem' is officially perceived and the political positions to which these perceptions give rise."[19] Whatever the case, it is clear that what Americans consider appropriate responses to dealing with crime changed substantially after the 1960s. Whereas prison was once seen as a last resort for offenders, it now represents one of the dominant strategies for dealing with the problems of crime and social disorder.

From Rehabilitation to Retribution

Criminal justice policies were not always as punitive as they are today. As recently as the 1950s and 1960s, most Americans held the optimistic view that offenders could be reformed and that it was the responsibility of the criminal justice system to do so. Individuals who committed crimes were seen as needing supervision, resocialization, and assistance in acquiring the necessary foundation for reentering society. It was widely believed that counseling, education, and job training were central to criminal desistance and that active intervention could have lasting effects.[20]

Finding empirical support for these intended effects, however, proved difficult. In fact, a series of studies conducted in the late 1960s and the early 1970s found the effects of prison programs to be variable at best, nonexistent at worst. A widely discussed and influential review by Robert Martinson in 1974 concluded that "nothing works" in the rehabilitation of offenders.[21]

As policy makers and the public grew increasingly dissatisfied with seemingly ineffective attempts at rehabilitation, an alternative orientation took hold. Crime policy increasingly emphasized punishment as an end in itself, distant from the broader corrections orientation of previous decades. In the extreme formulation of one influential observer, "Wicked people exist. Nothing avails except to set them apart from innocent people."[22] Replacing the mission of rehabilitation and reform came a rhetoric of containment and retribution, with the implication that crime was a problem to be managed by brute force.[23]

The Crisis of Indeterminate Sentencing

Indeed, an emphasis on containment dominated policy reform over the following decades, resulting in the passage of numerous state and federal acts to escalate the policing, prosecution, and imprisonment of offenders. One of the most influential changes to the system concerned sentencing policies. Throughout the twentieth century, virtually all states had followed a system of indeterminate sentencing, whereby judges were given substantial leeway in determining the strength of sanction, depending on a range of factors pertaining to the individual and the offense. Rather than assigning a fixed amount of time, judges would provide a minimum and maximum sentence, with the actual amount of time served depending on evaluations of the prisoner's rehabilitation in periodic reviews by parole boards. The indeterminacy of sentences was meant to provide incentives for inmates to follow rules and to demonstrate a commitment to reform. The possibility of early parole was intended as the carrot to accompany the stick of incarceration.[24] With increasing skepticism about rehabilitation, however, the rationale behind indeterminate sentencing came under sharp attack.

Conservative critics argued that the discretion afforded to judges and parole boards allowed for too much leniency: murderers could be sentenced to anything from one year to life in prison and, once in prison, they could be released for good behavior long before the completion of their sentences. Criticizing the current system as soft on crime, conservatives lobbied for mandatory sentencing policies that would impose fixed terms for specified crimes and stricter limits on early release.

Ironically, the crisis of indeterminate sentencing was also fueled by liberal critics, who argued that the large degree of discretion involved in sentencing decisions left the system wide open to the influence of discriminatory and arbitrary judgments. These critics called for the adoption of determinate sentencing as a means of making the criminal justice system fairer and more transparent.[25] Likewise, liberal critics rejected the rhetoric of rehabilitation as legitimating an ideology of social control, rather than a genuine service to offenders. The involuntary imposition of treatment was seen as a coercive means of subduing inmates, requiring that they submit not only to physical containment but to psychological containment as well.[26] According to this perspective, the process of designating individuals as "fit" or "unfit" to reenter society was morally bankrupt; instead, liberal critics called for the removal of these inherently subjective discretionary judgments and the instatement of fixed terms for specific offenses.

The aligned voices of liberals and conservatives created broad support for the widespread adoption of determinate sentencing structures. By the late 1990s, all fifty states had adopted mandatory minimum sentences, which mandate incarceration for particular offenses, and sentencing enhancements, which increase the certainty and severity of punishment when an offense is accompanied with specific behaviors or traits. In addition, eighteen states and the federal government adopted sentencing guidelines, which establish minimum and maximum penalties for offenses and provide exact measures for the effects of mitigating and aggravating circumstances. Finally, twenty-eight states and the District of Columbia adopted "truth in sentencing" policies that require that offenders not be released before 85 percent of their sentence has been served.[27]

The consequences of these policies were significant for the millions of individuals processed under this new regime. Whereas in the past, first-time or low-level offenders might have been placed on probation instead of in prison, new sentencing laws imposed stricter punishments for a broad range of offenses. The chances of receiving a prison sentence following arrest increased by more than 50 percent as a result of determinate sentencing laws. Likewise, the amount of prison time served increased substantially under new guidelines, with the average length of sentences served increasing by nearly 40 percent between the mid-1980s and the late 1990s.[28] Crime did not become more serious over this period, but punishment surely did.

A Formalization of Moral Order

Parallel to changing beliefs about the purpose of punishment, a new discourse about the causes of crime was simultaneously capturing popular attention. In part as a backlash against the "permissive" social and political agenda associated with the war on poverty, prominent conservative politicians and public intellectuals in the 1970s and 1980s offered a new public framing of the problem of moral order.[29] Against conceptions of crime as arising from social causes such as poverty and urban decay, these influential voices emphasized the core principles of personal responsibility and individual blame. President Ronald Reagan captured the emerging conservative consensus: "Choosing a career in crime is not the result of poverty or of an unhappy childhood or of a misunderstood adolescence; it is the result of a conscious willful choice."[30]

In this new formulation, crime was viewed not as an indicator of the failings of a social system but as a symptom of moral corruption. Conservative political commentator William Bennett and his coauthors, for example, located the root causes of contemporary urban crime in what they characterized as a growing problem of "moral poverty"—family breakdown, social disorganization, drug use, and the like—which had spawned a new generation of "selfish, impulsive, predatory propensities of morally impoverished street criminals."[31] Likewise, James Q. Wilson invoked a language of morality in characterizing the problem of illicit drug use: "Drug use is wrong because it is immoral."[32] Through the voices of these and other conservative critics, the war on poverty of the previous decade was gradually replaced by a rhetorical war on moral poverty.

As the locus of crime came to be increasingly situated within the individual, the task of identifying, segregating, and punishing suddenly appeared more tractable. According to one commentator, "The public, and public officials, are now less likely to view criminals as disadvantaged, ill-treated members of society who can be changed for the better. . . . If it seems criminals cannot be changed, and have only themselves to blame for their behavior, then the most pivotal compunctions against harsh dispositions have been swept aside. There is no compelling argument against incapacitating as many offenders as the system can accommodate for as long as possible."[33]

Where earlier decades had emphasized the situational factors that lead to crime—regular people caught in deplorable circumstances—new formulations set sharp distinctions between a law-abiding "us" and an unredeemable "them."[34] As David Garland argues, "Crime acted as a lens through which to view the poor—as undeserving, deviant, dangerous, different—and as a barrier to lingering sentiments of fellow feeling and compassion."[35] Reformulations of accepted wisdom about the causes of social problems and of the purposes of punishment together empowered the apparatus of the criminal justice system with the task of monitoring and enforcing "offending" behaviors that stretched beyond conventional categories of crime. What had begun as a movement to preserve public safety—to shield innocent victims from the lurking threat of danger—gradually led to a more expansive agenda encompassing more general displays of social disorder and moral transgressions.

Nowhere was this new moral order more apparent than in the war on drugs. Launched during the Reagan administration, the war on drugs focused national attention and federal resources on the problem of drug use and distribution, mobilizing vast public resources to combat this emerging social problem.[36] Although drug crimes had historically been a very small proportion of all convictions, the number of drug offenders admitted to prison skyrocketed during this period. Between 1980 and 1990, the annual number of drug offenders admitted to state prisons increased tenfold (see figure 1.3). In 1980, roughly one out of every fifteen offenders admitted to prison had been convicted of a drug crime; one decade later, this figure had jumped to one out of every three.[37] In fact, by the late 1990s, a higher proportion of state prison admissions were for drug

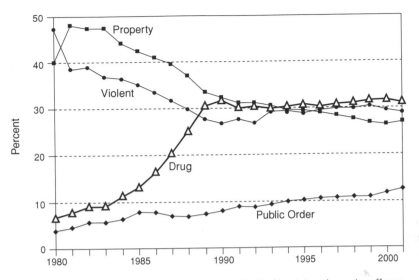

Figure 1.3   Percentage of sentenced prisoners admitted to state prisons, by offense type, 1980–2001. Data for 1980–1997 are from Bureau of Justice Statistics, 2000, "Correctional Populations in the United States, 1997." For years 1998–2001, data come from the National Corrections Reporting Program.

crimes than for violent crimes. In federal prisons, though representing a smaller proportion of inmates overall, the rise in drug offenders was even more dramatic, increasing from 16 percent of inmates in 1970 to more than 60 percent by 1993. Owing to the legacy of Reagan's domestic war, drug offenders have taken center stage in the federal prison system.

Though the war on drugs was a highly politicized initiative, the concern over illicit drug use did not materialize out of thin air. The use of heroin and cocaine increased significantly in the early to mid-1980s, and the introduction of crack cocaine was of serious concern. Further troubling, the homicide rate increased nearly 25 percent between 1985 and 1991, in part due to warring among rival drug marketers and the increasing use of handguns for protection and retribution.[38] It is therefore important to note that the rise in incarceration among drug offenders was influenced by a wider set of illicit activities linked to the drug trade. The twin problems of addiction and violence associated with illicit drugs took a heavy toll on communities already struggling with poverty, joblessness, and an array of social problems.

The criminal justice system offered one approach to restoring order in afflicted communities. Unfortunately, the criminal justice response appears to have been largely out of step with actual longer-term patterns of drug use and distribution. National surveys of drug use indicate that co-caine use rose markedly between 1983 and 1985, and then began a steep decline, leveling off in 1992. The number of crack users stabilized around 1988 and then decreased through the 1990s.[39] And homicide rates, including those associated with the drug trade, also stabilized and then fell steadily through the 1990s. As we can see in figure 1.3, however, the number of prison admissions for drug offenders rose sharply even as drug use was starting to decline.[40] Despite the fact that consumption of both powder cocaine and crack decreased substantially in the 1990s, as did violent crime associated with the drug trade, incarceration rates for drug offenders remained at peak levels.

Policies developed to fight the war on drugs have been intimately tied to changes in sentencing policies described earlier. Epitomized by the introduction of the Rockefeller drug laws in New York in the early 1970s, which imposed harsh mandatory prison sentences for drug offenders, drug convictions have been a major focus of determinate sentencing legislation. As a result, individuals convicted of drug crimes have been more substantially affected by the new sentencing guidelines than those convicted of any other type of crime: the chances of incarceration following a drug arrest increased by roughly 500 percent between 1980 and 1992, and the average length of sentences nearly doubled.[41] Although recently there has been some movement to divert drug offenders from criminal courts to drug courts and treatment programs, the number of drug offenders being processed through the criminal justice system remains immense.[42]

Apart from its general impact on rising incarceration rates, targeted enforcement associated with the war on drugs has had a large and disproportionate impact on African Americans. No single offense type has more directly contributed to contemporary racial disparities in imprisonment than drug crimes.[43] Between 1983 and 1997, the number of African Americans admitted to prison for drug offenses increased more than twenty-six-fold, relative to a sevenfold increase for whites (see figure 1.4). By 2001, there were more than twice as many African Americans as whites in state prison for drug offenses (139,700 versus 57,300). Though household surveys suggest that the vast majority of drug users are white (even with respect to cocaine), the brunt of drug prosecutions has fallen on African Americans.[44]

The war on drugs has been one of the most consequential developments in crime policy over the past thirty years, contributing substantially to the prison boom and reinforcing large racial disparities in incarceration. Though few studies have found prisons to be an effective strategy for reducing drug use—whether in terms of cost effectiveness or absolute crime

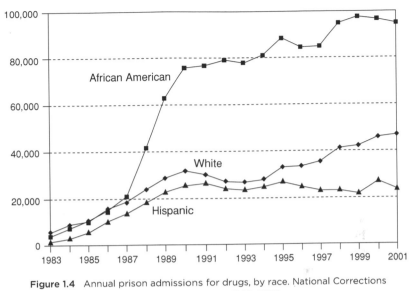

Figure 1.4   Annual prison admissions for drugs, by race. National Corrections Reporting Program, 1983–2001.

reduction—drug offenders remain the largest category of admissions to state and federal prisons.[45]

The war on drugs is undoubtedly the most important, but far from the only, manifestation of the new moral order guiding criminal justice policy. Indeed, while most people think of prison as a place for dangerous violent offenders, increasingly America's prisons are being used as a warehouse for social problems ignored by other public institutions. The proportion of prison admissions for property and violent crime—the "core" crimes—fell throughout the 1980s, as the percentage of admissions for both drug and public-order offenses steadily increased (see figure 1.3).[46] Small-time drug dealers, drug addicts, the homeless, and the mentally ill have been swept up in this cleansing of the streets. Whereas once prison was seen as a last resort for offenders, it now represents one of the dominant strategies for dealing with the problems of urban social disorder.

The increasing use of jails and prisons to manage the problems of petty crime has not been without cost. Though welfare benefits, homeless shelters, and mental health treatment centers lost funding over much of this period, spending on the poor has not decreased. Between 1977 and 2001, spending on corrections increased elevenfold, rising at roughly twice the rate of spending on education, hospitals and health care, public welfare, or interest on public debt.[47] The prison system—with annual budgets of $57 billion—has ironically become one of the largest providers of meals, shelter, and health care for the poor and indigent populations of our country.

The vast sweep of incarceration may have been effective as a temporary removal of disruptive elements of society. But it represents at best a short-term solution. Apart from the small number of offenders imprisoned for life, the vast majority are released back into the community after a few years of confinement. Today there are more than three times as many individuals being *released* from prison each year as the total number of prisoners held in 1970. As their numbers grow, the issue of offender reintegration becomes increasingly important. As we have seen, the criminal justice system actively abandoned the goal of rehabilitation after the early 1970s, emphasizing instead strict punishment as a mechanism of containment and retribution. The imposition of longer sentences further deflected attention from the point of release. And yet now, as a critical mass of offenders reach the completion of their prison terms each year, policy concern over the process of prisoner reentry has begun to grow. Indeed, the turn to prisoner reentry represents the next logical phase in the large social experiment that began roughly thirty years ago.

The Era of Prisoner Reentry

The transition from prison to society has long been recognized as a delicate process, during which offenders are set on a path toward either reform or recidivism. But the scale of reentry today poses qualitatively different concerns than in the eras prior to mass incarceration. In 2003, more than eight times as many inmates reentered society as in 1970 (see figure 1.5).[48] In the face of this swelling population flow, traditional modes of community reabsorption have been stretched thin.

The primary institutional apparatus charged with supervision of the reentry process are state departments of parole. In an earlier era of crime policy, parole was viewed as an integral part of the corrections process. Parole officers worked with offenders to find them stable housing and employment, and offered guidance and supervision through the reintegration process. According to a 1973 report of the National Advisory Commission on Criminal Justice Standards and Goals, "A parole staff has a specific task: to assist parolees in availing themselves of community resources.... Parole staff must also take responsibility for finding needed resources for parolees in the community."[49] Among other responsibilities, parole agents in the 1960s "tended to view their job as one of establishing relations with civic leaders, participating in voluntary associations, and making the acquaintance of local employers, all in the interest of

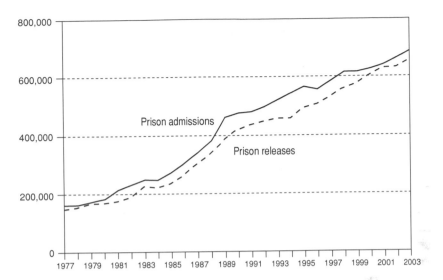

Figure 1.5 Admissions to and releases from state and federal prisons, 1977–2003.
Source: Bureau of Justice Statistics, 1998–2005, Prison and Jail Inmates at Midyear.

generating parolee job placements."[50] To be sure, the ideal and reality of parole services were not always aligned, with parole agents and agencies varying widely in the extent and effectiveness of their services.[51] Imperfect implementation notwithstanding, the stated function of parole was to oversee the process of reentry and to assist the ex-offender on his pathway to desistance.

With disillusionment in the ideal of rehabilitation, however, came a similar skepticism about the functioning of parole. Critics doubted that social services or employment assistance could have any meaningful impact on recidivism; they saw little use for a parole apparatus whose primary function was to support the seemingly failed mission of rehabilitation. Some called for the abolition of parole altogether.[52] As criminologist Jeremy Travis puts it, "Ironically, the rise in the number of prisoners has been accompanied by a loss of confidence in the institution entrusted with supervising their return."[53] In the midst of these shifting political priorities, budgets for the departments of parole fell substantially. Between 1985 and 1998, the annual budget for parole fell from $11,000 to $9,500 per capita. During roughly the same period, average caseloads for parole officers grew from 45 to 70 parolees, now more than twice the recommended supervision load. With such a high volume of offenders compared to parole staff, the ability of parole to affect the trajectory of reintegration (other than through reimprisonment) has dissipated. Thus, despite an eightfold increase in the scale of reentry, the states' capacity for regulating and overseeing this process markedly declined.[54]

Observations of parole transactions in recent times illustrate the perfunctory and formalized nature of supervision. As Jonathan Simon reports, "Parolees come in . . . a brief check is conducted on items like current address, contacts with police, and employment prospects, usually followed by a trip to the lavatory for a urine sample. Rarely [do] such interactions . . . last more than ten minutes."[55] Indeed, more than 80 percent of parolees meet with their parole officer for no more than fifteen minutes once or twice a month. Under these conditions, parole can function as little more than a weak mechanism of surveillance, issuing technical violations for revealed irregularities (missed meetings, positive drug tests, violating curfew, etc.), but providing little in the way of personalized supervision or support.[56] As one study of parole finds, "Instead of helping prisoners locate a job, find a residence, or locate needed drug treatment services, the new parole system is bent on surveillance and detection. Parolees are routinely and randomly checked for illegal drug use, failure to locate or maintain a job, moving without permission, or any other number of petty and nuisance-type behaviors that don't conform to the rules of parole."[57] Mirroring trends in the criminal justice system as a whole, contemporary parole practices have shifted from an emphasis on providing broad supports for the rehabilitation process to a more narrow set of monitoring and enforcement activities. Not surprisingly, this changing emphasis is reflected in the outcomes of those leaving parole: the proportion of parolees successfully completing their term without an arrest declined from 70 percent in 1984 to 44 percent in 1996.[58] The revolving door of prison is in large part fueled by the changing context of parole.

The withdrawal of state resources from the reentry process is most vivid in the case of parole, but has registered in the provisions of other public agencies as well. Beyond the more general retreat from social welfare—which has surely affected the resources available to the families and communities to which many ex-offenders return—specific restrictions have been placed on a wide range of government services for ex-offenders. Bans on entry into public housing, restrictions on public sector employment, limits on access to federal loans for higher education, and restrictions on the receipt of public assistance affect some or all ex-offenders, further constraining the range of possible supports.[59] Together with the curtailment of parole, the elimination of these broader sources of government support has created an environment for prisoner reentry in which offenders can rely on few public resources in making the transition from prison to home.

Absorbing Returning Prisoners

With only weak public institutions responsible for overseeing the transition of returning inmates, the burden of the reentry process falls largely on families, communities, and a patchwork of social service agencies. These resources can ease the transition, offering temporary housing and leads to jobs. Indeed, offenders with close personal ties demonstrate substantially better outcomes in the reentry process.[60] There is reason to believe, however, that, like government supports, this informal system has weakened in effectiveness over time. Longer periods of absence (due to increasing sentence length) are associated with weaker ties to family and community, as the barriers to communication and involvement are substantial. Strained or severed ties with family and friends reduce the availability of informal sources of support for the transition from prison to home. Further, the scale of reentry imposes heightened burdens on families and communities. The neighborhoods most affected by high levels of incarceration and ex-offender absorption are often those already struggling with serious problems of joblessness, single-parent families, and poverty. The churning of residents, mostly young men, between prison and home can further undermine the already tenuous social order that exists within these neighborhoods.[61] Thus, while family and community supports will always represent an important part of the reentry process, it is unlikely that these informal resources alone can effectively absorb the steady influx of returning offenders. Indeed, available statistics suggest that many ex-offenders are on their own: the California Department of Corrections, for example, estimates that on any given day 10 percent of the state's parolees are homeless; in Los Angeles and San Francisco, the proportion of parolees who are homeless is between 30 and 50 percent.[62]

Beyond the limited resources available to buffer the transition process, prisoner reentry is managed largely by market forces. Nowhere is this process more acute than in the labor market. Employment is widely considered a centerpiece of the reentry process, with the intuition that steady work can reduce the incentives of crime. Though the research findings on this question have been mixed, a number of careful studies do indicate a substantial effect of employment in reducing subsequent criminal involvement. A long-term follow-up of juvenile offenders, including extensive controls for individual predispositions, found that "job stability is central in explaining adult desistance from crime."[63] Likewise, a meta-analysis of studies measuring the impact of employment interventions on recidivism finds broad support for the notion that employment reduces crime.[64] These and other studies provide some indication that quality stable employment can play an important role in the pathway out of crime.

Consistent with this logic, nearly 80 percent of parole boards require "gainful employment" as a standard condition of parole.[65] Rates of joblessness among ex-offenders, by contrast, suggest that this condition is rarely met: up to a year after a release, roughly three-quarters of ex-offenders remain unemployed.[66] If unemployment is linked to recidivism, as the research above suggests, the widespread failures of prisoner reentry pose serious concerns for public safety.

A Case of Market Failure?

The labor market presents some particularly interesting puzzles from the perspective of prisoner reentry. On the one hand, the employment of ex-offenders can be viewed as a public good. When ex-offenders are employed, they have less reason to engage in crime; they impose fewer burdens on the families and communities that support them; and if they desist from crime, they impose fewer costs on the taxpayers who would otherwise fund their reincarceration. The public thus has an interest in promoting self-sufficiency and desistance among the ex-offender population through stable, long-term employment.

On the other hand, market forces do not themselves follow a logic of public interest. The employment of ex-offenders is regulated almost exclusively by the initiative and discretion of individual employers, but this group has no particular stake in the reentry process. In fact, quite to the contrary, employers have reason to use caution in considering job applicants with proven track records of breaking the law. Employers bear the costs of theft and violence in the workplace, as well as the more mundane problems of unreliable staff and employee turnover. To the extent that ex-offenders represent more costly hires along any of these dimensions, employers have reason to avoid applicants with prior criminal backgrounds. Indeed, given the possible risks individual employers bear in hiring ex-offenders, it is unlikely that the market will manage the problems of prisoner reentry on its own.

In reality, we know relatively little about how the market responds to ex-offenders. Employment rates alone cannot disentangle employer preferences from the many complicated factors that deter ex-offenders from finding or keeping jobs. Understanding the market functions, and market failures, related to prisoner reentry represents an important step toward policy development in this area.

To what extent do employers avoid applicants with criminal records? Does their reaction depend on the race of the applicant? What are the conditions under which employers may be more or less willing to hire ex-offenders? It is to these questions that we turn in the remainder of the book.

2 The Labor Market Consequences of Incarceration

In the year 2005:

135,000 people worked for Starbucks (worldwide);

1.5 million worked for McDonalds (worldwide);

1.8 million worked for Wal-Mart (worldwide);

2.2 million were housed in U.S. jails and prisons.[1]

Whereas once prisoners represented only a tiny fraction of the population, today the United States houses enough inmates to staff an entire global fast food empire. In addition to those currently behind bars, the number of prison veterans has likewise been growing at a rapid pace. The more than 600,000 inmates released each year could fill every one of the fast-food job openings created annually nearly five times over.[2] Though few direct ties exist between the criminal justice system and private industry, the extraordinary growth of the carceral sector has wide-ranging implications for broader labor market processes.

The functioning of labor markets is affected by both the supply of labor and the quality (or qualifications) of workers. Large-scale incarceration can affect both these dimensions, distorting labor market processes in unintended and unexpected ways. The large flow of individuals into and out of the prison system has complex effects, simultaneously concealing and creating inequalities in the labor market. Recognizing the range of economic effects associated with prison growth is the first step in accounting for the consequences of mass incarceration.

Concealing Inequality

The first and foremost function of the prison is one of containment. Warehoused in prison facilities, inmates are removed from their families and communities and set apart from the normal movements of society. But inmates are left out of more than just daily routines. In most cases, they become invisible to our official indicators of social and economic well-being, set apart from the normal accounting of social trends.

This insight can be credited to sociologist Bruce Western and his colleagues, who have provided the most comprehensive investigation to date of the "invisible inequality" associated with our prisons.[3] Government employment statistics typically limit their analyses to noninstitutionalized civilian workers.[4] Monthly reports of unemployment and labor force participation inform us of the health of our economy but ignore the large and growing numbers of the working-age population that sit idle in our prisons and jails. If we considered the more than two million inmates in our employment estimates, our conclusions about the state of the economy would grow steadily less optimistic. Indeed, Western and his colleagues reestimated national unemployment rates, employment-to-population ratios, and earnings with inmates counted among the nonworking. Their new estimates suggest that our official labor force statistics substantially underestimate rates of joblessness and economic inequality. In fact, while the free-market capitalism of America is often touted as the source of its low unemployment rates compared to those of Western Europe, this research suggests that the differential is largely a function of penal intervention. Adjusted estimates of joblessness, taking into account the prison population, indicate that U.S. employment rates are in fact much closer to those of Europe. Prison can thus be thought of as a "labor-market institution," disproportionately removing individuals from the bottom of the socioeconomic hierarchy who would likely otherwise be counted among the unemployed.[5]

Likewise, our understanding of racial disparities in economic outcomes may be heavily distorted by our prison population. Analysts have long touted the converging trends in wages among young black and white men as optimistic signs of the declining significance of race. What have been registered as gains in black economic progress in recent decades, however, largely reflect the substantial number of disadvantaged men who are simply overlooked by official statistics. According to Bruce Western and Becky Pettit, "apparent improvement in the economic position of young black men is...largely an artifact of rising joblessness fuelled by the growth in incarceration during the 1990s."[6] Our prisons thereby mask a substantial component of persisting racial disparities by "removing" the problem from our tracking systems.[7]

Creating Inequality

But prisons are not stationary institutions. The *stock* of prisoners at any given time is in part a function of the *flow* of individuals into and out of the prison system. The average duration of incarceration in state prison is roughly twenty-eight months, resulting in a steady churning of individuals from prisons back into the communities from which they came.[8] The large flow of inmates back into society and, for the most part, back into the active labor market, has implications for new forms of inequality not previously anticipated in discussions of the tough on crime approach.

Returning inmates face significant legal and social barriers to finding employment. While there is very little systematic research examining how returning inmates fare in their search for work, existing studies do suggest troubling results. Several studies of local or state inmate populations report that between 75 and 80 percent of parolees remain jobless up to a year after release from prison.[9] More controlled studies, following large samples over time and comparing them to otherwise similar individuals who have never been incarcerated, also show serious economic penalties following spells of incarceration. Sociologists Robert Sampson and John Laub, for example, using a rich set of longitudinal data from an early cohort of juvenile delinquents, find that incarceration has a strong and significant negative effect on later job stability, even after controlling for alcohol use, criminal activity, and prior criminal history.[10] Using longitudinal data on a more recent cohort of men, Bruce Western estimates that incarceration is associated with a 10 percent drop in wages and a flatter earnings trajectory than that of similarly skilled men who did not experience incarceration.[11] Indeed, it appears that America's prison policies impose penalties beyond those meted out in the form of criminal sentencing. Long after an individual completes his prison term, the labor market costs of incarceration continue to register.

Why do ex-offenders experience such bleak employment outcomes? The range of possible explanations can be distilled into three major categories.

(1) Selection. The kinds of people who wind up in prison don't really want to work, or don't have sufficient skills to find a job.

We can call this first explanation an argument about "selection effects"—the idea that prisons disproportionately "select" from the kinds of people that were never very willing or able to hold down legitimate jobs in the first place. Selection arguments suggest that incarceration has no independent effect on labor market outcomes, despite a correlation between the two. According to this perspective, if we were to eliminate the criminal justice system altogether, employment outcomes for this group would remain unchanged.

There are a number of reasons to believe that the employment problems of ex-offenders predate their incarceration experiences. Individuals who wind up in the prison system have on average low levels of education and spotty work histories, and many struggle with mental illness and substance abuse. At least a quarter to a third of inmates were unemployed at the time of their incarceration.[12] As I discuss in chapter 3, some research suggests that the employment outcomes of offenders change very little following an experience of incarceration, supporting the argument that the employment problems of this group are driven largely by initial selection into prisons, rather than by any direct consequence of penal intervention.

(2) Transformation. The experience of prison changes inmates in ways that make them less suited for the formal labor market.

In stark opposition to selection arguments, this second explanation suggests that the effects of prison actively undermine the employment prospects of ex-offenders by changing inmates in ways that make them less willing or able to hold down a job.[13] Periods of absence from the labor market leave large gaps in offenders' work histories, disadvantaging them relative to same-age nonincarcerated peers. Likewise, extended periods away from routines of work and skill building can leave inmates unprepared for stable economic activity. Incarceration may further damage an individual's ability to work through prolonged exposure to physical or psychological trauma endemic to prison environments. And finally, beyond its effects on the individual, prison can be extremely disruptive to social and familial ties, which are often central to finding a job.[14] Together, these arguments suggest that inmates are worse off when they leave prison than when they arrived, due to the range of disruptive and debilitating features of prison life.

The precise nature of the transformative effects of prisons remain poorly understood. Though numerous studies have documented the often physically and emotionally destructive impact of prison environments, others show prison as a stabilizing experience, an escape from the street and an opportunity to gain productive skills and schooling. Indeed, despite substantial cutbacks in funding for prison programming, more than half of all inmates participate in some additional schooling while in prison, with over a quarter completing their GED.[15] The jury is still out, then, on exactly what effect the experience of incarceration has on inmates. While a detailed investigation of these issues is beyond the scope of the present study (which seeks, rather, to assess the "credentialing effects" of incarceration, discussed below), future research should address these issues more systematically, as an understanding of the collateral consequences of incarceration also requires an accounting of the potential costs to human and social capital and the consequences for psychological well-being.

(3) *Credentialing. The stigma of incarceration imposes barriers to finding employment.*

I refer to this third explanation as the "credentialing effects" of incarceration, or the idea that inmates are formally classified in ways that make employers less likely to hire them.[16] According to this argument, mere contact with the criminal justice system can in itself impose significant economic costs, above and beyond any selective or transformative effects of incarceration. In the discussion below, I consider the ways in which exoffenders, marked by their criminal record, can become excluded from a wide range of formal and social opportunities. Chapter 4 then tests these propositions against competing selection arguments, assessing the relevance of credentialing effects to explaining the poor employment outcomes of ex-offenders.

The Negative Credential

The term "credential" has been variously defined as "proof of ability or trustworthiness," "authentication," or "official identification" ("a letter, badge, or other official identification that confirms [an individual's] position or status"). The credential offers official certification of an individual's formal rank or standing, conveying standardized information about the competencies and disposition of its bearer. We tend to think of the credentialing process only in its positive form, as a formal status that enables access and upward mobility. A college degree, a medical license, or an MBA are common examples of positive credentials that facilitate access to restricted social positions. What the case of the criminal record brings into bold relief, however, is that the credentialing of status positions can also take place in the opposite direction. *Negative credentials* are those official markers that restrict access and opportunity rather than enabling them. A criminal record is the archetypal negative credential (others with negative credentials include welfare recipients, those dishonorably discharged from the military, mental patients, and deportees). With a criminal record comes official state certification of an individual's criminal transgressions; a wide range of social, economic, and political privileges become off-limits. Further, just as positive credentials offer the informal rewards of social status and generalized assumptions of competence, negative credentials confer the inverse: social stigma and generalized assumptions of untrustworthiness or undesirability.

The credentialing effects of criminal conviction can result in both legal and social exclusion. In the context of labor markets, formal exclusion is imposed through the web of federal and state laws that restrict ex-offenders from a range of labor market activities. Fully thirty-three states, as well as the District of Columbia, impose some kind of legal restriction on public employment following a felony conviction.[17] All states place at least certain restrictions on occupational licenses for individuals with criminal records, with the number of barred occupations increasing substantially over time.[18]

In certain cases the logic of these occupational restrictions is straightforward—individuals with a history of violent crime are clearly inappropriate candidates for employment in child care institutions or schools. In many other cases, however, legal restrictions on ex-offenders have far less connection to apparent safety concerns. In some states, for example, ex-offenders are restricted from jobs as septic tank cleaners, embalmers, billiard room employees, real estate agents, plumbers, eyeglass dispensers, and barbers.[19] Blanket restrictions on these occupations, with no attention to individual circumstances or qualifications of the applicant in question, demonstrate the wide-ranging consequences of the criminal credential, extending even to some of the most basic forms of low wage work.

Legal restrictions on ex-offenders are not equally felt across the population. Blacks, who represent a disproportionate share of ex-offenders, face a correspondingly disproportionate share of the legal penalties. Moreover, many of the restricted jobs are in occupations traditionally important for African Americans. The public sector, for example, has in the past played a central role in black social mobility. These career jobs become largely off-limits, however, for the growing number of blacks with conviction records. Likewise, hospitals, which have been a major source of low-wage job growth, especially for blacks, are often the target of employment bans for ex-offenders. The large numbers of blacks returning from prison, therefore, face an ever-shrinking pool of eligible jobs from which to transition out of crime.[20]

In some states, the courts have considered arguments against employment bars on individuals with criminal records on the grounds that they have a "disparate impact" on African Americans. In 1975, the Eighth Circuit Court of Appeals struck down an employer's bar on hiring ex-offenders under the doctrine of disparate impact (*Green v. Missouri Pacific Railroad Co.*). The court's ruling stated, "We cannot conceive of any business necessity that would automatically place every individual convicted of any offense . . . in the permanent ranks of the unemployed. This is particularly true for blacks who have suffered and still suffer from the burdens of discrimination in our society."[21] Though this ruling offers a strong precedent for eliminating blanket restrictions on employment for individuals with criminal backgrounds, other rulings having come to very different conclusions. In a 1989 ruling (*EEOC v. Carolina Freight Carriers Corp.*), the presiding judge concluded, "If Hispanics do not wish to be discriminated against because they have been convicted of theft, then they should stop stealing."[22] Arguments over disparate impact remain inconsistent across jurisdictions, with little guidance from the higher courts as to when and where the use of criminal records in employment or licensing decisions can constitute disparate impact. Meanwhile, legal restrictions on the employment of ex-offenders continue to expand, further empowering the criminal credential as an instrument of labor market exclusion.

But the criminal credential has implications well beyond the relevant legal jurisdiction. In seeking to understand the barriers to employment facing ex-offenders, we must account not only for the formal barriers they face but also for the social consequences of the conviction. While the former requires a simple inventory of state and federal laws, the latter requires a more in-depth analysis of the ways in which a criminal record influences social judgments about the character and competence of its bearer. Some occupational licenses, for example, while not officially off-limits to ex-offenders, become so in practice because of a general requirement that license holders demonstrate "good moral character." Though character requirements do not automatically preclude ex-offenders from becoming license holders, criminal background information is often invoked as evidence of general disrepute.[23] Likewise, even where occupations may be legally accessible, employers may be reluctant to hire ex-offenders. Surveys find that 60 to 70 percent of employers would not knowingly hire an ex-offender. Employers appear to view a criminal history as a sign of poor work habits and an indicator of "lack of honesty and trustworthiness," closing doors to ex-offenders regardless of their specific qualifications or circumstances.[24] In parallel (but inverse) fashion to the positive credentials of a college degree or professional membership, the criminal credential conveys generalized information to employers about the skills and disposition of presenting job applicants. According to a dissenting opinion written by Chief Justice Earl Warren in *Parker v. Ellis* (1960), "Conviction of a felony imposes a *status* upon a person which not only makes him vulnerable to future sanctions through new civil disability statutes, but which also seriously affects his reputation and economic opportunities."[25]

Indeed, in the aftermath of the prison boom, employers are now more conscious of the criminal backgrounds of their workers than ever before. They are increasingly likely to ask job applicants about their criminal histories and substantially more likely to conduct official criminal background checks to verify applicants' reports.[26] The state's massive certification system is not going unused.

A Credential Society

The legitimacy of the criminal credential and its increasing use in the regulation of social goods is unique neither in form nor in function. As a society, we are moving toward a stratification regime wherein key opportunities and resources are increasingly allocated on the basis of formally designated status positions. Instead of relying on ascribed markers to determine social ranking, individuals are increasingly sorted by formal institutions and the credentials they bestow. In his seminal book, *The Credential Society*, Randall Collins discusses the movement toward the credentialization of status positions, with higher education, occupational licensure, and professional membership increasingly regulating access to privileged positions. Growing numbers of jobs require at least a bachelors degree; doctors must have a medical license; lawyers must be admitted to the state bar association; plumbers and electricians must be certified by state boards. These credentials, which are assumed to provide standardized information about the abilities and dispositions of their holders, are used as the formal basis for authorizing membership within a particular occupational class.[27]

Table 2.1. Ascribed and achieved markers of social differentiation

Source of differentiation	Positive	Negative
Ascriptive markers	White	Black
Achieved credentials	College degree	Criminal record

The implications of this broad system of credentials are best understood when placed in contrast to more traditional, ascriptive bases of social differentiation. Table 2.1 presents a stylized diagram illustrating categories of inequality determined through ascription and credentialing, in both positive and negative forms.[28] In this simple example, relative to an implicit baseline of equality, white skin provides an ascriptive basis of advantage, while a college degree confers the official legitimacy of a positive credential. Conversely, black skin represents an ascriptive basis for social marginality, while the criminal credential represents an official rationale for exclusion across a wide range of social domains.[29]

Several important points are illustrated here. First, the move from ascriptive markers to achieved credentials is in part characterized by a shift toward a formalization of status distinctions. Ascriptive categories such as race are largely social classifications, created and reinforced through social interactions and historical conventions. Though ascriptive modes of stratification in the past (and in other societies) have been regulated by official categorization (e.g., the feudal lord, the Brahmin caste, blacks under Jim Crow), contemporary forms of ascription typically operate through social designation. While these characteristics can nevertheless evoke real material (dis)advantages, such categories are rarely formalized as markers of rights or opportunities. Rather, social mechanisms of reproduction regulate the preservation of privilege, with initial (dis)advantages impeding or facilitating subsequent achievements.

Unlike ascriptive sources of stigma, credentials represent highly formalized status distinctions, granted or imposed through a bureaucratic process of selection and classification. Designated institutions such as universities, licensing boards, and courts have vested authority to regulate the credentialing process. Credentials themselves are then used to formally regulate opportunity (e.g., eligibility for an occupation) and as tools of informal classification, signaling a credential holder's social status and desirability. The specific case of the criminal credential fits neatly into this typology. Like other negative credentials, the criminal credential imposes limits on eligibility for a range of social goods and carries with it a powerful source of stigma. In addition to formal barriers, then, the negative credential of a criminal record conveys generalized information about the disposition of its bearer in ways that further limit access to opportunities.

A second element of contrast between ascription and credentialing centers around the legitimacy with which each is viewed. As a modern society, we self-consciously privilege credentials over ascribed characteristics as the explicit basis for allocating rewards. Overt social distinctions based on race, gender, national origin, or other ascribed characteristics have become increasingly censured in recent years.[30] To be sure, prejudice and discrimination persist along each of these dimensions, but public displays of hostility toward such groups are subject to widespread disapproval, and instances of unequal treatment are proscribed by law. Indeed, the social and political legitimacy of conventional sources of social stigma has largely eroded.

The same is not true of credentials, which retain high levels of moral legitimacy. Credentials operate on the basis of what is perceived to be a regulated and largely meritocratic process of allocation, unlike ascriptive characteristics, which are assigned at birth. Credentials are thus viewed as a reasonable basis on which to determine status and access to opportunity. With respect to the specific case of the criminal credential, individuals are routinely—and legally—denied access to jobs, housing, educational loans, welfare benefits, political participation, and other key social goods solely on the basis of their criminal background. Although rules vary across states as to when and where such restrictions apply, it is clear that the range of opportunities that become off-limits to those with criminal records enable a powerful form of social disenfranchisement.[31] The legitimacy of these status characteristics is reinforced by assumptions of personal initiative (or personal culpability) in the acquisition of the credential and by the institutional authority with which the credentials are granted or imposed. It is the legitimacy of the credential that gives it its unquestioned influence.

Finally, despite the distinctiveness of these sources of differentiation, the content of ascriptive traits and achieved credentials often reveals substantial overlap. Particularly in cases where the certification of a particular status is largely overlapping with other status markers (e.g., race, gender), public assumptions about who is and is not a credential holder may become generalized or exaggerated. As discussed earlier, because blacks are so strongly associated with the population under correctional supervision, it becomes easy to assume that any given young black man is likely to have—or to be on his way to acquiring—a criminal record.[32] Invoking this formal category, then, can legitimate forms of social exclusion that, based on ascriptive characteristics alone, would be more difficult to justify.[33] In this way, negative credentials make possible a new rationale for exclusion in ways that reinforce and legitimate existing social cleavages.

Help Wanted

In the late 1960s and early 1970s, certain states, concerned about the lingering stigma attached to ex-offenders, passed legislation to protect ex-offenders from discrimination by employers. Though criminal records continued to be disseminated by state and local agencies, and employers retained the right to inquire into a job applicant's criminal background, these laws attempted to regulate the impact of this stigmatizing information. Laws in states such as Wisconsin, New York, and Hawaii caution employers that a criminal record may be considered in employment decisions only if the nature of the crime directly relates to the specific responsibilities of the job in question.[34] In these states, then, ex-offenders hold the status of a protected category, similar to that of racial minorities and other groups protected under Title VII of the Civil Rights Act. The decision to dismiss an applicant simply on the basis of a criminal record would be legally considered employment discrimination. The degree to which employers continue to discriminate against ex-offenders, even in the face of specific legal protections, is an important focus of the empirical analysis presented in chapter 4.

To some, the idea of describing an employer's decision not to hire an ex-offender as discrimination is naïve and short-sighted. The word "discrimination" carries the connotation of irrational, mean-spirited, prejudice-driven decision making. While some forms of discrimination are consistent with this description, discrimination can also be motivated by simple attempts at rational economic assessments. In the case of ex-offenders, employers may perceive numerous risks associated with these hires, thus motivating a rejection of ex-offender applicants regardless of the employer's personal feelings about ex-offenders as a group. We know, for example, that ex-offenders have on average lower levels of education, less work experience, and a higher incidence of substance abuse and mental health problems than members of the general population.[35] Each of these characteristics is arguably related to worker quality, and in some cases may be difficult to observe directly. Moreover, to the extent that the past is a strong predictor of the future, a conviction conveys some information about the likelihood of future illegal, dangerous, or debilitating forms of behavior. Employers thus have reason to be concerned about hiring ex-offenders.

Others would argue that employers hold exaggerated or outdated concerns about the ex-offender population. Whereas the mental image conjured up by reference to an ex-offender may be a violent murderer or rapist, the largest share of individuals being released from prison today are drug offenders, many of whom were incarcerated for first-time or non-violent offenses. Indeed, the composition of inmates has changed substantially as the net of criminal justice intervention has widened. Individuals leaving prison today are older, less likely to have been convicted of a violent offense, and more likely to be first-time offenders than those leaving prison in the early 1980s.[36] To the extent that the frequency and severity of criminal activity are among those components of the criminal character associated with labor market productivity, changes in the composition of inmates over the past three decades may have affected the relationship between incarceration history and worker quality.

At the same time, the costs of a poor hire are potentially much greater than the costs of overlooking a high-quality applicant, suggesting that even an exaggerated assessment of the specific risks posed by ex-offender employees may represent the most rational strategy. While this research does not attempt to evaluate the validity of employers' concerns, it recognizes that any policy designed to promote the employment of ex-offenders will have to address the real and perceived risks facing employers who hire individuals with criminal records.[37] Indeed, in chapter 7 I investigate the specific concerns employers may have in considering applicants with criminal records. Legal mandates notwithstanding, if employers' concerns are not addressed, the prospects for ex-offender employment will likely remain woefully inadequate for the growing influx of returning inmates actively seeking work. While lawmakers and the general public may see benefits in the employment of ex-offenders, it is the employer's assessment of the costs and benefits associated with such hires that will determine whether and how the credential of a criminal record will be invoked as a basis for hiring decisions.

Taking Stock

This chapter began by describing the complex array of labor market consequences that follow from our current system of mass incarceration: Prisons conceal inequality by removing disadvantaged workers, while simultaneously creating inequality by deepening the disadvantages these workers possess. The negative credentialing effects of incarceration trigger a range of legal and social restrictions on employment, creating substantial barriers to achieving economic self-sufficiency.

The rapid growth in prisons has likewise produced a heightened awareness of those most likely to be housed there. Assumptions about the criminality of young black males—based on real or distorted associations—may intensify negative reactions toward this group, coloring the reception of even those African Americans (the majority) who remain crime free.

A final question left unresolved in this discussion is to what degree these arguments hold in real employment situations. Certainly we can imagine many ways in which the stigmas of incarceration and minority status produce all sorts of debilitating barriers. But there is not a lot of direct evidence as to whether or to what degree they actually do. Debates about the consequences of incarceration have been obscured by a lack of reliable, credible evidence. In large part, this omission is the result of inadequate measurement techniques for detecting the causal effects of incarceration, leaving the field open for wild speculation. In the following chapter, I discuss the methodological complexities inherent to the measurement of racial and criminal stigma and propose an experimental field methodology as a tool well-suited to contribute to this important discussion.

3 Measuring the Labor Market Consequences of Incarceration

Figuring out just how to study the effects of incarceration is indeed complex. Questions of causality and generalizability plague research in this area, making it difficult to establish strong claims about the relationship between criminal justice contact and subsequent employment opportunities. Some researchers argue that incarceration has only a negligible impact on future employment outcomes, with observed disparities resulting largely from the preexisting characteristics of offenders themselves. Others posit a direct and significant effect of criminal sanctions on postrelease employment and earnings. Resolving the conceptual and empirical claims in this debate is critical to understanding the impact of our criminal justice policies and to developing informed responses to the problems posed by large-scale incarceration and release.

The empirical core of this book takes one step toward resolving this debate by conducting a field experiment on the effects of a criminal record for employment outcomes. Why a field experiment? Experiments offer a powerful technique for addressing questions of causality, central to understanding whether a criminal record itself (as opposed to any other associated characteristics of offenders) produces the negative employment outcomes we observe. Locating the experiment within the context of real-life job searches increases our ability to generalize the results to a broader population of interest.

Of course, an experiment is only one of a number of available approaches to investigating the labor market consequences of incarceration. Before addressing the experimental method in detail, I first consider the broader range of methodological strategies and dilemmas relevant to studying the labor market consequences of incarceration.

An Emerging Field of Research

Until recently, the links between prison and work had not been a major focus of research by sociologists or criminologists. In part because of data limitations, and in part because of traditional boundaries between research on the criminal justice system and research on labor markets, studies of the employment consequences of incarceration remained few and far between. Fortunately, what literature does exist draws from a diversity of approaches, allowing for a wide-ranging discussion and critique of the techniques available for studying these issues. With research in this area now garnering more interest, this discussion can also serve as a guide to incomplete or unanswered questions for future work to address.

The four primary methods that have been used in the existing research literature include surveys of employers, ethnographic studies of the jobless, statistical analyses of employment patterns, and experimental studies of hiring behavior. While no single method can offer an exhaustive assessment, together they provide multiple complementary perspectives on the barriers to employment facing ex-offenders.[1] The following discussion considers each approach in turn, focusing on each method's ability to address the key concerns of causality (does incarceration *cause* poor employment outcomes?) and generalizability (can we generalize from the results of the study to the larger population of interest?). After considering the range of methodological approaches, I then turn to an in-depth discussion of the experimental audit methodology, an approach that, despite its infrequent use in studies of employment, offers a number of unique advantages for evaluating the causal effects of racial and criminal stigma.

Non-experimental Methods for Studying the Labor Market Consequences of Incarceration

Surveys of Employer Attitudes

In seeking to understand whether employers are willing to hire ex-offenders, one straightforward approach is simply to ask them. Indeed, a handful of employer surveys have explored these issues and have found, for the most part, a strong reluctance on the part of employers to hire applicants with criminal histories.[2] Economist Harry Holzer estimates that fully two-thirds of employers would not knowingly hire an ex-offender; other employer surveys have come to similar conclusions. The barriers to employment facing ex-offenders are thus readily apparent in the frank negative reactions expressed by employers.

The primary advantage of survey techniques for measuring employer attitudes is the ease with which large numbers of diverse employers can be recruited for participation. In addition to enhancing the generalizability of the survey results, the large sample sizes afforded by survey techniques allow researchers to look for patterns in employer attitudes across a range of relevant characteristics. For example, some survey research suggests that employer attitudes vary by type of occupation, with sales and clerical jobs placing greater restrictions on ex-offenders than do operative or laborer positions.[3] Likewise, as I show in chapter 7, surveys can explore variation in employers' attitudes according to a range of employer characteristics (e.g., size of firm, race of employer, racial composition of workforce) and applicant characteristics (e.g., race, type of crime, type of sanction). With relatively little additional cost, surveys can investigate a wide range of issues relevant to employers' attitudes, practices, and experiences regarding hiring ex-offenders. Indeed, few other methods offer the scope of information that surveys can provide.

The main limitation of survey research stems from its reliance on accurate reporting by respondents. Though employers in general do not seem reluctant to express negative views about hiring ex-offenders, as the above discussion suggests, there remains some ambiguity in interpreting exactly how employer attitudes may correspond to subsequent behavior.[4] Small differences in question wording can yield substantially different estimates, leaving some uncertainty as to the substantive conclusions to be drawn. Though most recent surveys have found fairly consistent negative attitudes about hiring ex-offenders, a 1979 review of eleven employer surveys found wide variation in the reported attitudes of employers, ranging from a low of 6 percent to a high of 51 percent of employers who were unwilling to hire ex-offenders.[5] This wide range of employer responses leaves substantial ambiguity as to how strong or prevalent employers' reluctance to hire ex-offenders may be. One possible explanation for the discrepancies across surveys is that they reflect a genuine ambivalence on the part of employers. Indeed, employers may be reacting to multiple, competing concerns, including but not limited to their need for labor and their concern about the potential for trouble in hiring ex-offenders. Each of these concerns may be more or less salient at different times (e.g., in tight/slack labor markets), perhaps leading to fluctuation in survey responses. At the same time, when responses differ across items or across surveys, it becomes difficult to assess whether changing response patterns reflect real variation in attitudes or whether they are simply an artifact of question wording. Rather than comparing results across distinct studies, then, a more reliable use of employer surveys looks to repeated item use to assess variability across contexts or changes in attitudes over time based on a common measurement tool. Survey results serve better as measures of *relative* preferences than as reliable estimates of absolute employer demand.

A second disadvantage of survey research is its limited ability to capture racial attitudes that may bear upon or interact with attitudes about ex-offenders. Because race is such a sensitive topic, especially to employers, it is difficult to elicit honest and accurate self-reports. As a result, few of the surveys investigating employer attitudes about ex-offenders have included race as a topic of consideration.[6] Though there exist techniques thought to increase the accuracy of survey measures of racial attitudes, even the subtle priming of race can be sufficient to distort survey responses in ways that mask racial concerns.[7]

Surveys can thus offer a valuable overview of the range of concerns employers have in considering ex-offender employees. Translating measures of employer attitudes into actual hiring outcomes and assessing how these outcomes may vary by race, however, typically require additional measures from an alternative methodological approach.

Interview-Based and Ethnographic Accounts

Turning from the perspectives of employers to the experiences of job seekers, research using in-depth interviews or ethnography—a method based on detailed, firsthand observation—provides rich and textured accounts of some of the struggles ex-offenders experience as they attempt to reestablish lives and jobs on the outside. Mercer Sullivan's study of youth involvement in crime and work, for example, based on in-depth interviews and extensive observation of the lives and communities of roughly forty black, Hispanic, and white youths, finds some direct evidence for the harmful effects of criminal sanctions. Indeed, several of the young men in his study experienced employment difficulties that appeared to be directly related to their criminal justice involvement. "Gaspar Cruz lost one job that he had held for a year after his employer found out that he had been in jail . . . Miguel Tirado lost four different jobs in the course of a six-month period during which he had to make weekly court appearances. He did not want to tell his employers that he had to go to court and could not otherwise explain his absences."[8] These cases point to both the stigma and disruption associated with criminal justice interventions. Though other young men in Sullivan's study were able to find work through ex-offender employment services or personal networks, those who did not have access to such resources struggled to find steady jobs.

Other studies, while not focused primarily on the experiences of ex-offenders, have touched on themes of crime and employment as they emerge in the lives of their subjects. Most of the twenty-six young black men in Alford Young's interview-based study had experienced brushes with the law, the effects of which Young views as crushing for their future job prospects. "Nothing created as great a stigma for them than the possession of a criminal record. Each knew very well that a record was a severe detriment to finding work."[9] Likewise, Mitchell Duneier's study of mainly unhoused street vendors in New York City documents the importance of the criminal justice system in the lives of the men he studied, more than a third of whom had spent time in state or federal prison for drug-related crimes. Duneier explains, "After [the completion of their sentences], they are released and come directly to the streets. In most cases, family ties have been shattered by their past behavior. Neither state nor federal prisons are organized to help ex-convicts make smooth transitions into homes and jobs." With few resources at their disposal, many of these men make their way to the streets, cobbling together a subsistence in the informal economy.[10]

These accounts offer thick description of their subjects' lives, helping to piece together stories with numerous interconnected threads. The richness of ethnographic work provides nuance and detail that helps us to visualize the complicated pathways of any individual life. At the same time, however, this complexity rules out simple conclusions about the net impact of any single factor. Sullivan, for example, emphasizes the detrimental effects of formal criminal sanctions, while at the same time acknowledging the many personal characteristics that also impeded ex-offenders' chances at finding and keeping a job. "They found themselves hampered by their involvement in crime and the criminal justice system *and* by the personal habits developed during years of being out of work, out of school, and on the streets."[11] Likewise, Duneier is appropriately cautious in drawing conclusions about the rocky path of prisoner reentry. After considering the harmful absence of social services available to men leaving prison, he cautions, "At the same time ... we must also acknowledge some uncertainty as to the extent to which these [structural] forces are determinative in the outcome of any life. ... Individual factors also have an influence."[12] Indeed, the multiple disadvantages present in the lives of each of these subjects–including histories of drug or alcohol abuse, unstable housing, poor social supports, and a criminal record— make difficult any attempt to isolate the effect of a single causal variable.

Statistical Analyses of Employment Trajectories

As one means of disentangling the complicated web of influences that affect individual life trajectories, a third line of research relies on statistical techniques to identify reliable patterns in the experiences and outcomes of individuals with varying characteristics. Large-scale longitudinal surveys, for example, which track individuals at regular intervals over a number of years, allow researchers to observe changes in labor market outcomes associated with time spent in prison. As with the other approaches discussed in this chapter, research in this area has been limited. Few large-scale surveys include information about both labor market experiences and criminal justice involvement, thus constraining the availability of data for investigations of the relationship between the two. Nevertheless, a handful of studies have been able to exploit available data resources to conduct relevant analyses. For the most part, these studies have focused on unemployment and earnings as primary indicators of the economic consequences of arrest or incarceration. Statistically controlling for the social and demographic characteristics associated with both incarceration and employment (such as educational attainment, age, race, marital status, and region), these analyses attempt to isolate the effects of criminal justice contact on subsequent labor market outcomes.

The weight of the evidence from this line of work suggests a significant decline in employment following spells of incarceration, consistent with the notion that contact with the criminal justice system imposes lingering negative consequences. Economist Richard Freeman, for example, using longitudinal survey data on a cohort of young men with rich controls for schooling, labor market experience, marital status, and drug/alcohol use, estimates that youth incarceration is associated with a 25 to 30 percent decline in average annual weeks worked.[13] Though roughly a third of this effect can be attributed to recidivism (or return incarceration), there remains a substantial drop in employment associated with the lasting effects of incarceration. Sociologists Bruce Western and Katherine Beckett find that youth incarceration reduces employment by more than 5 percent, with effects that continue to register ten to fifteen years later. Adult incarceration is associated with nearly twice as large an effect on employment, though these effects diminish substantially over the subsequent five years.[14] This and other research supports the perspective that criminal sanctions are associated with lower levels of employment and earnings. (Several notable exceptions are discussed below.)

To date, few quantitative studies investigating the consequences of incarceration have included sufficient numbers of minority sample members to explore possible differences in the effects of incarceration by race. The small body of existing research arrives at varied and inconclusive results.[15] Incarceration thus appears to be strongly related to labor market outcomes, but it is not clear whether or how these effects may vary by race.

This existing research has been instrumental in demonstrating the strong association between incarceration and a range of labor market outcomes. The large sample sizes allow researchers to statistically control for many of the competing explanations for employment difficulties (e.g., low levels of education, lack of work experience), and nationally representative samples allow researchers to generalize more readily to the population of interest. At the same time, however, certain fundamental limitations of survey data leave the conclusions of this research vulnerable to criticism. First, it is difficult, using survey data, to rule out the possibility that unmeasured differences between those who are and are not convicted of crimes may drive the observed results. Though statistical models attempt to control for relevant differences between groups, survey data rarely provide adequate measures of the many hypothetical differences that could account for observed disparities between groups. High levels of substance abuse, poor interpersonal skills, and behavioral problems, for example, represent just a few of the many characteristics (virtually untestable using survey data) that lead ex-offenders to be differentially selected into incarceration and likewise to lead them to struggle in finding work.

Consistent with these selection arguments, a few studies have found little or no effect of incarceration once the characteristics of individual offenders were adequately controlled. These studies have typically used administrative data to track individuals before and after incarceration, matching records of employment and earnings from unemployment insurance files with records from state or federal departments of corrections. Comparing preincarceration employment with employment rates several years after the completion of a prison term, several researchers conclude that the observed association is instead largely determined by unmeasured individual characteristics that predispose those in prison to poor employment outcomes.[16] The findings of these authors stand in stark contrast to the literature discussed earlier that asserts a strong link between incarceration and poor employment outcomes. It thus remains an open question whether and to what extent incarceration causes employment difficulties.

Unfortunately, survey research is poorly equipped to offer a definitive answer. The Achilles heel of the survey methodology is its inability to escape from the problems of selection that plague research in this field.[17]

A second, related limitation of survey research is its inability to identify specific mechanisms. From aggregate effects we can infer plausible causal processes, but these are only indirectly supported by the data. Because numerous mechanisms could lead to the same set of outcomes, we are left unable to assess the substantive contribution of any given causal process. As discussed in chapter 2, a range of mechanisms could account for the employment problems of ex-offenders, including the credentialing effects of incarceration; legal barriers to employment; the loss of human capital; institutional trauma; the disruption of social and familial ties; the influence on social networks; and, of course, the possibility that all incarceration effects may be entirely spurious.[18] Without direct measures of these variables, it is difficult to discern which, if any, of these causal explanations may be at work.

Experimental Approaches to Studying Criminal Stigma

As a means of directly testing the mechanisms by which incarceration exerts its effects, a few researchers have turned to an experimental approach. Experimental methods provide a powerful means of isolating some of the causal pathways through which incarceration may affect employment. Though very few studies have made use of these techniques for studying the effects of criminal sanctions, the approach represents one of the most effective strategies for establishing causal effects in this and other domains. In particular, experimental methods can help us separate arguments about the credentialing effects of a criminal record from the selection arguments discussed earlier.

Traditional experiments typically begin with clearly defined "treatment" and "control" conditions to which subjects are randomly assigned (random assignment helps to remove the influence of any respondent characteristics that may affect the outcomes by breaking the link between respondent characteristics and selection into treatment conditions). All other environmental influences are carefully controlled. A specific outcome variable is then recorded to test for differences between groups. Often subjects are not told the purpose of the experiment to ensure a naïve or "natural" reaction to the experimental condition.

Field experiments blend experimental methods with field-based research, relaxing certain controls over environmental influences in order to better simulate real-world interactions. While retaining the key experimental features of matching and random assignment important for inferences of causality, this approach relies on real contexts (e.g., actual employment searches, real estate markets, consumer transactions) for its staged measurement techniques. Field experiments of this kind, also referred to as audit studies, were pioneered in the 1970s when the Department of Housing and Urban Development conducted a series of audits to test for racial discrimination in real estate markets.[19] The approach has since been applied to numerous settings, including mortgage applications, housing markets, negotiations at a car dealership, and hailing a taxi.[20] In the case of employment, two main types of audit studies offer useful approaches: correspondence tests and in-person audits.

Correspondence Tests

The correspondence test approach, so named for its simulation of the communication (correspondence) between job applicants and employers, relies on fictitious matched résumés submitted to employers by mail or fax. In these studies, two or more résumés reflecting equal levels of education and experience are prepared. The experimental condition (e.g., criminal record, race) of the fictitious applicant is then signaled through one or more cues; for example, a criminal record may be signaled by reporting work experience gained within a correctional facility, or by listing one's parole officer as a reference (see chapter 4 for a discussion of this specific example). Experimental and control conditions are randomly varied across résumé types over the course of the study (i.e., a criminal record is assigned to résumé A for half the employers and to résumé B for the other half); this is to ensure that any differences between résumés will not be correlated with the measured effects of a criminal record or race. Reactions from employers are then typically measured by written responses (to staged mailing addresses) or callbacks (to voice mail boxes) for each applicant.

Though most correspondence studies have been used to investigate racial discrimination in employment, there have been a limited number of studies that have adopted an experimental approach to the study of criminal stigma. The most notable in this line of research is a classic study by Richard Schwartz and Jerome Skolnick in which the researchers prepared four sets of résumés to be presented to prospective employers for an unskilled hotel job. The four conditions included: (1) an applicant who had been convicted and sentenced for assault; (2) an applicant who had been tried for assault but acquitted; (3) an applicant who had been tried for assault, acquitted, *and* had a letter from the judge certifying the applicant's acquittal and emphasizing the presumption of innocence; and (4) an applicant who had no criminal record. Employers' interest in candidates declined as a function of severity of the criminal record, though in all three criminal conditions—even with a letter from the judge "certifying the finding of not guilty and reaffirming the legal presumption of innocence"—applicants were less likely to be considered by employers than the non-criminal control.[21] The findings of this study suggest that *mere contact* with the criminal justice system can have significant repercussions, with records of "arrest," "conviction," and "incarceration" conveying a stigma differing in degree but not kind. Several later studies, both in the United States and in other countries, have extended Schwartz and Skolnick's design.[22] Each of these studies reports the similar finding that, all else being equal, contact with the criminal justice system leads to worse employment opportunities.

The advantage of the correspondence test approach is that it requires no actual job applicants (only fictitious paper applicants). This is desirable for both methodological and practical reasons. Methodologically, the use of fictitious paper applicants allows researchers to create carefully matched applicant pairs without needing to accommodate the complexities of real people. The researcher thus has far more control over the precise content of treatment and control conditions. Practically, the reliance on paper applicants is also desirable in terms of the logistical ease with which the application process can be carried out. Rather than coordinating job visits by real people—creating the possibility of applicants getting lost or contacting the employer under unfavorable circumstances (such as when the employer is out to lunch or busy with a customer)—the correspondence test approach simply requires that résumés be sent out at specified intervals. Additionally, the small cost of postage and faxes is trivial compared to that involved in hiring people to pose as job applicants.

While correspondence tests do have many attractive features, there are also certain limitations of this design that have led some researchers to prefer the in-person audit approach. Because correspondence tests rely on paper applications only, all relevant target information must be conveyed without the visual cues of in-person contact. In testing the effects of certain characteristics, such as gender or ethnicity, researchers can easily convey the necessary information using gender-specific or ethnically identifiable names.[23] In the case of age discrimination, several studies have relied on high school graduation dates to convey the applicants' ages.[24] In testing the effects of race, by contrast, written materials provide a more limited resource. One recent correspondence test measuring racial discrimination, for example, was criticized for its attempt to use racially distinctive names to signal the race of applicants. In this study names like "Jamal" and "Lakisha" signaled African Americans, while "Greg" and "Emily" were associated with whites. While these names are reliably associated with their intended race groups, some critics argued that the more distinctive African American names are also associated with lower socioeconomic status, thus confounding the effects of race and class. Indeed, mother's education is a significant (negative) predictor of a child having a distinctively African American name.[25] The use of names to test for black-white differences, then, is complicated by the social context in which racially distinctive names are situated. Directly assessing these connotations/associations is an important first step in developing the materials necessary for a strong test of discrimination.[26] Perhaps in part the result of these difficulties, the field experiment–based research on the effects of a criminal record has generally overlooked the role of race as a conditioning variable.[27] This is an unfortunate limitation of existing research, given that nearly half of all returning inmates today are African American.

Another important limitation of the correspondence test method relates to the types of jobs available for testing. The type of application procedure used in correspondence tests—sending résumés by mail—is typically reserved for studies of administrative, clerical, and other white-collar occupations. The vast majority of entry-level jobs, by contrast, require in-person applications. For jobs such as busboy, messenger, laborer, or cashier, a mailed-in résumé would appear out of place. Schwartz and Skolnick's study addressed this problem by presenting applications to employers through an intermediary—a researcher posing as an employment counselor. This "mediated audit" approach provides one strategy for presenting unskilled applicants to employers; but it requires the introduction of an added layer of fiction, which may detract from the realism of the experiment. Recall also that Schwartz and Skolnick's study included only a single job type (an unskilled hotel job). By contrast, for most low-wage employment, in-person application procedures are the standard and preferred approach. While in-person audit studies also face a restricted range of job openings (see appendix 4A), in-person application procedures typically allow for a substantially wider pool than can be achieved through paper applications alone.

In-Person Audit Studies

The use of in-person audits, as opposed to mail-in résumés, represents a more elaborate simulation of the hiring process.[28] These audits involve the use of matched pairs of individuals (called testers) who pose as job applicants in real job searches. Applicants are carefully matched on the basis of age, race, physical appearance, interpersonal style, and any other characteristics to which employers may respond in making hiring decisions. As with correspondence tests, résumés are constructed for each applicant that reflect equal levels of schooling and work experience. In addition, testers must receive intensive training and supervision to ensure that their interactions with employers convey comparable information. Though in-person audits are time-consuming and require high levels of supervision, the approach offers several advantages over correspondence studies. In-person audits provide a clear means of signaling race; they allow for a wide sample of entry-level job types; and they provide the opportunity to gather both quantitative and qualitative data, with information on whether or not the applicant gets the job as well as how s/he is treated during the interview process. Indeed, one of the attractive features of the in-person audit design is its ability to measure a wide range of outcome variables. While the primary outcome variable is typically a quantitative indicator of positive response by the employer (a callback or job offer), the audit process can also detect a number of more subtle indicators of differential treatment. In some cases, for example, testers are channeled into jobs other than the ones originally advertised (e.g., jobs requiring less customer contact or more manual labor). In other cases, employers may make revealing comments in the course of a conversation or interview. Tracking the level of attention, encouragement, or hostility testers elicit can provide important information about the experiential aspects of the job-seeking process. Indeed, by observing the kinds of treatment testers receive in their ongoing job searches, one can identify the experiences that may lead certain workers to become discouraged from seeking work altogether.

Experimental approaches to studying hiring behavior thus provide a number of appealing features. Random assignment of a criminal record across applications allows for a strong test of the effect of criminal status on employers' decisions. At the same time, the real-life contexts of actual job searches increases the generalizability of the results. We can thus draw strong conclusions about the actual hiring behavior of real employers. It is important to note, however, that conclusions about employer behavior are based on aggregate patterns rather than individual employers. Because the standard design of an audit study for research purposes typically includes no more than a single audit per employer, *it is not possible to draw conclusions about the discriminatory tendencies of any given employer.* Indeed, even in the complete absence of discrimination, an employer confronted with two equivalent candidates will choose the dominant group applicant (e.g., the white applicant or the nonoffender) 50 percent of the time. Using a single test of each employer, therefore, does not allow for individual-level assessments of discrimination; only by looking at systematic patterns across a large number of employers can we determine whether hiring appears to be influenced by race or other stigmatizing characteristics.[29] The point of research-based audit studies, therefore, is to assess the prevalence of discrimination across the labor market, rather than to target particular sites of discrimination.

For those readers interested in the nuts and bolts of audit design, I include a lengthy discussion in appendix 4A. For the remainder of this chapter, I turn to a consideration of the possible critiques of the audit methodology. Indeed, while the audit methodology is widely considered the gold standard for measuring employment discrimination, it has several vulnerabilities that deserve careful consideration.

Critiques of the Audit Method

While most researchers view the audit methodology as the most effective means of measuring discrimination, the approach is not without its critics. Economist James Heckman is among the most vocal, particularly when the methodology is used to study the effects of race. Heckman's primary criticism focuses on the problems of effective matching.[30] The validity of an audit study relies on its success in presenting two otherwise equally qualified job applicants who differ only in one key characteristic (e.g., race, criminal background). Given the vast number of characteristics that can influence an employer's evaluation, however, it is difficult to ensure that all such dimensions have been effectively controlled. Fortunately, in testing for the effect of a criminal record (or other nonembodied characteristics), random assignment of the treatment condition can effectively address these concerns. Because testers are able to alternate serving in each condition (e.g., with and without the criminal record), any remaining differences within the tester pairs effectively cancel out over the duration of the study. The same individuals serve as both treatment and control, ensuring that any other fixed characteristics of the testers will be randomly distributed across conditions. Characteristics such as race, however, cannot be experimentally assigned. Instead, researchers must rely on effective selection and matching to construct audit pairs that represent comparable candidates with respect to all relevant characteristics—something that, according to Heckman, leaves substantial room for bias. Heckman's primary critique focuses on the problem of unobservables—those characteristics "unobservable to the audit study [researchers], but... at least somewhat visible to the prospective employer and acted on in hiring . . . decisions." According to Heckman, blacks and whites (at the population level) may differ in the average and/or distribution of important characteristics. As an example, consider a hypothetical case in which whites on average have a faster response time in interview interactions than blacks. That is to say, the delay in seconds between a question posed by an interviewer and the initiation of response is shorter on average for whites than for blacks. (To be sure, response times are just one potential example, and I emphasize that it is a case that to my knowledge has no empirical basis. Heckman himself does not suggest any concrete examples of potentially relevant unobservables that could affect hiring outcomes; but it is instructive to consider a concrete hypothetical case for the purpose of clarity.) Because any difference in response time would be extremely subtle, it may not be immediately recognizable to researchers; and may even register for employers only at a subliminal level. Nevertheless, if this trait produces an incremental advantage for the individual with a faster response time—because he is perceived as sharper or more engaged—we may mistake the employer's response for discrimination when in fact nonracial evaluations are driving the differential response.

A related problem emerges if blacks and whites differ on key characteristics, not on the average, but in the level of dispersion. To continue with the same example, imagine a case in which blacks and whites each have a mean response time of 0.5 seconds, but blacks demonstrate greater heterogeneity along this dimension than whites. Differential results may then be observed depending on the overall qualifications of the testers relative to the requirements of the job. If testers are highly qualified for the positions they apply for (which tends to be the case in audit studies), differential dispersion on any key variable will favor the group with lower dispersion (because a smaller proportion of applicants in the low-dispersion group will be at the low end of the tail relative to a high-dispersion group).

Heckman's critique raises some important considerations and encourages a more rigorous scrutiny of the audit methodology. In each case, it is worth considering when and how these concerns can be effectively addressed. Heckman's primary concern is that if, on average, blacks and whites differ in the mean or variance on any unobserved productivity-related variable, estimates from matched-pair studies will be biased by design. If auditors were randomly drawn from the population and matched on a rote basis according to readily measurable characteristics, this critique would surely be valid. It is a mistake, however, to assume that the researcher is at a necessary disadvantage relative to the employer in identifying productivity-related characteristics. In fact, the researcher is her/himself an employer in the planning and implementation of an audit study. The job of a tester is not an easy one, and finding a suitable team to complete this type of project requires extensive screening and careful selection. The job requires solid writing skills (for the written narratives that follow each audit); good communication skills (to communicate the necessary information in an interview and to make a favorable impression on the employer); high levels of motivation (to keep up day after day); reliability (to conduct and report each test accurately); navigation skills (to find locations throughout the city); and an endless number of other qualifications. Thus, apart from the more explicit traits of height, weight, race, and age, researchers must search for testers who can perform well in an intensely demanding position.[31] As an employer, the researcher must identify subtle cues about applicants that indicate their ability to perform. Whether or not these cues are explicit, conscious, or measurable, they are as present in a researcher's evaluation of tester candidates as they are for employers' evaluations of entry-level job applicants. Like other employers, researchers are affected by both objective and subjective/subconscious indicators of applicant quality in their selection and matching of testers in ways that should ultimately improve the nuanced calibration of test partners.

A related concern of Heckman's has to do with the possibility that matching (even when done successfully) may itself produce distortions in the hiring process. Because audit partners are matched on all characteristics that are most directly relevant to the hiring process (education, work experience, physical appearance, etc.), employers may be forced to privilege relatively minor characteristics simply in order to break the tie. "By taking out the common components that are most easily measured, differences in hiring rates as monitored by audits arise from the idiosyncratic factors, and not the main factors, that drive actual labor markets."[32] If employers care only marginally about race or criminal background but are confronted with two applicants equal on all other dimensions, this single characteristic may take on greater significance in that particular hiring decision than it would under normal circumstances, when evaluating real applicants who differ on multiple dimensions.

Again, this critique is important, though in this case it is one that can be addressed more easily. If the only outcome of interest in an audit study is whether or not an applicant gets the job, Heckman's concerns become directly relevant. If forced to choose a single hire, employers will use whatever basis for differentiation exists, whether that particular attribute is valued highly or not. Audit studies that measure callbacks as an outcome variable, by contrast, avoid situations in which employers must choose only one applicant. In fact, the employers in this study interviewed an average of eight applicants for each entry-level job they filled.[33] If race and criminal background represent only minor concerns for employers, we would expect both members of an audit pair to make it through the first cut. To the extent that race or criminal background figures prominently even in these early rounds of review, we can infer that this characteristic has been invoked as more than a mere tie breaker. In these cases, the evidence of race-based (or criminal record–based) decision making is quite strong.

A third important critique of the audit methodology points to the problem of experimenter effects, or the possibility that the expectations or behaviors of testers can influence the audit results in nonrandom ways. For example, if a tester expects to be treated poorly by employers, he may appear more withdrawn, nervous, or defensive in interactions. The nature of the interaction may then create a self-fulfilling prophecy in which the tester experiences poor outcomes, but for reasons unrelated to the exper- imental condition (e.g., his criminal record). Indeed, the possibility of experimenter effects represents one of the most serious threats to the validity of the audit experiment. While there is no way to conclusively rule out the possibility of experimenter effects, several precautions can be taken to minimize the problem. First, effective training and super- vision are critical to the successful implementation of an audit study. Testers must be so familiar with their assumed profiles and the audit protocol that appropriate responses to employer queries become almost automatic. Extensive role playing, videotaped interviews, and practice audits help testers to become comfortable with their roles and to gain important feedback on their performance. Likewise, during the course of the fieldwork, daily debriefings and regular troubleshooting sessions are critical to identify any potential problems or to refine the protocol in ways that best suit the specifics of the study. Finally, after the fieldwork is completed, it is possible to conduct an indirect check on the problem of experimenter effects. Typically, a number of tests are conducted with little or no in-person contact, because the employer either is not present or does not have time to meet with the applicant. By comparing audit outcomes for testers who did and did not interact with employers, we can assess the degree to which in-person interaction leads to a different distribution of results. If testers are acting in ways that fulfill their expec- tations of discrimination, we would expect outcomes for those tests con- ducted with interaction to show greater evidence of differential treatment than those without. If the results are equivalent, or show weaker evidence of differential treatment, we can be more confident that experimenter effects are not driving the results. In appendix 4A I discuss such a comparison from the results of the audit experiment presented in chapter 4.

Critiques of the audit methodology point out the possible vulnerabilities of this approach and remind us that the experimental design on its own does not automatically protect against threats to the internal or external validity of the results. Indeed, audit studies require painstaking planning and supervision in order to simulate real-world hiring interactions within the framework of a carefully controlled experiment. At the same time, with sufficient care and attention to detail, it is possible to anticipate and address many of the potential problems that can arise in the design and implementation of an audit study. When properly implemented, audit studies can provide among the most rigorous measures available for assessing the effects of a criminal record and race on employment outcomes.

Conclusion

While no research method is without flaws, careful consideration of the range of methods available helps to match one's research question with the appropriate empirical strategy. The body of research investigating the labor market consequences of incarceration includes surveys of employers, interview-based and ethnographic work, statistical analyses, and field experiments. Each of these approaches provides a unique vantage point from which to assess the possible effects of incarceration; across the range of perspectives—from job seeker to employer, micro to macro—we can begin to piece together a more complete assessment of the pathways from prison to work.

In the following chapters, I discuss the specific design and results of an audit study testing for discrimination on the basis of race and criminal background in Milwaukee. Despite its complexities, the audit method remains one of the most effective approaches to measuring discrimination in real-world settings. By participating in actual job searches, and by simulating the application process of real job seekers, we can get as close as possible to the interactions that produce discrimination in contemporary labor markets. While the audit design cannot address all relevant aspects of labor market disadvantage, it can provide strong and direct measures of discrimination at the point of hire, a powerful mechanism regulating the broader array of labor market opportunities.

4 The Mark of a Criminal Record

Incarceration is intended to serve as punishment for individuals who have broken the law. And yet, there is reason to believe that the punishing effects of prison do not end upon an inmate's release. Rather, information about an individual's experience with the criminal justice system can be widely accessed by prospective employers, landlords, and creditors, extending the reach of the criminal justice system into the wider arenas of domestic and business affairs. To the extent that this information results in the exclusion of ex-offenders from valuable social and economic opportunities, individuals face what is akin to double jeopardy: being punished more than once for the same crime.

As it turns out, however, assessing the impact of a criminal record is not altogether straightforward. On the one hand, it's not hard to imagine that a prison record would itself carry a weighty stigma, with members of the general public (employers included) reluctant to associate or work with those bearing this mark of ill-repute. On the other hand, criminal offenders aren't typically the image of the model employee. It's certainly possible that the poor employment outcomes of ex-offenders stem from the personal characteristics of the offenders themselves rather than from any official record of criminal conviction. Poor work habits, substance abuse problems, or deficient interpersonal skills may be sufficient to explain the employment disadvantages of ex-offenders without any added impact of a formal state sanction. Simply observing that ex-offenders do worse in the labor market than nonoffenders does little to help us understand why.

Given the difficulties inherent to evaluating the impact of incarceration through conventional measures, I set out to investigate this issue by constructing an experiment. I wanted to bracket the range of personal characteristics associated with ex-offenders in order to hone in on the causal impact of a criminal record.[1] The experimental audit methodology allowed me to do just that. Using this approach, I pose the question: Given two equally qualified job applicants, how much does a criminal record affect the chances of being selected by an employer? In answering this question, we can begin to understand the ways in which the official marker of a criminal record shapes and constrains important economic opportunities.

Study Design

As discussed in the previous chapter, the basic design of an experimental employment audit involves sending matched pairs of individuals (called testers) to apply for real job openings in order to see whether employers respond differently to applicants on the basis of selected characteristics. The current study included four male testers, two blacks and two whites, matched into two teams—the two black testers formed one team, and the two white testers formed the second team (see figure 4.1).[2] The testers were college students from Milwaukee who were matched on the basis of age, race, physical appearance, and general style of self-presentation. The testers were assigned fictitious résumés that reflected equivalent levels of education and work experience. In addition, within each team, one auditor was randomly assigned a criminal record for the first week; the pair then rotated which member presented himself as the ex-offender for each successive week of employment searches, such that each tester served in the criminal record condition for an equal number of cases. By varying which member of the pair presented himself as having a criminal record, unobserved differences within the pairs of applicants were effectively controlled.

I identified job openings for entry-level positions (jobs requiring no previous experience and no education beyond high school) from the Sunday classified advertisement section of the *Milwaukee Journal Sentinel*. In addition, I drew a supplemental sample from Jobnet, a state-sponsored Web site for employment listings that was developed in connection with the W-2 Welfare-to-Work initiatives.[3] I excluded from the sample those occupations with legal restrictions on ex-offenders, such as jobs in the health care industry, work with children and the elderly, jobs requiring the handling of firearms (e.g., security guards), and jobs in the public sector.

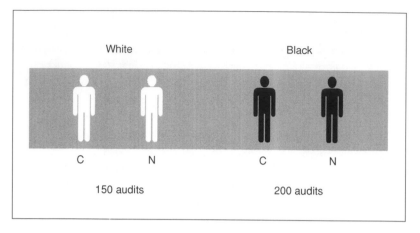

Figure 4.1 Audit design. C = criminal record; N = no criminal record.

Of course, any true estimate of the collateral consequences of incarceration would also need to take account of the wide range of employment fully off-limits to individuals with felony convictions.

Each week I randomly assigned the audit pairs fifteen entry-level job openings. The white pair and the black pair were assigned separate sets of jobs, with the same-race testers applying to the same jobs. One member of the pair applied first, with the second applying one day later (randomly varying whether the ex-offender was first or second). A total of 350 employers were audited during the course of this study: 150 by the white pair and 200 by the black pair. Additional tests were performed by the black pair because black testers received fewer callbacks on average, and there were thus fewer data points with which to draw comparisons. A larger sample size enables the calculation of more precise estimates of the effects under investigation.

Immediately following the completion of each job application, testers filled out a six-page response form that coded relevant information from the test. Important variables included type of occupation, metropolitan status, wage, size of establishment, and race and sex of the interviewer. Additionally, testers wrote detailed narratives describing the overall interaction, and recording any comments made by employers (or statements on application forms) specifically related to race or criminal records.

It is important to note that the study focused only on the first stage of the employment process. Testers visited employers, filled out applications, and proceeded as far as they could during the course of one visit. If testers were asked to interview on the spot, they did so, but they did not return to the employer for a second visit. The primary outcome of interest, then, is the proportion of applications that elicited callbacks from employers. Individual voice mail boxes were set up for each tester to record employer responses. If a tester was offered the job on the spot, this was also coded as a positive response.[4] I focus only on this initial stage of the employment process because it is the stage likely to be most affected by the marker of a criminal record. Early on, employers have the least individualizing information about the applicant, and are thus more likely to generalize on the basis of group-level (stereotyped) characteristics. As a parallel case, for example, a recent audit study of age discrimination found that 76 percent of the measured differential treatment occurred at this first stage of the employment process.[5] Given that a criminal record, like age, is a highly salient characteristic, it is likely that as much, if not more, of the overall effect of criminal stigma will be detected at this stage.

A second advantage of the callback—rather than the job offer—as our key outcome variable is that it does not require employers to narrow their selection down to a single applicant. At the job offer stage, if presented with an ex-offender and an equally qualified nonoffender, even employers with little concern over hiring ex-offenders would likely select the applicant with no criminal record, arguably a safer choice. Equating the two applicants could in fact magnify the impact of the criminal record, as it becomes the only remaining basis for selection between the two.[6] The callback, by contrast, does not present such complications. Typically employers interview multiple candidates for entry-level positions before selecting a hire. In fact, in a subsequent survey employers in this study reported interviewing an average of eight applicants for the last entry-level position filled. At the callback stage, then, employers need not yet choose between the ex-offender and nonoffender. If the applicants appear well-qualified, and the employer does not view the criminal record as an automatic disqualifier, both can make it past this initial round of review.

Tester Profiles

In developing the tester profiles, I emphasized characteristics that were both numerically representative and substantively important. The criminal record consisted of a felony drug conviction and eighteen months of served prison time.[7] I chose a drug crime (as opposed to a violent or property crime) because of its prevalence, its policy salience, and its connection to racial disparities in incarceration. The effects I report here may, of course, differ for other types of crimes.[8]

In assigning the educational and work history of testers, I sought a compromise between an accurate representation of real offenders and a background that made the applicants attractive to employers. Most audit studies of employment have created tester profiles that include some college experience, so that testers will be highly competitive applicants for entry-level jobs and so that the contrast between treatment and control group is made clear.[9] In the present study, however, postsecondary schooling experience would detract from the representativeness of the results. More than 70 percent of federal and nearly 90 percent of state prisoners have no more than a high school degree (or equivalent). I therefore chose to give testers a high school diploma, representing the largest category of offenders.[10]

There is little systematic evidence concerning the work histories of inmates prior to incarceration. Overall, 77 percent of federal and 67 percent of state inmates were employed prior to incarceration. There is, however, a substantial degree of heterogeneity in the quality and consistency of work experience during this time.[11] In the present study, I assigned testers favorable work histories, with steady work experience in entry-level jobs and nearly continual employment (until incarceration). In the job prior to incarceration (and, for the control group, prior to the last short-term job), testers reported having worked their way from an entry-level position to a supervisory role.[12] Although a supervisory position surpasses the modal occupational attainment for high school graduates (with or without criminal records), this feature was added to the tester profiles in order to make them more competitive applicants. The solid job histories of these applicants should affect the results in a conservative direction, offering cues about the tester's reliability and competence that may offset some of the negative associations of a criminal background.

The testers participated in an intensive training program to become familiar with the details of their assumed profile and to ensure uniform behavior in job interviews. The training period lasted for one week, during which testers participated in mock interviews with one another and practice interviews with cooperating employers. The testers were trained to respond to common interview questions in standardized ways and were well-rehearsed for a wide range of scenarios that emerge in employment situations. Frequent communication between the testers and me throughout each day of fieldwork allowed for regular supervision and trouble-shooting in the event of unexpected occurrences.

Design Issues

There are a number of complexities involved in the design and implementation of an audit study. Appendix 4A provides an overview of the general problems of implementation associated with research of this kind. In addition, there were several specific dilemmas posed in the development of the current study that required substantial deliberation. First, in standard audit studies of race or gender, it is possible to construct work histories for test partners in such a way that the amount of work experience reported by each tester is identical. In the present study, however, one applicant has spent eighteen months in prison. It was therefore necessary to manipulate the work histories of both applicants so that this labor market absence did not bias the results.[13] The solution opted for here was for the ex-offender to report six months of work experience gained while in prison (preceded by twelve months out of the labor force, representing the remainder of the total prison time). The nonoffender, on the other hand, reported graduating from high school one year later (thereby accounting for twelve months) and, concurrent with his partner's six months of prison work time, working for a temporary agency doing similar low-skill work. Thus, the actual amount of work experience was equivalent for both testers. The effect of having the nonoffender graduate from high school one year later should impose a conservative bias, as graduating from high school late may indicate less motivation or ability.

A second major difference from audit studies of race or gender is that criminal status is not something that can be immediately discerned by the employer. The information had to be explicitly conveyed, therefore, in order for the interaction to become a "test." In most cases, the tester was given the opportunity to communicate the necessary information on the application form provided, in answer to the question "Have you ever been convicted of a crime?"[14] In the 26 percent of cases where the application form did not include a question about criminal history, however, it was necessary to provide an alternative means of conveying this information. In the present study, testers provided two indirect sources of information about their prior criminal involvement. First, as mentioned earlier, the tester in the criminal record condition reported work experience obtained while in the correctional facility. Second, the tester listed his parole officer as a reference (calls to whom were recorded by a voice mail box).[15] These two pieces of evidence provided explicit clues to employers that the applicant had spent time in prison. Both of these strategies are used by real ex-offenders who seek to account for gaps in their work history by reporting work experience in prison and/or who wish to have their parole officer vouch for their successful rehabilitation. Pilot tests with employers in a neighboring city suggested that this strategy was an effective means of conveying the criminal record condition without arousing suspicion. Additional investigation into the effect of providing unsolicited information about the applicant's criminal history is provided in appendix 4A.

Contextual Matters

This study was conducted in the metropolitan area of Milwaukee, Wisconsin. Milwaukee has a profile common to many major American cities, with respect to population size, racial composition, and unemployment rate.[16] In addition, Wisconsin has more expansive fair employment regulations than most states, including explicit protections from discrimination for individuals with criminal records. Employers are cautioned that crimes may be considered only if they closely relate to the specific duties required of the job, however shocking the crime may have been. If anything, then, this study represents a strong test of the effect of a criminal record. We might expect the effect to be larger in states where no such legal protection is in place.

The fieldwork for this project took place between June and December 2001. During this time, the economic condition of the metropolitan area remained quite stable, with unemployment rates ranging from a high of 5.2 percent in June to a low of 4.5 percent in September.[17] It is important to note that the results of this study are specific to the economic conditions of this period. It has been suggested in previous research that the level of employment discrimination corresponds closely to the tightness of the labor market.[18] Certainly the economic climate was a salient factor in the minds of these employers. During a pilot interview, for example, an employer mentioned that a year earlier she "would have had 3 applications for an entry-level opening; today [she gets] 150." Another employer for a janitorial service mentioned that previously the company had been so short of staff that they had to interview virtually everyone who applied. The current conditions, by contrast, allowed them to be more selective.[19] After the completion of this study the unemployment rate continued to rise. It is likely, therefore, that the effects reported here may understate the impact of race and a criminal record during periods of economic recession.

As mentioned earlier, the job openings for this study were selected from the Sunday classified section of the *Milwaukee Journal Sentinel* and from Jobnet, a state-sponsored Internet job service. All job openings within a twenty-five-mile radius of downtown Milwaukee were included, with 61 percent of the resulting sample located in the suburbs or surrounding counties and only 39 percent in the city of Milwaukee. Because a limited area was covered by this project, the distribution of jobs does not accurately represent the extent to which job growth has been concentrated in wider suburban areas. According to a recent study of job growth in Milwaukee, nearly 90 percent of entry-level job openings were located in

Table 4.1. Distribution of entry-level positions.

Job title	%	Job title	%
waitstaff	18	Delivery driver	9
Laborer/warehouse	17	Cashier	7
Production/operators	12	Cook/kitchen staff	5
Service	11	Clerical	5
Sales	11	Mangagerial	2

Note: An excluded "other" category combines the remaining 3 percent of job titles.

suburbs and outlying counties, with only 4 percent of full-time openings located in the central city.[20] The average distance from downtown in the present sample was twelve miles, with a substantial number of job openings located far from reach by public transportation. Again, testers in this study represented a best-case scenario: all testers had their own reliable transportation, allowing them access to a wide range of employment opportunities. For the average entry-level job-seeker, by contrast, the suburbanization of low-wage work can in itself represent a major barrier to employment.

As in other metropolitan labor markets, the service industry has been the fastest-growing sector in Milwaukee, followed by retail and wholesale trade and manufacturing.[21] Likewise, the sample of jobs in this study reflect similar concentrations, though quite a range of job titles were included overall (see table 4.1). The most common job types were for waitstaff, laborers, warehouse workers, and production workers or operators. Although white-collar positions were less common among the entry-level listings, a fair number of customer service, sales, clerical, and even a handful of managerial positions were included.[22]

Figure 4.2 presents some information on the ways employers obtain background information on applicants. In this sample, roughly three-quarters of employers asked explicit questions on their application forms about the applicant's criminal history. Generally this was a standard question, "Have you ever been convicted of a crime? If yes, please explain."[23] Even though in most cases employers are not allowed to use criminal background information to make hiring decisions, a vast majority of employers nevertheless requested the information. A much smaller proportion of employers (27 percent) actually performed official background checks.[24] As discussed above, criminal background checks are becoming far more frequent—estimated at over 50 percent, and rising—and thus this figure is likely to represent a lower-bound estimate of the number of background checks today.

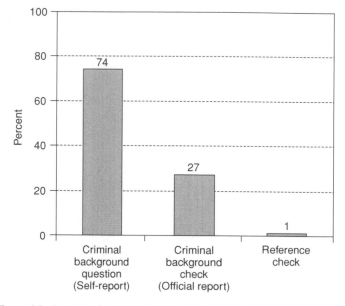

Figure 4.2 Sources of background information on job applicants. These are nonexclusive categories and are thus not meant to sum to 100.

Finally, I recorded reference checks with the belief that, for applicants with criminal records, having former employers or a parole officer willing to vouch for the reliability and competence of the individual would be critical. Additional voice mail boxes were set up for references, so that each application could provide numbers for two functioning references. As it turns out, however, employers paid virtually no attention to references. Over the course of the 350 audits completed, only four employers checked references. Employers would frequently tell testers, "I'll just check your references and then give you a call," or leave messages saying, "I'm going to call your references, and then I'd like you to come in for a training," and yet no calls were registered (the voice mail system was set up in such a way that even hang-ups could be detected).

This finding emphasizes the point that employers do not go out of their way to solicit nuanced information about applicants for entry-level jobs. Rather, it is up to the applicant to convey the important information on the written application or during a brief interview. It is possible that a larger number of employers do check references at a later stage of the employment process. By this point, however, the ex-offender has already likely been weeded out of the pool under consideration.

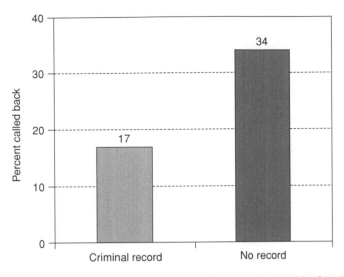

Figure 4.3 The effect of a criminal record on employment opportunities for whites. The effect is large and statistically significant ($p < .01$).

The Effect of a Criminal Record for Whites

To what extent are ex-offenders weeded out at the initial stages of the employment process? To answer this question, I begin with an analysis of the effect of a criminal record among whites. White nonoffenders can serve as our baseline in the following comparisons, representing the presumptively nonstigmatized group, as opposed to blacks and those with criminal records. Given that all testers presented identical qualifications, the differences experienced among groups of testers can be attributed directly to the effects of criminal status. Figure 4.3 shows the percentage of applications submitted by white testers that elicited callbacks from employers, by criminal status. As illustrated in the figure, there is a large and significant effect of a criminal record, with 34 percent of whites without criminal records receiving callbacks compared to only 17 percent of whites with criminal records. A criminal record thus reduces the likelihood of a callback by 50 percent.[25]

There were some fairly obvious examples documented by testers that illustrate employers' strong reaction to the signal of a criminal record. In one case, a white tester in the criminal record condition went to a trucking service to apply for a job as a dispatcher. The tester was given a long application, including a complex math test, all of which took nearly forty-five minutes to fill out. During the course of this process, there were several details about the application and the job that needed clarification, some of which involved checking with the supervisor about how to proceed. No concerns were raised about the applicant's candidacy at this stage. When the tester turned the application in, the secretary brought it into a back office for the supervisor to look over. The tester was instructed to wait, with the implication that he would likely be interviewed on the spot. When the secretary came back out, presumably after the supervisor had had a chance to look over the application more thoroughly, he was told the position had already been filled. Though no concerns had been raised up until that point, and all signs indicated a willingness to consider the applicant for a job, once the application had been submitted (and the criminal record revealed), the position quickly became unavailable. Similar episodes were not infrequent. Often testers reported seeing employers' levels of responsiveness change dramatically once they had glanced down at the criminal record question.

Clearly, the results here demonstrate that a criminal record closes doors in employment situations. Many employers seem to use the information as a screening mechanism, without attempting to probe deeper into the possible context or complexities of the situation. As we can see here, in 50 percent of cases, employers were unwilling to consider equally qualified applicants simply on the basis of their criminal background.

To be sure, this is not true of all employers in all situations. There were, in fact, some employers who seemed to prefer workers who had been recently released from prison. One owner told a white tester in the criminal record condition that he "liked hiring people who had just come out of prison because they tend to be more motivated, and are more likely to be hard workers [not wanting to return to prison]." Another employer for a cleaning company attempted to dissuade the white nonoffender tester from applying because the job involved "a great deal of dirty work." The tester with the criminal record, on the other hand, was offered the job on the spot. It seems, then, that certain kinds of jobs are viewed as appropriate for ex-offenders. On average, however, as we have seen, a criminal record reduces employment opportunities substantially.

The Effect of a Criminal Record for Blacks

Turning from white to black, this study next investigates whether the effect of a criminal record differs depending on the race of the applicant. Most research investigating the differential impact of incarceration on blacks has focused on the differential *rates* of incarceration and how those rates translate into widening racial disparities. In addition to disparities in the rate of incarceration, however, it is also important to consider possible racial differences in the *effects* of incarceration. Very little of the existing literature to date has explored this issue, and the theoretical arguments remain divided as to what we might expect.

On the one hand, there is reason to believe that the signal of a criminal record should be less consequential for blacks. Pervasive racial stereotypes include strong associations between race and crime, regardless of official criminality.[26] If employers view all blacks as potential criminals, they are likely to differentiate less between those with official criminal records and those without. Actual confirmation of criminal involvement will seem redundant, whereas evidence against it will be discounted. In this case, the outcomes for all blacks should be worse, with less differentiation between those with criminal records and those without.

On the other hand, the effect of a criminal record may be worse for blacks if employers, already wary of black applicants, are even more gun-shy when it comes to those with proven criminal tendencies. The literature on racial stereotypes also tells us that stereotypes are most likely to be activated and reinforced when a target matches on more than one dimension of the stereotype.[27] Although employers may have learned to keep their racial attributions in check through years of heightened sensitivity around issues of employment discrimination, when combined with knowledge of a criminal history, negative attributions are likely to intensify. Given these competing predictions, a direct comparison of the effects of a criminal record for blacks and whites proves useful.

The results presented in figure 4.4 confirm the severe disadvantage associated with a criminal record, with the chances of a callback to a black applicant reduced by more than 60 percent. Moreover, the effect of a criminal record appears more pronounced for blacks than whites. While the ratio of callbacks for nonoffenders relative to offenders for whites is 2 to 1, this same ratio for blacks is nearly 3 to 1.[28] Because the absolute number of callbacks is low, the standard errors around these estimates are too large to detect statistical significance in the interaction between race and a criminal record (though see chapter 6). Nevertheless, this evidence is suggestive of the way in which associations between race and crime may affect interpersonal evaluations. Employers' apprehension about applicants with criminal records appears to grow when confronted with black ex-offenders. Despite the fact that these testers were bright, articulate college students with effective styles of self-presentation, the cursory review of entry-level applicants leaves little room for these qualities to be noticed. Whether due to fear, anxiety, or mere discomfort, employers' doors appear to close quickly when confronted with a black ex-offender.

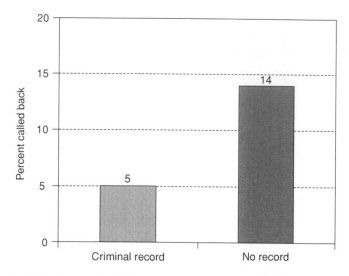

Figure 4.4   The effect of a criminal record on employment opportunities for blacks. The effect is large and statistically significant ($p < .01$).

The intensity of the race-crime association has been vividly demonstrated in laboratory experiments conducted by social psychologists. A common finding to this line of research is that responses to criminal offenders grow consistently more negative when the criminal or the criminal act is associated with African Americans. For example, one relevant study asked police officers and juvenile probation officers to read and respond to a vignette describing an adolescent who had allegedly committed a crime. The race of the adolescent was left unstated, but a randomly selected half of the subjects were primed with unconscious images of words associated with African Americans. In the race-prime condition, officers were more likely to rate the juvenile offender as more mature, more culpable, and warranting harsher sanctions than in evaluations of the same file without the race prime. Unconscious activation of racial cues was thus sufficient to affect the interpretation of the criminal act, skewing evaluations toward more negative attributions and more serious punishment.[29] In another study, subjects were asked to review evidence from a crime in order to assess the defendant's guilt. When the defendant was presented as an ethnic minority, subjects were subsequently better able to recall incriminating evidence and less able to recall exonerating evidence than subjects presented with ethnically nondescript (but otherwise identical) targets. The strong associations between race and crime facilitate the processing and encoding of stereotype-consistent information, leading subjects to differentially attend to the full range of evidence. This "confirmation bias" thus places a greater burden on the amount or salience of information needed to overcome stereotyped associations.[30] A criminal record can thus confirm negative stereotypes against blacks, overriding the many positive indicators of applicant quality presented by the testers. In the present study, because the interaction between race and crime does not reach conventional levels of statistical significance, this conclusion remains tentative. As we will see in chapter 6, however, the consistency of these effects suggests that the results represent more than a random statistical artifact.

Conclusion

Even as the official term of punishment comes to an end, prior contact with the criminal justice system imposes lingering effects on job seekers. The finding that ex-offenders are one-half to one-third as likely as equally qualified nonoffenders to be considered by employers is clear evidence of the barriers to employment imposed by a criminal record. Like a high school diploma or an occupational license, the credential of a criminal record provides an official marker of status and suitability for employment that can be used as an easy screening mechanism by employers. Even in the absence of any other discrediting information, this official marker carries significant weight.

Further, as vast racial disparities have become emblematic of our criminal justice system, the findings of this study suggest that black ex-offenders may be doubly disadvantaged: not only are blacks more likely to be incarcerated than whites; according to the findings presented here, they may also be more strongly affected by the stigma of a criminal record.[31] Previous estimates of the consequences of mass incarceration may therefore underestimate its impact on racial disparities.

The implications of this study point to a large and growing population of ex-offenders unable to secure even the most basic kinds of low-wage work. With more than 650,000 ex-offenders returning from prison each year, existing problems of prisoner reentry are likely to amplify over time. The social costs of high unemployment among this group—manifested by high rates of recidivism and additional burdens to families, communities, and public agencies—are cause for serious public concern. At the same time, it would be unrealistic to expect private employers to open their doors to ex-offenders solely in the interest of the public good. Employers face tough decisions in hiring workers. They are often confronted with large numbers of applicants and little time to sort through them; they bear the costs of employee turnover and theft; and they are potentially liable if someone on their staff harms a customer or fellow employee. All of these considerations (no matter how remote the actual risks may be) point to the rationality of employers' reluctance to hire applicants with criminal records. The bridging of this impasse between public interest and private costs represents a major dilemma for policies promoting successful prisoner reentry. Market forces clearly appear insufficient to manage the problems of prisoner reentry alone.

···   ···   ···

APPENDIX 4A.   METHODOLOGICAL CONCERNS

The first part of this appendix provides a general orientation to the nuts and bolts of designing and implementing an in-person audit study. It addresses the selection and matching criteria necessary for ensuring high-quality and well-aligned applicant pairs, training and supervision requirements, outcome measures, and the ethics of audit research. The second part of the appendix discusses a number of design issues specific to the Milwaukee study and presents additional details into the strategies for assessing possible threats to the validity of the experiment.

The Implementation of an In-Person Audit Study

Matching: The selection of testers who will play the role of job applicants is one of the most critical components in the design of an employment audit and one of the most time intensive. Testers must be chosen based on personal attributes that make them individually well-qualified to perform what can be a highly demanding job requiring a substantial degree of autonomy; but they must also be chosen based on personal attributes that make them a good match for another well-qualified individual (their test partner). Taking into account the wide range of characteristics employers may pay attention to in evaluating applicants, testers should be matched on concrete factors, such as age, height, weight, and level of education, in addition to more subjective criteria: articulateness, ease of personal interaction, physical attractiveness, and nonverbal communication style. Though the relevance of these characteristics may vary by job type or employer, they are all nevertheless potentially influential in hiring decisions and thus must be considered in deciding on potential matches. Taking all these considerations into account, it is not unusual to interview between eighty and a hundred applicants for each tester hired.

The matching process itself is an art as much as it is a science (an issue that has provoked criticism by some).[32] While there exist a number of psychometric scales to measure personality attributes, verbal ability, and so on, there are certain intangible qualities that are arguably more important in making a first impression. Including a wide range of external evaluators (individuals not directly involved in the research project) can provide important feedback about the holistic impressions formed by each potential tester and the degree of similarity between proposed pairs.

Note that audits of contexts other than employment require less attention to physical appearance and personality characteristics. Housing audits and audits of consumer markets, for example, are typically based on a far narrower (and easier to control) set of tester characteristics. Likewise, requirements are less stringent when treatment conditions can be randomly assigned. In testing the effects of a criminal record, for example, testers can alternate which individual presents himself as the ex-offender over the course of the study, thus evening out any unobserved differences within the tester pair. If one tester is slightly more attractive, for example, in certain cases he will be a slightly more attractive offender and in other cases a slightly more attractive nonoffender. Any individual differences will even out if each tester serves in the treatment and control condition in an equal number of cases.[33] In testing the effects of race, by contrast, the treatment condition cannot be randomly assigned. The quality of the matches thus becomes extremely consequential, as race can be fully confounded with any other individual characteristic. To the extent that differences will persist, researchers should err in the direction of choosing black testers with slightly more desirable attributes. Results will then represent a conservative test of discrimination, essentially providing a lower-bound estimate.

Constructing résumés: Once tester pairs have been matched, they are assigned résumés reflecting equal levels of education and experience. Substantial thought must go into choosing high schools and neighborhoods that have similar reputations and student/resident compositions; likewise, work histories must be developed to reflect not only equal amounts of prior work experience but also similar types of work experience.[34] In addition to pretesting résumés to assess their comparability, ideally résumé types can be assigned independent of treatment condition (e.g., any given résumé will be used by both black and white testers, to control for any unmeasured differences). In some cases, the résumé will be the only point of contact between the tester and the employer (e.g., in cases where the person in charge of hiring is not present at the time of the test, and the tester leaves a résumé); it is thus important that all relevant information be effectively conveyed on this single-page document.

Training: No matter how carefully matched two testers may be, they can act as successful audit partners only if they learn to interact with employers in similar ways. A wide range of questions can come up in the course of a conversation or interview with an employer, and testers must be prepared to share similar information and communicate similar types of profiles in their descriptions of (fictitious) past experiences. Before starting actual fieldwork for an audit study, testers typically participate in an extensive training period during which they rehearse the content of their profile, and the appropriate way to phrase answers to interview questions, and work on aligning their responses with those of their test partner. Training can consist of videotaped mock interviews, practice interviews with cooperating employers, and practice audits with real employers. In addition to the initial training period, daily debriefings with testers can help to identify problems that may arise, or additional content that needs rehearsing.

Problems of implementation: With any field experiment, the unpredictabilities of the real world often interfere with carefully planned research designs. Traffic can back up (or public transportation can break down), making it impossible for one tester to make it to an employer at the specified time; a job can get filled in between the time the two testers come to apply; a tester may run into someone he knows during an audit; an employer may know the manager of a fictitious job listed on the testers' résumé. The key to maintaining the integrity of the experimental design lies in the ability to respond quickly to unexpected happenings and to constantly tweak the protocols to take account of new situations. In cases where the protocol appears not to have been fully (or effectively) implemented, the test should be cancelled. While it is impossible to catalogue the countless number of potential disruptions that may arise, researchers must be vigilant throughout the course of the study. Effective and continual supervision of the testing process is one of the most important elements of a successful audit study.

Supervision: The quality of the data from an audit study depends on the degree to which testers effectively follow the established protocol. And yet evaluating testers' performance is difficult, since the majority of the testers' work is completed with no direct supervision. In order to monitor the quality of the testing process, a number of formal procedures can be put into place. First, immediately following each visit to an employer, testers are typically required to fill out an extensive summary form, including a large number of close-ended questions (e.g., job title, race/gender/ age of interviewer, whether screening tests were required, whether they were asked about criminal background, etc.). In addition, testers write a lengthy open-ended narrative, describing their contact with the employer and the content of interactions they had during the test. These summary forms allow researchers to monitor the relative experiences of tester pairs and to identify any anomalies in the testing experiences that may confound measurement of the treatment variable. Second, the researcher (or project manager) should be available for debriefings with each of the testers following the completion of each day's work. When something unexpected occurs, the project manager should be contacted immediately. Third, weekly group meetings can be useful to allow testers the opportunity to brainstorm together about how to make the logistics of testing as efficient and controlled as possible. And finally, spot checks of tester performance can provide helpful tools for surveillance and continued training. For example, researchers can arrange for testers to apply for jobs with employers who, unbeknownst to the testers, are in collaboration with the researcher, to allow for an external assessment of their performance. Arranging for hidden cameras to record these spot checks can then provide an additional training tool, as the audit team can watch and discuss the videotapes to identify differences in presentation style within tester pairs. The vast majority of problems that arise in the course of fieldwork for an audit study are relatively minor and can be resolved quickly, provided effective monitoring. It is only when problems continue unchecked that they can pose a significant threat to the validity of the research.

Testing for litigation versus research: One common question asked about the audit methodology concerns how it can be used to reduce the problems of discrimination. The audit method was initially designed for the enforcement of antidiscrimination law. Testers were used to detect racially discriminatory practices among real estate agents, landlords, and lenders, providing the evidence necessary to pursue litigation.[35] Audit studies for research purposes, by contrast, are oriented not toward a specific intervention, but rather to obtaining accurate measures of the prevalence of discrimination across a broad sector or metropolitan area. The difference between these two types of studies is further reflected in the study design. Testing for litigation requires multiple audits of the same employer (or real estate agent, etc.) to detect consistent patterns of discrimination by that particular individual and/or company. Testing for research, by contrast, typically includes no more than a single audit per employer, with discrimination detected through systematic patterns across employers, rather than repeated acts of discrimination by a single employer. The distinction here is important in what we can tell from audit studies intended for research purposes. As discussed in chapter 3, it is not possible to draw conclusions from research-based audit studies about the discriminatory tendencies of any given employer. Only by looking at systematic patterns across a large number of employers can we determine whether hiring appears influenced by race or other stigmatizing characteristics. The point of research-based audit studies, therefore, is to assess the prevalence of discrimination across the labor market, rather than to intervene in particular sites of discrimination. Nevertheless, although the objective is different, research audit studies provide important information about discriminatory practices that can support calls for strengthening antidiscrimination policy or other policy initiatives designed to protect vulnerable workers.

Ethics of audit research: Discussions of audit studies inevitably lead to questions about the ethics of such research. Audit studies require that employers be unwittingly recruited for participation and then led to believe that the testers are viable job candidates. Contrary to the ethical standards for research established by the federal government, this design does not allow for the use of informed consent by research subjects for participation and often avoids debriefing subjects after the study's completion. How then are audit studies permitted to take place? As it turns out, there are specific criteria that regulate waivers of informed consent, and a well-designed audit study can arguably meet each of them. Below I provide a discussion of the relevant concerns and potential solutions to the ethical problems posed by research of this kind.

The use of deception in social science has long been met with suspicion. While individual researchers may feel they can clearly distinguish between appropriate and improper research practices, examples from the past indicate that researchers' individual judgments may not always conform to the standards of the discipline.[36] Because of past transgressions, legislation concerning the use of human subjects now governs all social science research and includes, as one of its fundamental criteria, the use of informed consent from all research participants.[37] In the case of audit studies, however, the nature of the research requires that subjects remain unaware of their participation, and the condition of informed consent therefore cannot be met.

While current federal policy governing the protection of human subjects strongly supports the use of informed consent, there is recognition that certain types of research that fail to obtain formal consent can be deemed permissible. According to the regulations, a Human Subjects Institutional Review Board (IRB) "may . . . waive . . . informed consent provided (1) the research involves no more than minimal risk to human subjects; (2) the waiver or alteration will not adversely affect the rights and welfare of the subjects; (3) the research could not practicably be carried out without the waiver or alteration; and (4) whenever appropriate, the subjects will be provided with additional information after participation."[38] Each of these conditions can arguably be satisfied in the context of audit studies of discrimination. While there are potential risks to subjects, reasonable efforts can be made to reduce the costs to subjects and thereby impose only minimal risk.

Most audit research poses two primary potential risks to subjects: (1) loss of time; and (2) legal liability. In the first case, subjects are asked to evaluate a pair of applications submitted by phony applicants. Time spent reviewing applications and/or interviewing applicants will therefore impose a cost on the subject. Most employment audit studies limit their samples to employers for entry-level positions—those requiring the least intensive review—in part to minimize the time employers spend evaluating phony applicants. Entry-level positions are typically filled on the basis of cursory overviews of applications and limited personal contact. Contact with subjects is thus minimal, consisting of requesting an application and/or answering a few brief questions. Audits of higher-skill jobs, by contrast, impose a greater burden on employers, as the hiring process for such positions typically requires a greater investment of time and effort.[39]

A second potential risk posed by audit research is the potential for employers and/or firms to be held liable for discrimination if evidence were to be publicly released as to their performance in the audit. In fact, as mentioned above, the evidence provided by audit studies intended for research cannot support claims of discrimination against any individual employer. Nevertheless, efforts must be taken to protect employer identities so that even association with a study on discrimination cannot be made. To this end, identifying information should be kept in a secure location, and any publicly released publications or presentations should omit all identifying characteristics of individuals and firms.

The issue of debriefing subjects following the completion of the audit study is a complicated one. Though typically IRB protocol supports the debriefing of subjects whenever possible, in certain cases acknowledging the occurrence or nature of a research study is deemed undesirable. It could be argued, for example, that subjects could be placed at greater risk should their behavior, as a result of the audit study, fall under greater scrutiny by superiors. For human resource personnel or managers who are thought to be discriminating, the consequences may be more serious than if no attention were brought to the audit whatsoever. While the chances that negative consequences would result from this research in any case are very small, some IRB committees take the view that eliminating the debriefing stage is the most prudent strategy. The purpose of audit research is *not* to harm individual employers. Rather, the research seeks to improve our understanding of the barriers to employment facing stigmatized groups in their search for employment.

As a final matter, it should be emphasized that the ethics of audit research is not only of concern in a university context. The legal standing of testers has likewise received close scrutiny by the courts. In fact, the issue of testing has reached the highest judicial body, with the United States Supreme Court upholding the standing of testers in a 1982 decision.[40] A more recent ruling by the Seventh Circuit Court again upheld the standing of testers in cases of employment discrimination, broadening their endorsement of this methodology. In each of these rulings, the courts have been primarily concerned with the use of testing for pursuing litigation against realtors or employers (rather than for pure research, as is the case here). Implicit in these holdings, however, is the belief that the misrepresentation involved in testing is worth the unique benefit this practice can provide in uncovering discrimination and enforcing civil rights laws. According to former EEOC chairman Gilbert Castellas, "Using employment testers in a carefully controlled manner is an important tool for measuring the presence or absence of discrimination. If we can shed light on barriers to fair hiring in entry-level jobs, which are the gateway to self-sufficiency and economic independence, we will have made an important step in assuring equal opportunity for everyone."[41] Indeed, despite certain burdens imposed by audit studies, the ultimate benefit from research of this kind extends far beyond the contribution of a single study. Rigorous and realistic measurement of discrimination is fundamental to understanding and addressing persistent barriers to employment facing members of stigmatized groups.

Specific Dilemmas in Designing the Milwaukee Study

Here I discuss some of the limitations of the audit methodology and ways in which findings from an experimental design may conflict with real-life contexts.

Limits to Generalizability

The Reporting of Criminal Backgrounds

In the present study, testers in the criminal record condition were instructed to provide an affirmative answer to any question about criminal background posed on the application form or in person. Employers are thus given full information about the criminal background of this applicant. But how often do real ex-offenders offer such complete and honest information? To the extent that ex-offenders lie about their criminal background in employment settings, the results of this study may overestimate the effect of having a criminal record. If employers do not know, then surely a criminal record can have no influence on their hiring decisions.

Before starting this project, I conducted a number of interviews with parolees and men with criminal records. When asked how they handled application forms, the majority of these men claimed to report their criminal record up front. There are a number of reasons motivating this seemingly irrational behavior. First, most men with criminal records believe that the chance of being caught by a criminal background check is much larger than it actually is. Although a majority of employers did not perform background checks on all applicants, at least at the time this study was conducted, there was the perception that this practice was widespread. Second, most men coming out of prison have a parole officer monitoring their reintegration. One of the most effective mechanisms of surveillance for parole officers is to call employers to make sure their parolees have been showing up for work. If the individual has not reported his criminal history, therefore, it will soon be revealed. There is thus a strong incentive for parolees to be up-front in their reporting.[42]

A second source of information on this issue comes from interviews with employers. In a second stage of this project, the same sample of employers were interviewed about their hiring practices and experiences (see chapter 7). During these conversations, the employers were asked to report what percentage of applicants over the past year had reported a prior conviction; and, among those employers who performed official criminal background checks, what percentage of applicants were found to have criminal records. According to the employers, roughly 12 percent of applicants over the past year reported having a prior record on their application form. Of those employers who perform official background checks, an average of 14 percent of applicants were found to have criminal records. The disparity between self-reports and official records, therefore, is a minimal 2 percentage points. In fact, one manager of a national restaurant chain mentioned that sometimes applicants report *more* information

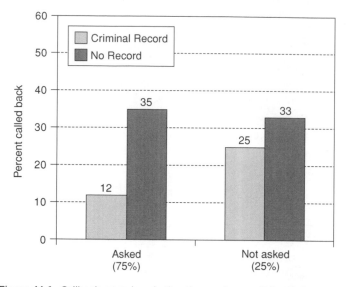

Figure 4A.1   Callback rates, by whether the employer solicited information on criminal history. These data are based on white applicants only.

than they need to: although the question on his application form only asked about felony convictions over the past year, this employer revealed that applicants sometimes report misdemeanors and felony convictions from several years back. Whatever the reason, there seems to be evidence that far more ex-offenders report their prior convictions than rational actor models might predict. Although surely some ex-offenders do lie on their applications, there is reason to believe this is far from the norm.

A related issue of study design concerns the reporting of criminal background even when not solicited by the employer. Recall that roughly 25 percent of employers do not ask explicit questions on their application forms about an applicant's criminal history. In order to make sure the experimental condition was known to all employers, testers also reported work experience in the correctional facility and listed their parole officer as a reference. Although this strategy was chosen to reflect a composite profile of a number of real ex-offenders, in no way does this represent a modal application procedure. In most cases, if employers do not ask about (or check) criminal histories, they will never know. It is possible that conveying the information artificially caused the level of measured discrimination to be inflated. To investigate this concern, a direct test is possible. Figure 4A.1 presents the callback rate for employers who did and those who did not solicit information about prior convictions. As is clear from this graph, employers who did not solicit information about criminal histories were much less likely to use the information in their hiring decisions. The disparity in treatment of ex-offenders versus nonoffenders among employers who did request the information (12 versus 35 percent) is more than twice as large as that among employers who did not ask (25 versus 33 percent). In terms of its correspondence to the real world, therefore, providing unsolicited information about criminal backgrounds did little to affect employer responses.

The Representativeness of Testers

Testers in this study were bright, articulate college students with effective styles of self-presentation. The interpersonal skills of the average inmate, by contrast, are likely to be substantially less appealing to employers. The choice of testers in this respect was deliberate, as a means of fully separating the signal of a criminal record from other correlated attributes to which employers may also respond. It is nevertheless important to consider the extent to which these testers can be considered accurate representatives of the ex-offender experience. On the one hand, it may be the case that the testers in this study represent a best-case scenario. Because their interactional style does not correspond to that of a stereotypical criminal, employers may be more willing to consider them as viable candidates despite their criminal background. In this case, the present study design would underestimate the true effect of a criminal record. On the other hand, for individuals with poor interpersonal skills, a criminal record may represent just one additional—but less consequential—handicap to the already disadvantaged candidate. If this is the case, the effect of a criminal record may be overestimated by the testers in the present study.

One approach to investigating this problem is to analyze those applications submitted with no personal contact with the employer (as was the case with over 75 percent of the applications submitted in this study). In these cases, the interpersonal skills of the testers should have no influence on the employer's consideration of the applicant. In the analysis reported in figure 4A.2, we see that the effect of a criminal record *among whites* is even greater in the absence of personal contact than in the overall findings reported earlier. Personal contact appears to mediate the effect of a criminal record for whites, reducing its negative impact. These results are suggestive of the former hypothesis: the interpersonal skills of testers in the present study, to the extent that they are noticed by employers, serve to weaken the effect of a criminal record for a white applicant. At the same time, however, the effects of personal contact appear to work quite differently in the case of blacks, for a variety of possible reasons discussed

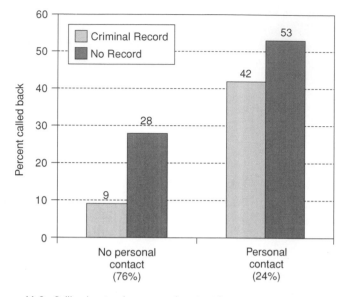

Figure 4A.2 Callback rates, by personal contact between tester and employer. These data are based on white applicants only.

in chapter 6. Because we cannot discern the exact cause of this interaction, it is difficult to know whether the mismatch between testers' real characteristics and the profiles they presented may have played a role. Judging by the testers' experiences, employers reacted more often with surprise when noticing the criminal record among the white testers than the black testers, suggesting that, if anything, the white testers were more at risk of distorting reactions as a result of their articulate and clean-cut style of self-presentation. If this is the case, the estimates reported here are likely represent a lower-bound estimate of the true effect of a criminal record.

Sample Restrictions

The present study was intended to assess the effect of a criminal record on employment in entry-level jobs. In order to obtain a sample of such positions for use in this study, however, it was necessary to impose certain sample restrictions on the categories of entry-level employment to be included. The degree to which these restrictions affect the generalizability of these findings to real employment searches therefore warrants careful consideration.

Virtually all employment audits have relied on samples of job openings identified through ads in metropolitan newspapers. Although want ads provide an easily accessible listing of job vacancies, research on actual job search behavior demonstrates that only a minority of jobs are found through this source. Holzer estimates that only roughly 20 to 25 percent of search time is spent on contacts generated by newspaper advertising, with friends and relatives and direct contact of firms by applicants representing much more common sources of new employment.[43]

Though it would be preferable to include job vacancies derived from representative sources, it is difficult if not impossible to map the network of informal contacts that lead to most job opportunities. Instead, researchers have relied on sources that allow for systematic and consistent sampling schemes, despite the reduction in representativeness. Fortunately, there is compelling research to suggest that the restricted sample provides a more conservative estimate of discrimination. Firms that wish to discriminate, it is argued, are more likely to advertise job openings through more restrictive channels than the metropolitan newspaper, such as through referrals, employment agencies, or more selective publications. Indeed, this argument is indirectly supported by research showing that minorities are more successful in job searches generated by general newspaper ads than through other means.[44] Further, pilot audits conducted by the Fair Employment Council in Washington, D.C., also indicate lower rates of discrimination against minorities in jobs advertised in metropolitan newspapers than in those advertised in suburban newspapers or in employment agencies.[45]

The present study, therefore, following previous audit studies, relies on a random sample of job openings from advertised sources (the *Milwaukee Journal Sentinel* and Jobnet). Prior to sampling, the following additional restrictions were imposed (for reasons discussed below):

- no hiring through employment agencies;
- no education requirements beyond a high school degree;
- no public sector positions;
- no health care positions;
- no jobs related to the care of children or the elderly; and
- no jobs whose announcements explicitly stated that security clearance is required.

The restrictions with the largest effect on my sample are those related to employment agencies and the health care industry. Employment agencies are becoming increasingly dominant in regulating the market for entry-level labor. Between 35 and 40 percent of jobs advertised on Jobnet (the Internet employment bulletin) were "temporary to permanent" positions through an employment agency. There exists quite a bit of literature on the quality of temporary employment and the treatment of workers hired through employment agencies. An audit of employment agencies, however, warrants an independent study, given the very different hiring procedures used in such establishments.[46]

The elimination of health care positions from my sample was due to the extensive legal restrictions in this sector barring the employment of individuals with criminal records (such restrictions also apply to occupations involving care for children or the elderly and many public sector positions). This sample constraint eliminated a huge number of jobs otherwise available to entry-level job seekers without criminal records. The health services sector represents 8.3 percent of total employment in Wisconsin, and a much larger share of new employment. Hospitals alone were the fourth largest employers in the Milwaukee region in 1995. These are some of the highest-wage jobs in the service sector.[47]

Other occupations were likewise eliminated from the sample, not because of blanket legal restrictions, but because their job announcements explicitly stated that applicants must pass a criminal background check and/or that security clearance was required. Although it is not clear that blanket exclusion of all criminal convictions in these cases is defensible under the law, the employers' policies are made fairly explicit. While one cannot always assume that stated policies will be enforced, in the case of criminal records, these jobs are unlikely to demonstrate much variance.

A true estimate of the collateral consequences of a criminal record on employment opportunities would take into account the large number of jobs formally closed to ex-offenders (rather than just those demonstrating a preference for or against applicants with criminal records). The estimates produced from the audits, therefore, represent only part of the overall effect of a criminal record of the likelihood of finding employment.

Experimenter Effects

As discussed in chapter 3, a potential weakness of the audit methodology is that the expectations or behaviors of testers can influence the outcome of results in nonrandom ways. In the course of this research, it became apparent that testers may in fact (unconsciously) behave differently depending on the experimental condition. With respect to the criminal record condition, several testers commented that they felt irrationally bad about themselves when presenting themselves as ex-offenders. If it is the case that these feelings made them more self-conscious and/or more reticent or nervous when speaking with employers, then this behavior in itself may lead to spurious outcomes. These psychological reactions were most pronounced at the start of the study. One tester, for example, reported feelings of discouragement and frustration that he had had very few responses from employers. For a successful, bright college student, the change in status to a young black criminal was extreme, and the difference in treatment he received seemed to take a toll. Fortunately, after gaining more experience with the project, this tester (and others) seemed to feel more comfortable in their interactions and better able to perform in their assigned roles.

The psychological experiences of testers can certainly influence the outcome of audit studies. It is unlikely, however, that they are the driving force behind the results reported from this study. As noted earlier, in a vast majority of cases (76 percent) testers had little if any contact with employers. Given that a majority of callbacks were made on the basis of applications submitted with little or no personal contact, the internal disposition of the tester is unlikely to exert much of an effect. The finding that personal contact actually served to weaken the effect of a criminal record (see figure 4A.2) provides further evidence that the friendly, appealing qualities of the testers were apparent to employers even among applicants in the criminal record condition.

APPENDIX 4B.

Table 4B.1. Logistic regression of the effects of criminal record and race on applicants' likelihood of receiving a callback.

	Coefficient	Robust standard error
Criminal record	−0.99	0.24***
Black	−1.25	0.28***
Criminal record*black	−0.29	0.38

Note: Standard errors are corrected for clustering on employer ID in order to account for the fact that these data contain two records per employer (i.e., criminal record vs. no criminal record). The model also controls for location (city vs. suburb) and contact with the employer, variables that mediate the relationship between race, crime, and employer responses.

5 The Mark of Race

In December 2002, the EEOC filed a lawsuit in a Wisconsin Federal Court against the Target Corporation, alleging discrimination against black job applicants at nearly a dozen Wisconsin stores. In depositions for the lawsuit, Target employees admitted to routinely destroying the job applications of black individuals who attended job fairs held at several Milwaukee universities.[1]

Examples of blatant forms of discrimination appear sporadically in a blitz of media attention. As much as these examples provide vivid illustration of lingering forms of racial bias, they simultaneously reinforce the notion that acts of discrimination in contemporary America are rare events committed by unusually malevolent actors. Under more typical circumstances, direct discrimination in America appears to have all but disappeared. Indeed, the presence of prominent black athletes, actors, and politicians provides an image of an open door to opportunity for blacks, one no longer conditioned by the stigma of skin color. In his book *Creating Equal: My Fight Against Racial Preferences,* Ward Connerly (sponsor of the successful proposition in California to end affirmative action) argues that liberals cling to a misguided belief in the persistence of racism, characterized by the "need to believe that Rosa Parks is still stuck in the back of the bus, even though we live in a time when Oprah is on a billboard on the side of the bus."[2] Perhaps, then, periodic examples of discriminators "caught in the act" represent only extreme aberrations. Dramatic cases of discrimination may get extensive publicity even if they represent rare occurrences overall.

On the other hand, contemporary forms of discrimination may simply be more subtle and covert, leading to less frequent detection and awareness by the general public. In the contemporary United States, social and legal proscriptions against discrimination are strong, placing pressure on potential discriminators to conceal their motives in ways that are consistent with norms of colorblindness. Employers (or other gatekeepers) who retain preferences for or against members of a particular race thus face strong incentives to mask their discriminatory actions behind nonracial justifications. It could be the case, then, that discrimination remains fairly routine in certain contexts, despite infrequent public exposure.[3]

Debates about the contemporary relevance of discrimination have been ongoing for many years, but few systematic measures are available to adjudicate among competing positions. The methodology used in this study provides one opportunity to carefully assess the impact of race on hiring decisions.

The Declining Significance of Race as an Explanatory Variable

Much has changed in American race relations since the middle of the twentieth century. The civil rights movement brought with it a wave of reform, undermining the previously entrenched racialized allocation of opportunity. Historic legislative and court decisions banning segregated schools and discrimination in employment and public accommodations and others extending the franchise created a new horizon of opportunities for African Americans. Antidiscrimination law and affirmative action provided the twin vehicles for the enforcement and promotion of equal opportunity for America's racial minorities, spurring an unprecedented growth of black upward mobility.[4] With the shifting legal context, the social context of discrimination was transformed dramatically as well. Whereas in 1940 fewer than half of Americans believed that blacks should attend the same schools as whites or have the same chances of getting a job, by 1970 the balance had shifted toward an endorsement of the principles of racial equality; by 1995 more than 95 percent of Americans would support the ideals of racial integration and equality of opportunity.[5] In the wake of this historic transformation, many grew confident that American society had moved beyond the fault lines of race. Lingering signs of racial inequality could be viewed as the eroding vestiges of the previous era rather than as the continuing product of contemporary racial injustice.

Prominent intellectuals of the post-civil rights era were quick to document this transformation. Most notably, in 1978, William Julius Wilson published the now-classic treatise on black America, *The Declining Significance of Race*, in which he skillfully argued that the problems facing African Americans in the modern industrial period had more to do with class than race. Discrimination, Wilson argued, was no longer paramount in shaping the outcomes of blacks; rather, a lack of jobs, caused by structural changes in the economy, represented the fundamental source of black—and other groups'—disadvantage. Wilson's book clearly picked up the developing zeitgeist. Indeed, in the thirty years since its publication, we have seen a notable decline in attention to the problems of racial discrimination in academic and policy discussions.[6]

Consistent with notions of a "declining significance of race," racial disparities on a number of key indicators have diminished or disappeared since the 1960s. Rates of high school graduation have narrowed to just a few percentage points difference, and the black-white test score gap appears to be following a similar trajectory.[7] These improvements in the human capital attainment of blacks, along with a liberalization of opportunity, have facilitated greater performance in the labor market, with blacks becoming increasingly well-represented in occupational sectors previously dominated by whites, along with a shrinking of the wage gap through 1980.[8]

Despite visible improvements, however, blacks continue to lag behind whites on key dimensions of inequality. Particularly among those at the bottom half of the distribution, rapid gains beginning in the 1960s slowed, and in some cases reversed, during the 1980s and 1990s. Even at the high point of economic expansion in the late 1990s, when unemployment rates were dropping steadily for all groups, black men were still more than twice as likely to be unemployed as their white counterparts. Over time blacks, and young black men in particular, have become increasingly likely to drop out of the labor market altogether when faced with the prospect of long-term unemployment or marginal employment opportunities.[9]

How can we explain these persistent racial disparities? The truth of the matter is that the employment problems of blacks are vastly overdetermined. There are far more factors contributing to black employment problems than would be necessary to produce the trends we observe: the manufacturing sector declined; jobs moved from the central city; black test scores have lagged behind those of whites as the demand for cognitive skills has increased; blacks have less effective social networks for finding work; black men face increasing competition from women and immigrants.[10] Interestingly, in this litany of possible explanations, rarely nowadays do we hear mention of the oldest and most basic interpretation. Does discrimination continue to contribute to the employment problems of African Americans?

According to most Americans, the answer is no. The majority of white Americans believe that a black person today has the same chance at getting a job as an equally qualified white person, and only a third believe that discrimination is an important explanation for why blacks do worse than whites in income, housing, and jobs.[11] Mainstream public opinion thus favors the idea that discrimination is of vanishing importance, at least as a direct cause of present-day inequalities.

Scholarly opinion likewise remains divided on the question of discrimination. Social psychologists have extensively documented the subtle distortions that take place when race is involved in the course of reasoned evaluations. Despite the widespread conscious endorsement of racial equality, deep-seated stereotypes about the intelligence, work ethic, criminality, and cultural dispositions of various groups continue to frame our evaluations and decision making in social situations.[12]

In contrast to social psychological research that shows a strong persistence of racial stereotypes and discrimination, a growing body of research in sociology and economics has challenged the notion that contemporary labor market outcomes are influenced by race. Wilson's work, mentioned earlier, highlights the importance of structural changes in the economy that, although race neutral, have disproportionately affected poor and working-class blacks. More recent work has moved from structural to individual explanations, emphasizing the growing importance of skill in today's economy and the persistent black-white skill gap as a key source of contemporary racial disparities. A series of influential studies, for example, indicate that once relevant individual characteristics—in particular, cognitive ability—have been accounted for, racial disparities in wages among young men narrow substantially or disappear.[13] This line of research has reinforced the view that the vast majority of the employment problems of young minority men can be explained by skill or other individual deficiencies, rather than by any direct effect of discrimination. Economist James Heckman summarizes this position most clearly: "Most of the disparity in earnings between blacks and whites in the labor market of the 1990s is due to differences in skills they bring to the market, and not to discrimination within the labor market," and he goes on to describe discrimination as "the problem of an earlier era."[14]

Have we conquered the problems of racial discrimination? Or have acts of discrimination become too subtle and covert for detection? These questions are difficult to answer using standard techniques of observation and analysis. Here again, then, the field experiment becomes an optimal tool for examining the prevalence of labor market discrimination. By observing the outcomes of equally qualified job applicants in the context of real job searches, we can make strong inferences about the direct effects of race on labor market outcomes.

Research Design

The design of the present study is not typical of the matched-pair tests used to study racial discrimination. Remember from the previous chapter that black testers and white testers applied to separate sets of employers over the course of the study. One tester on each team presented evidence of a criminal record. While this approach is not as efficient in detecting racial discrimination, it can nevertheless produce unbiased estimates. The black pair and the white pair used *identical* sets of résumés in their job searches (something that would not have been possible in cross-race pairings, because test partners must present unique information). The levels of education, work experience, and résumé content and format are thus identical (rather than merely similar) across the black and white teams.[15] Further, jobs were randomly assigned across the two tester pairs, ensuring a comparable distribution of employers visited by each pair over the course of the study.[16] Over a large enough sample of jobs, therefore, this design is effective in identifying differential employment experiences among equally qualified black and white job seekers.

Racial Comparisons in Hiring Outcomes

As in the previous chapter, results are based on the proportion of applications submitted by each tester that elicited callbacks from employers. The previous chapter focused on the effect of a criminal record for blacks and whites separately. This chapter now brings the results together to investigate the overall impact of race on hiring outcomes. Looking at the callback rates for black and white tester pairs side by side, the importance of race becomes vividly clear (figure 5.1). Among those without criminal records, blacks were less than half as likely to receive callbacks as equally qualified white applicants (14 vs. 34 percent). This implies that young black men needed to work more than twice as hard (apply to twice as many jobs) to secure the same opportunities as whites with identical qualifications. Even more striking, the powerful effects of race rival even the strong stigma conveyed by a criminal record. In this study, a white

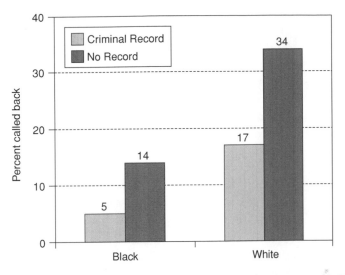

Figure 5.1 The effects of race and criminal record on employment opportunities. Both effects are large and statistically significant ($p < .01$).

applicant *with a criminal record* was just as likely to receive a callback as a black applicant *without* any criminal history (17 vs. 14 percent); the difference is not statistically significant.[17] Despite the fact that the white applicant revealed evidence of a felony drug conviction, and despite the fact that he reported having only recently returned from a year and a half in prison, employers seemed to view this applicant as no more risky than a young black man with no history of criminal involvement. Racial disparities have been documented in many contexts, but here, comparing the two effects side by side, we are confronted with a troubling reality: being black in America today is just about the same as having a felony conviction in terms of one's chances of finding a job.

Often in presentations of this research, there has been an audible gasp from the audience when I display these results. Could the effect of race really be so large? The magnitude of these effects stands in striking opposition to the prevailing wisdom that such blatant forms of discrimination have become vanishingly rare. It's tempting then to think that there is something peculiar about this study, or about the time and place in which it was conducted, which offers an exaggerated view. For one thing, Milwaukee was, at the time this study was conducted, the second most segregated city in the country, implying great social distance between blacks and whites, with possible implications for the results of the audit study. If race relations are more strained in Milwaukee than in other parts of the country, then the effects of race presented here may be larger than what would be found in other urban areas. In fact, however, the magnitude of the race effect found here falls squarely within the range found in previous audit studies.[18] An audit study in Washington, D.C., for example, found that blacks were 24 percentage points less likely to receive a job offer than their white counterparts, a finding strikingly similar to the 20 percentage point difference (between white and black nonoffenders) found here.[19]

Likewise, a recent field experiment by Marianne Bertrand and Sendhil Mullainathan finds large effects of race among employers in Boston and Chicago. In this study, the researchers mailed résumés to employers in the two cities using racially identifiable names to signal race. Their sample was restricted to listings for sales, administrative support, and clerical and customer service positions. Despite the narrower range of occupations and the higher level of qualifications presented in this study, these authors find clear evidence of racial bias. White male names triggered a callback rate of 9.19 percent, compared to 6.16 percent among black male names. The ratio of callbacks for whites to blacks (1.5), while smaller than the ratio of callbacks for white and black nonoffenders from this study (2.4), strengthens our confidence that Milwaukee is not the only city in which race continues to matter.[20]

Each of these studies reinforces the conclusion that race represents an extremely powerful barrier to job entry. The matched designs allow us to separate speculation about applicant qualifications (supply-side influences) from the racial attributions or biases of employers (demand-side influences). While these studies remain silent on the many supply-side factors that may also contribute to the employment difficulties of young black men, they speak loud and clear about the significance of employer demand in shaping the opportunities available to young black and white job seekers. Before applicants have an opportunity to demonstrate their capabilities in person, a large proportion are weeded out on the basis of a single categorical distinction.

Driving While Black: Associations between Race and Crime

I received a call from Andre at about two o'clock one afternoon. He was calling me from his cell phone, sitting in the back of a police car. The police had stopped him at a freeway entrance on the way to one of his audit assignments. Though Andre hadn't committed any traffic violation, the police explained they were looking for someone who matched his description ("a black man, between the ages of 21-25 . . . "). Andre was instructed to step out of his car and asked to take a seat in the back of the police vehicle. Passersby craned their necks to catch a glimpse of the latest apprehended criminal. The police asked him a long series of questions, and called in his information to the station to have his background thoroughly checked. In the end, the police were satisfied that Andre wasn't their guy and they let him go. Andre had spent over an hour in the back of that police car.

We often hear popular accounts of the problems of "driving while black," the phenomenon of blacks being pulled over for arbitrary police checks, with the implication that any black man is automatically suspect.[21] Over the course of the fieldwork for this study, I witnessed some of these episodes firsthand. The young men serving as testers in my field experiment were bright college kids, models of discipline and hard work; and yet in the course of their daily lives, they were at times mistaken for the troublemaker types featured on the nightly news. Particularly in casual encounters—such as while driving or when entering a place of business—there sometimes seemed little they could do to signal their distance from the black male stereotype.[22]

On several occasions, for example, black testers were asked in person (before submitting their applications) whether they had a prior criminal history. For these employers, a young black man immediately aroused concern about criminal involvement, and this issue took center stage before getting to matters of education, work experience, or qualifications. None of the white testers, by contrast, was asked about his criminal history up front.[23] These experiences are consistent with Elijah Anderson's account of the suspicion with which young black men are often viewed. According to Anderson, "the anonymous black male is usually an ambiguous figure who arouses the utmost caution and is generally considered dangerous until he proves he is not."[24] Overcoming this initial stereotype becomes one of the first challenges facing the young black male job applicant, particularly in low-wage labor markets where fewer objective indicators (e.g., a college degree, related work history, etc.) are available for, or relevant to, the evaluation.

The effect of race demonstrated here is in part memorable by virtue of its contrast with the effect of a criminal record. Seeing the two categories side by side drives home just how much race matters in employment contexts, with being black viewed as tantamount to being a convicted felon. These effects, however, should by no means be seen as independent.

In an era of mass incarceration, where one in three young black men will wind up in prison, there is reason to associate blacks with criminal activity. High levels of incarceration cast a shadow of criminality over all black men, implicating even those (in the majority) who have remained crime free.

Racial stereotypes of black criminality are further fueled by media coverage of crime, which tends to depict criminal episodes in a heavily racialized context. A study of local television news in Chicago, for example, found that the *largest share* of news stories featuring blacks (on any topic) portrayed blacks as the perpetrators of violent crimes.[25] More often than news about Oprah Winfrey or Michael Jordan (Chicago residents), and more often than news about the thousands of black corporate leaders, professionals, and community organizers in the city, stories about blacks become newsworthy when they have broken the law.

Of course, the frequency of coverage focusing on black criminals does have some basis in reality. Higher arrest rates for blacks will logically translate into greater news coverage of black criminals. But direct comparisons of local crime reports with corresponding arrest rates do not support a straightforward explanation. In one study, for example, researchers compared news reports about crime in the Los Angeles metro area with arrest rates from the California Department of Corrections. Their findings indicated that blacks were 75 percent more likely to be represented as perpetrators in crime reports than their actual arrest rate would have predicted. White offenders, by contrast, were shown on television about 25 percent *less* than their arrest rate would have predicted.[26] Existing racial disparities in criminal justice involvement are thus often exaggerated in the news, with blacks more often—and whites less often—shown in custody than actual crime statistics reveal to be true.

Other studies of race and crime in the news have found media coverage of black criminals to be skewed not only in frequency, but also in kind. A study by Richard Entman and Andrew Rojecki found that news coverage of blacks in custody was more likely to present mug shots (as opposed to a live image, or an image taken prior to arrest), or images of the suspect in handcuffs and under the physical restraints of a white police officer than was true of coverage of whites in custody. Moreover, in coverage of individuals accused of violent crimes, local news broadcasts were nearly twice as likely to provide an on-screen name for whites (47 percent) than for blacks (26 percent). According to the authors, "The presence of the accused's name provides a sense of his or her individual identity. Its absence may suggest that individual identity does not matter, that the accused is part of a single undifferentiated group of violent offenders: just another Black criminal."[27] The more menacing and less individualized images of black suspects provide vivid "evidence" in support of racial stereotypes depicting blacks as dangerous, violent, and criminal.

With roughly 70 percent of Americans identifying television as the source of "most of your news about what's going on in the world today," media distortions of the frequency and severity of offending among blacks can have important consequences for how Americans think about race and how they think about crime.[28] To begin with, the vast overrepresentation of black criminals in the news is linked to distorted images of the race-crime connection. A 1991 survey, for example, asked, "Of all the people arrested for violent crimes in the United States last year, what percent do you think were black?" The modal response to this question was 60 percent, an exaggeration by roughly one-third of the actual proportion at that time.[29] Similarly, an experiment in which individuals were shown a short news clip describing a murder—in which the race of the alleged perpetrator was not identified—found that over 40 percent of subjects falsely recalled having seen a black perpetrator.[30] When the most common image of blacks on TV is that of the criminal offender, the associations between race and crime become virtually automatic.[31]

Indeed, images of blacks as violent or crime prone are among the most salient dimensions of contemporary stereotypes about African Americans. The associations remain deeply embedded in the unconscious and can affect cognitive processing and behavior even of those individuals who consciously repudiate racial stereotypes or discrimination.[32] Social psychological experiments have found that subjects are more likely to interpret ambiguous actions as threatening when the actor is portrayed as African American.[33] Subjects instructed to shoot potentially armed targets in a video game are quicker to do so when the target is African American.[34] Through some combination of higher crime rates, media distortions, and cultural biases, race has become a powerful heuristic with which to assess danger.[35] Particularly in interactions that contain some ambiguity or in decisions made under pressure, evaluations are easily colored by these pervasive (and largely unconscious) stereotypes about black aggressiveness or threat.

Findings such as these suggest that the characteristic of criminality is readily ascribed to blacks. Consequently, even blacks with no history of criminal involvement are likely to suffer some of the same penalties as do ex-offenders of any race. Despite the lack of official conviction record, their job candidacy is nevertheless suspect by virtue of membership in a group with high incarceration rates and pervasive images of criminality.[36] This is not to say that employers are indifferent to a criminal record among blacks. As we saw in the previous chapter, blacks if anything suffer a larger penalty for a criminal record than whites. What this research suggests, by contrast, is that even without an official marker of criminality, blacks are viewed as high-risk employees. Once again, then, we return to one possible far-reaching consequence of our crime policies: steeply rising incarceration rates among blacks cast a shadow of criminality across the black population. The effects of race shown in this study should not be thought of as unrelated to employers' concerns about crime. Rather, it seems to be the case that blacks with or without criminal records are likely to be viewed by employers with suspicion.[37]

Reconciling Competing Measures of Discrimination

If employment discrimination is indeed as great a problem as the results of this and other field experiments suggest, how can we reconcile this conclusion with competing evidence demonstrating a small or nonexistent wage gap between equally qualified blacks and whites? As mentioned earlier, recent analyses of large-scale survey data indicate that, after statistically controlling for a wide range of individual characteristics (cognitive ability, in particular), most or all of the wage gap between young black and white men can be eliminated.[38] The implication of this line of research is that discrimination plays little role in determining the economic attainment of young men. How then can we account for the substantial evidence of discrimination indicated by the audit results?

To make sense of the discrepancies, it is first important to keep in mind that the employment relationship is characterized by a number of discrete decisions, including: hiring, wage setting, promotion, and termination. Discrimination may affect all, none, or some of these decisions. Varying incentives or constraints characteristic of different employment decisions can mediate the emergence of discrimination in important ways. For example, there is reason to believe that decisions about whom to interview and whom to hire may be more susceptible to discriminatory bias than those decisions made at later stages of the employment relationship. Both economic theories of statistical discrimination and social psychological theories of unconscious bias predict that discrimination will be most pronounced when objective information about the target is limited or unreliable.[39] Indeed, the amount of information employers have about applicants at this point of introduction is at a minimum. We would expect, then, that whether exerted consciously or not, underlying assumptions about race and productivity will be most likely to color evaluations of blacks at earlier stages in the employment process (i.e., hiring) than at later stages (i.e., wage setting/termination decisions), when more objective performance indicators become available.[40] Likewise, we would expect to see the effects of discrimination reflected in differential employment rates rather than wage rates.

In addition to information asymmetries that affect employers' perceptions about workers, workers' perceptions of employer decision making are likewise most limited at the point of hire. Uncertainty about the competing applicant pool, about the employer's preferences, and about the job itself make acts of discrimination particularly difficult to detect at the initial point of contact. At later stages, by contrast, workers have more information with which to compare their treatment to that of others in comparable positions. Employers concerned about detection, or even accusations of discrimination, will thus be safer eliminating black applicants early on.

Finally, aside from the distinct conditions that characterize different stages of the employment process, it is important also to consider their interdependence. The presence of discrimination in labor markets can itself produce distortions in the search behavior of job seekers in ways that mask its aggregate consequences. Minority job seekers may avoid generalized job searches, instead limiting their efforts to job sectors or employers thought less likely to discriminate. These dynamics can lead to longer search or wait times for minority job seekers, even if not reflected in ultimate wage offers. The barriers or constraints of discrimination can also add to the psychic costs of a job search, which may lead some to drop out of the labor market altogether.[41] To the extent that discrimination increases joblessness among blacks—whether due to constraints on labor market entry or discouragement from participation—any measure of wage earners will reflect a more select sample of blacks. Trends in labor force participation indeed show high levels of labor force nonparticipation among young black men, and a growing black-white disparity in rates of joblessness.[42] Because individuals who are not working and not looking for work are excluded from standard economic analyses, increases in labor force nonparticipation among blacks can substantially distort conventional measures of racial wage disparities.[43] According to sociologists Bruce Western and Becky Pettit, "By 1999, the high rate of black joblessness inflated black relative earnings by between 7 and 20% among working age men, and by as much 58% among young men."[44] According to this and other analyses, black-white wage equality is in large part an artifact of decreasing labor force participation among the most disadvantaged young black men. Without effectively accounting for the processes that precede labor force participation—such as discrimination, discouragement, incarceration, or other sources of selection—wage estimates can account for only one incomplete picture of the larger employment process.

Discrepancies between wage estimates and measures of discrimination at the point of hire may then reflect one (or both) of two processes. First, incentives to discriminate at the point of hire are greater than those at later stages, due to information asymmetries that affect both employer and worker perceptions. In this case, estimates of hiring discrimination and wage estimates may both represent accurate reflections of discrimination at different stages of the employment relationship. Second, discrimination at the point of hire may distort wage estimates by contributing to the large numbers of young black men who are unemployed or who drop out of the labor force altogether. In this case, wage estimates reflect only the more "select" members of the black population, artificially reducing the contrast with less select white workers. In either scenario, discrimination at the point of hire remains an active barrier to employment for young black men. Indeed, the magnitude of the results shown here, rivaling the effects of a felony conviction, suggest that barriers to labor market entry continue to represent a serious constraint on the achievement of economic self-sufficiency among young black men today.[45]

Conclusion

By focusing on discrimination at the point of hire, this study uncovers an important and much underinvestigated source of racial disadvantage in the low-wage labor market. Blacks are less than half as likely to receive consideration by employers than equally qualified whites, and black nonoffenders fare no better than even those whites with prior felony convictions. The sheer magnitude of these findings underlines the continuing significance of race in employment decisions.

This research cannot identify the precise source of employers' reluctance to hire blacks. Indeed, it is difficult if not impossible to get inside employers' heads to determine what combination of conscious or unconscious considerations may lead to the racial preferences we observe. This chapter considers the influence of high incarceration rates among blacks—and its amplification in the media—as one possible source of racial bias. Indeed, the available evidence points to the pervasiveness of images associating blacks with crime, and the power of these images to strengthen negative feelings about blacks as a group. It may be the case, then, that increasing rates of incarceration among blacks, and its disproportionate coverage in the media, heighten negative reactions toward African Americans generally, irrespective of their personal involvement in crime.

   While the true concerns underlying employers' decisions are difficult to discern, the prima facie evidence shows that race carries important meaning to employers and can often represent the sole basis for dismissing a candidate. According to the results presented here, black men must work at least twice as hard as equally qualified whites simply to overcome the stigma of their skin color. Rather than being merely a problem of the past, direct racial bias continues to shape employment outcomes in ways that contribute to persisting racial inequality.

6 Two Strikes and You're Out: The Intensification of Racial and Criminal Stigma

Jerome arrived at a branch of a national restaurant chain in a suburb twenty miles from Milwaukee. He immediately sensed that he was the only black person in the place. An employee hurried over to him, "Can I help you with something?" "I'm here about the job you advertised," he replied. The employee nodded reluctantly and went off to produce an application form. Jerome filled out the forms, including information about his fictitious criminal history. He was given a math test and a personality test. He was then instructed to wait for the manager to speak with him. The manager came out after about ten minutes, looked over Jerome's application, and frowned when he noticed the criminal history information. Without asking any questions about the context of the conviction, the manager started to lecture: "You can't be screwing up like this at your age. A kid like you can ruin his whole life like this." Jerome began to explain that he had made a mistake and had learned his lesson, but the manager cut him off: "I'll look over your application and call if we have a position for you."

Black testers in the criminal record condition routinely met with frustration in their searches for employment. Even when an interview appeared to be going well, once the employer became aware of the criminal record, things often seemed to go downhill from there. On a few occasions, as in the case described above, employers were fairly straightforward in communicating their disapproval. In others, employers avoided the issue altogether, seeking rather to terminate the interview quickly and move on to other, more suitable candidates. In most cases, though, we can only indirectly interpret employers' reactions by observing their ultimate hiring decisions. Across the span of these decisions, we see a strong aversion to both blacks and ex-offenders, and an even stronger aversion toward applicants bearing both characteristics. Indeed, the extremely low callback rate among black ex-offenders (5 per 100 applications) suggests that the combination of minority status and a criminal record results in almost total exclusion from this labor market. While being black or having a criminal record each represent a strike against the applicant, *with two strikes, you're out.*

The limited number of employers audited in this study prevents us from making strong claims about the reliability of this interaction in the full sample; there are, however, some revealing patterns that emerge from further investigation. In this chapter, I look at how the effects of race and criminal background differed depending on degree of personal contact, location, and occupation. The patterns discerned here more clearly illustrate the intensification of stigma that results when blackness and criminal background are combined.

Two Strikes and You're Out

Why might we expect the combined effects of race and criminal background to be larger than the sum of each effect on its own? What is it about the association between race and crime that generates such strong reactions? According to social psychological research, the activation and application of stereotypes can be triggered both by characteristics of the individual being evaluated and by the context in which the evaluation takes place. With respect to the individual being evaluated, we know that the more closely an individual matches along multiple dimensions of a stereotype, the more powerfully that stereotype will be activated.[1] Racial stereotypes triggered by the appearance of a young black man (already containing an age, race, and gender profile) are further intensified by the revelation of his criminal past. Subtle and perhaps unconscious concerns about black applicants are at once confirmed, weakening any incentive to give a young black man the benefit of the doubt.

Among young white men, by contrast, the reaction is likely to be quite different. Because whites do not fit the stereotypical profile of a criminal, employers may be more willing to overlook a single prior conviction.[2]

A young white man with a criminal background can more convincingly explain that he made a regrettable mistake and has learned his lesson. His prior criminal involvement is then interpreted as an isolated incident rather than an internal disposition. Of course, as we've seen, whites also pay a significant penalty for having a criminal background; but based on the results shown earlier, and confirmed in the analyses presented below, a criminal conviction for a white man does not generate the same level of intensity as it does when presented by a young black male.

At the same time, it is also important to recognize variation in the activation of stereotypes across social contexts. While both race and criminal background show strong effects in all segments of the labor market, particular types of employers or employment interactions generate distinct patterns of responses. In the following discussion, I illustrate the ways in which these differences in reactions to racial and criminal stigma affect employment outcomes in various contexts.

In each of the following comparisons, I look first at the outcomes for white testers, followed by a discussion of the differences in effects for blacks. As in previous comparisons, whites can provide a baseline measure of the outcomes for all applicants with a given set of human capital characteristics. Adding race to this picture—and the interaction of race and criminal record—then demonstrates the often sharp contrast between these groups.

Personal Contact

> Bill, one of the white testers, applied in person at a furniture sales company. The owner of the company was on-site to look over Bill's completed application. The owner read through the application, looked Bill up and down, then looked back at the application. "So it says here you were at the Winnebago Correctional Facility," he stated matter-of-factly, but clearly looking for an explanation. "Yes, I served time for a drug conviction. I made a big mistake in my life and I'm looking to move on," Bill gave the scripted response. The owner looked at him for a moment, seemed satisfied, and went on to ask Bill some questions about his work experience and interests. "Well, you seem okay to me," the owner concluded. Bill seemed to have made a positive impression, despite the awkward beginning.

Stereotypes act in part as guides for individual assessments. When we encounter a stranger, we take note of their age, gender, and race, for example, often before learning anything specific about them as individuals. Each of these characteristics provides clues that help us to form an immediate assessment of the unknown person before we begin the more time-consuming task of acquiring distinguishing information. When an individual seems to neatly fit into a coherent stereotypical category—for example, a young black male with a criminal record—a wealth of inferences about that individual becomes automatically available. The stereotype provides a framework through which to filter the acquisition of subsequent information.[3]

Working against first impressions, one-on-one contact can provide the opportunity to supply personal information that is inconsistent with stereotyped expectations. Through the course of interaction, personalizing information can be passed on, slowly replacing generalizations based on group membership with more nuanced information specific to that individual.[4] A closer look at the ways in which personal contact between testers and employers shaped the outcome of the audits can help us to infer the meanings attached to race and criminal records in the minds of employers and how these views are attenuated or intensified in the course of direct interaction. Though the design of this audit study does not permit direct comparisons of employer treatment by race (because black and white testers visited separate employers), the overall picture demonstrates the substantially different ways in which black testers—in particular those with criminal records—were evaluated in interactions with employers.

Given that this audit study tested only the first stage of the employment process, a majority of tests were completed without significant personal contact with the employer. Testers were instructed to ask to speak to the person in charge of hiring, but often this person was unavailable or appeared only briefly to instruct the tester to fill out the application and wait for a callback. In these cases, only the most superficial indicators are available to the employer when making decisions about which applicants to consider.

In about a quarter of the audits, by contrast, testers had the opportunity to engage in extensive discussions with employers. Whether in the form of an official interview or merely an informal conversation about the job, these interactions allowed testers to demonstrate their highly effective interpersonal abilities and to convey an image of general competence. Comparing the outcomes of testers who did and did not interact with employers allows us to assess to what extent employers notice and utilize interpersonal cues in evaluating entry-level job applicants. Particularly in the case of applicants with criminal records, where stereotypical images

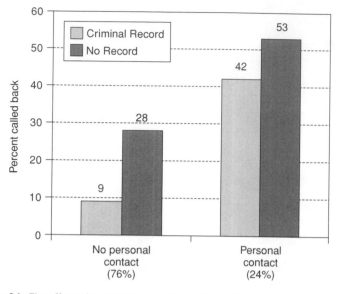

Figure 6.1 The effect of a criminal record for white applicants, by level of personal contact. The main effects of criminal record and personal contact for white applicants are statistically significant ($p < .01$). The interaction between criminal record and personal contact is marginally statistically significant ($p = .07$).

are likely to dominate an employer's evaluation, the presentation of a friendly or trustworthy demeanor may be especially important.

As it turns out, personal contact did go a long way in reducing the negative effects of a criminal record; but these effects differed substantially by race. Figure 6.1 presents the percentage of callbacks received by white testers by criminal status and personal contact. Personal contact here includes conversations with employers and/or formal interviews, as recorded by testers on their postapplication data sheet.[5] We can see here that personal contact is associated with a much higher likelihood of receiving a callback for all white testers. When testers had the opportunity to interact with employers, the rate of callbacks for nonoffenders nearly doubled, and that for ex-offenders was nearly five times as great. Correspondingly, the effect of a criminal record diminishes in those cases where testers had the opportunity to interact with the employer. Indeed, the penalty associated with a criminal record drops from 70 percent to 20 percent among testers who had personal contact with the employer. Presenting personal indicators that are at odds with the stereotypical profile of a criminal appears to offset the strong negative reactions otherwise activated by a criminal record. For employers concerned that ex-offenders will be aggressive or uncouth, personal contact can effectively attenuate these associations,

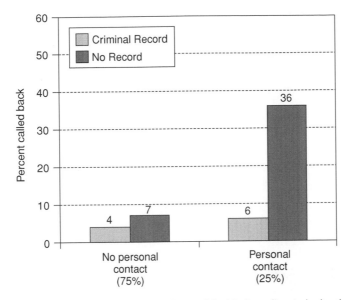

Figure 6.2 The effect of a criminal record for black applicants, by level of personal contact. The main effects of criminal record and personal contact for black applicants are statistically significant ($p < .01$). In a model including an interaction between the two, the main effect of a criminal record becomes insignificant, while the interaction term demonstrates a large and marginally statistically significant negative effect ($p < .06$).

offering the applicant a better chance to demonstrate his true capabilities.[6]

Of course, we must also acknowledge the possibility that there may be something specific about these firms that makes them more responsive to all applicants. Employers who are experiencing acute labor shortages, for example, may be those who tend to be present to conduct on-the-spot interviews (as a strategy to fill vacancies more quickly). This would result in an association between personal contact and hiring probabilities in the absence of any mediating effects. As we will see below, however, the fact that personal contact has a very different effect for black testers suggests that the interaction itself—rather than merely the types of employers likely to interact—does in fact have a direct effect on hiring outcomes.

Figure 6.2 presents the percentage of callbacks received by black testers in each condition. The picture is strikingly different. On the one hand, as in the case of whites, personal contact does increase the likelihood of a callback for blacks *without* criminal records. In fact, black nonoffenders were five times as likely to receive a callback if they had had personal contact, whereas whites were only about twice as likely. In this respect, interpersonal cues certainly seem to strengthen the applicant's case, perhaps mediating initial negative racial stereotypes.[7] Indeed, in one interview for a delivery job at an upscale cabinetry store, the employer asked Jerome, one of the black testers, whether he had a criminal record. After being told "no," the employer told the tester he was "just the sort of person we're looking for." Jerome had made a good impression on the employer and, with reassurance of his clean background, appeared to have assuaged any of the employer's lingering concerns.

In contrast to blacks with clean records, personal contact did little to improve the outcomes of black ex-offenders. Indeed, quite different from the situation with white applicants, where personal contact increased the likelihood of a callback for all testers and narrowed the gap between those with and without criminal records, for black applicants, personal contact actually widens the disparities. As we can see in figure 6.2, among those who had no contact with the employer, black testers with criminal records were roughly 40 percent less likely to be called back than those without criminal records. Among those who did have personal contact, by contrast, there was more than an 80 percent difference. Black ex-offenders are thus substantially worse off relative to nonoffenders when they have the opportunity to interact with employers. Far from the payoff we saw to white ex-offenders following conversations with employers, black ex-offenders fall ever further behind.

Before making too much of this finding, it is important to remember that these three-way interactions are based on small sample sizes. Although black testers completed 200 audits in total (or 400 tester-visits), only 38 tester visits resulted in a callback. As a result, the actual proportions in these figures are based on small sample sizes: the number in each of these cells is 7, 10, 3, and 18, respectively. Small fluctuations in the number of callbacks among black ex-offenders, therefore, could make large differences in the comparison of effect sizes. Despite the small sample sizes, the interactions between race, criminal record, and personal contact are statistically significant.[8] In this case, then, the disparity is unlikely to be due to simply to chance.

Even though these testers were bright, articulate, and personable, these traits appear insufficient to overcome the intense negative attributions that accompany the combination of blackness and criminal background. Although whites with criminal records seem to benefit a great deal from personal interaction with employers, this type of interaction does nothing to improve the chances for blacks with criminal histories. Even a bright, friendly demeanor appears immaterial relative to the profound stigma associated with race and criminal involvement.

City and Suburban Location

> After returning from a day of testing, Darrell reflected on the site of a job he'd just applied for. "There's nothing in Franklin but white people and prisoners." Franklin, a suburb on the outskirts of Milwaukee, was indeed a very white part of town. Apart from the population housed in the Franklin Correctional Facility, very few blacks live or work nearby. It is in suburbs like these where job growth in the Milwaukee metropolitan area is most rapid. The residents in the suburbs of Milwaukee clearly look different from those in the city; and the urban job seekers who make their way to these locations are often made to feel their difference.

A great deal of sociological literature has described the vast inequalities in employment between city and suburb.[9] Changes in the spatial distribution of job growth have been highly consequential for the employment prospects of urban job seekers, as job development has primarily occurred outside the city in areas generally less accessible to central city residents. Indeed, a recent survey of employment in the Milwaukee metropolitan area found that more than 90 percent of recent job growth was in the outlying areas, compared to only 4 percent of new jobs in the central city of Milwaukee.[10] These trends are in sharp contrast to the location of job seekers who are far more heavily concentrated in the city. In 2001 the ratio of persons seeking work relative to full-time job openings in the central city of Milwaukee was close to 8 to 1, compared to a ratio of just over 3 to 1 for the county as a whole.[11]

Previous research has suggested that the "spatial mismatch" between job growth and job seekers has been an important source of minority disadvantage.[12] It is not clear from the available literature, however, whether the obstacles to employment are created by physical distance alone, or whether those employers located far from minority populations actively seek to avoid minority workers.[13] On the one hand, the concentration of job growth in suburban areas, paired with high levels of residential segregation, implies a growing distance between black urban residents and emerging job opportunities. The cost of transportation to these jobs is often prohibitive, particularly for entry-level jobs for which compensation is minimal. Even among those willing to make the journey, information about job opportunities in the distant suburbs is less likely to make its way to central city residents. These barriers of access—including both transportation and information—reduce the pool of black applicants for suburban jobs, with a corresponding reduction in black employment overall.[14]

This first explanation remains silent on the issue of employer prefer-ences. Racial segregation in housing and social networks contributes to segregated applicant pools, with employers simply drawing from the pool that is available. Other interpretations of the spatial mismatch hypothe-sis, by contrast, argue that firm location is directly related to a preferred applicant type. Employers who wish to avoid disadvantaged populations are more likely to locate themselves far from the central city. Previous research, for example, has shown a deep reluctance among suburban em-ployers to hire racial minorities, openly expressing concerns about the characteristics of black men from the central city. According to one sub-urban employer quoted in a study by William Julius Wilson, "We have some problems with blacks . . . I find that the blacks aren't as hard work-ers as Hispanics and—or the Italian or whatever. . . . The black kind of has a, you-owe-me kind of an attitude." Another reported a similar sentiment, "They tend to laziness . . . I think people are willing to give them a chance and then it's like they really don't want to work."[15] As a more system-atic investigation, economist Harry Holzer investigated characteristics of employers related to the likelihood of hiring a black worker for a recent noncollege job opening. Controlling for the racial composition of the ap-plicant pool, suburban employers were significantly less likely than those in the city to hire an African American.[16] According to these and similar studies, "the problem isn't space. It's race."[17]

With respect to criminal records, there is a small amount of evidence pointing in the opposite direction. Holzer found suburban employers to be somewhat less resistant to hiring applicants with criminal records (and less likely to conduct criminal background checks) than their coun-terparts in the city.[18] It may be the case that central city employers more often encounter ex-offenders among their applicant pool and are there-fore more sensitized to concerns about criminal backgrounds. Whatever the case, we have little concrete information about how employers in various parts of a metropolitan area respond to job applicants of varying characteristics. In fact, because of limitations in existing data sources, it has been difficult to tease out the elements of supply and demand (or space and race) that produce the observed patterns.

Among the biggest limitations, studies of spatial mismatch have been plagued by the problems of selection, or the possibility that residents of the central city may differ from suburban residents in important unob-served ways that make them less employable.[19] If this is the case, the problems of mismatch have less to do with the location of jobs and job seekers and more to do with the quality of workers located near and far from new job growth. Researchers have used creative techniques in attempts to control for selective migration and individual background characteristics.[20] Available data sources, however, are typically limited in the number and quality of control variables available, leaving open the possibility of spatial misattribution.

The design of the audit study offers a novel approach to the study of spatial mismatch. Job seekers are matched on neighborhood of residence, mode of transportation (private vehicle), source of information about job openings (classified ads), and all job-relevant characteristics. Within this model, therefore, the effects of transportation, information, and individual selection are effectively controlled; we can then assess the degree to which employer preferences for blacks, whites, and ex-offenders vary by location. The extensive controls in the current study design are perhaps overly conservative. Suburban employers with strong preferences against workers from the central city are likely to advertise through informal networks or local suburban newspapers rather than in the major metropolitan newspapers, and thus are less likely to show up in our sample. Likewise, many suburban employers are located far from the reach of public transportation, further constraining the opportunities of job seekers who do not have their own cars. We would expect, then, that the results found here may understate the degree to which suburban employers resist certain applicant types.

Starting again with whites, figure 6.3 presents callback rates by criminal status and location. The results here indicate that the overall demand for employment is substantially higher in the suburbs and surrounding counties than in the city of Milwaukee. Among white testers with and without a criminal record, the likelihood of a callback is significantly greater in suburban areas; in fact, the rate of callbacks among white ex-offenders in the suburbs is approximately equal to that of white nonoffenders in the city. Location, therefore, is highly consequential with respect to the likelihood of finding employment. Furthermore, these results indicate that the effect of a criminal record is smaller among suburban employers than among those in the city. The move from city to suburb corresponds to drop in the penalty of a criminal record from 70 to 45 percent. Though this interaction does not reach statistical significance in the present sample, the magnitude of the effect is nevertheless worthy of consideration. While a criminal record remains a major barrier in all contexts, suburban employers appear to be somewhat less put off by evidence of a white applicant's criminal history than are city employers. This finding is consistent with evidence from Holzer's study that suburban employers are less likely to screen for criminal background information in their recruitment of noncollege workers. It is also consistent with general

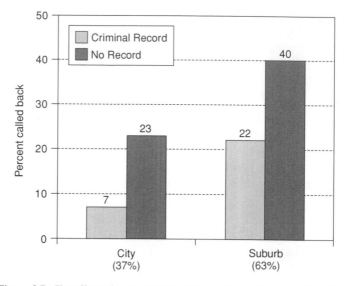

Figure 6.3 The effect of a criminal record for white applicants, by location. The main effects of criminal record and location (city vs. suburb) for white applicants are statistically significant ($p < .01$). The interaction between the two is not statistically significant.

arguments about labor supply, according to which the higher overall demand for workers among suburban employers should lead to less differentiation on the basis of worker characteristics (such as a criminal record). Whatever the case, it appears that the problem of spatial mismatch for white ex-offenders is not indicative of employer tastes. Though suburban jobs may be more difficult to access for ex-offenders from the city due to limited and costly public transportation, for those that make it into the applicant pool their chances of selection improve substantially.

Once again, however, we see a different story emerge for black job seekers. In fact, for blacks, the higher demand for workers in the suburbs appears to offer little benefit. In figure 6.4, we see that, moving from city to suburb, the increase in callbacks for black nonoffenders is less than 50 percent (compared to a jump of almost 100 percent among white nonoffenders). Among blacks with criminal records, on the other hand, the move from city to suburb actually lowers the likelihood of a callback. In fact, the interaction between race and criminal record becomes statistically significant among suburban employers, with black ex-offenders facing substantially worse prospects in suburban job searches than the additive effects of race and criminal record would predict.[21] Far from benefiting from the tighter labor market in the suburbs, black ex-offenders fare espe-

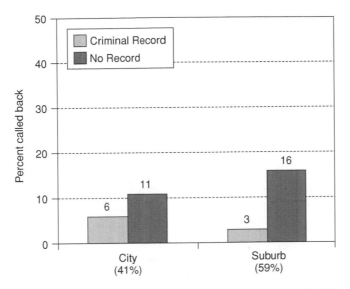

Figure 6.4 The effect of a criminal record for black testers, by location.
The main effect of a criminal record for black applicants is statistically
significant ($p < .001$) whereas the main effect of location (city vs. suburb)
is not. There is a large and statistically significant positive interaction
between city location and criminal record, indicating the substantial
advantage to black ex-offenders in the city over the suburbs ($p < .05$).

cially poorly in suburban job searches.[22] The net result of these disparate
effects is a widening of the criminal record effect for suburban employment. In contrast to whites, for whom the effect of a criminal record was
less pronounced among suburban employers, among blacks, the ratio of
callbacks for nonoffenders compared to offenders is less than 2:1 in the
city, but more than 5:1 in the suburbs. Callback rates remain, nevertheless,
quite low for blacks in the city; but among those city employers willing to
hire blacks, a criminal record presents less of an obstacle than it does in
the suburban context. Though suburban employers are somewhat more
likely than their city counterparts to consider black nonoffenders, they
all but close their doors to black applicants with criminal histories.

The interaction between race, criminal record, and location suggests
some interesting insights into the relative preferences of city and suburban employers. While suburban employers are generally more responsive
to applicants of all kinds—reflecting the tighter labor market in suburban
areas—this rule does not apply to blacks with criminal records. Spatial
mismatch, therefore, is unlikely to be the consequence solely of physical distance between employers and job seekers. Suburban employers do
exert different preferences for low-wage workers, with black ex-offenders

ranking well at the bottom of their queue. Once again we see that the combination of race and criminal record has an effect far more powerful than does either attribute on its own. In the case of suburban employers, being black *or* an ex-offender may be tolerable, but the combination of the two represents almost full grounds for exclusion. As in the case of personal contact above, the "two strikes and you're out" phenomenon applies in the context of suburban employment as well.

Occupational Category: The Case of Restaurant Jobs

A third domain in which tester experiences differed was across occupational categories. Job types varied substantially in terms of the profile of workers needed, from physical stature (for jobs involving lifting and carrying) to knowledge of Milwaukee roads (for delivery drivers) to an outgoing friendly demeanor (for sales jobs). The norms and expectations of workers across occupational categories may likewise affect relative openness to minority applicants or applicants with criminal records.

One notable difference among occupational types was the relative frequency with which applicants were asked about their criminal histories. Among six major occupational categories, restaurant jobs stood out in particular as the least likely to request criminal history information on application forms (see figure 6.5). In fact, among restaurant jobs included in this sample, just over half included questions about the applicant's criminal background, compared to more than 75 percent in all other occupational categories.[23] It is worth considering how this and other distinctive characteristics of restaurant jobs may affect the hiring patterns of blacks and ex-offenders.

Restaurant jobs have high rates of turnover and offer low fixed wages (with the assumption that a majority of the employee's compensation will come from tips). The combination of these conditions often leads to the

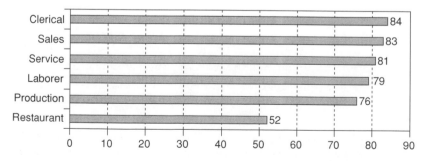

Figure 6.5 Percentage of applications requesting criminal background information.

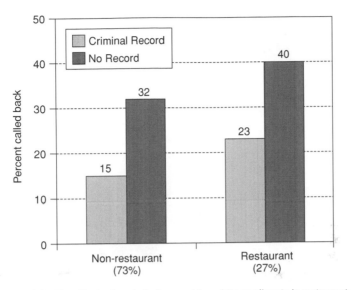

Figure 6.6 The effect of a criminal record for white applicants in restaurant and nonrestaurant jobs. The main effect of a criminal record is statistically significant ($p < .001$) whereas the main effect of restaurant occupation and the interaction between the two are not statistically significant.

casting of a wide recruitment net and lower restrictions on candidacy. Indeed, among white testers, restaurant jobs offered one of the highest rates of callbacks for those both with and without criminal records. Employers often seemed eager to hire applicants right away and were perhaps therefore less put off by information about their criminal past.

Figure 6.6 presents the callback rates for white testers by criminal status for restaurant and nonrestaurant jobs. As we can see, rates of callbacks were higher among restaurant jobs for white applicants with and without criminal records, and, likewise, the gap between applicants with and without criminal records is somewhat smaller than in other occupational types. The outcomes for blacks were markedly different (see figure 6.7). Restaurant jobs were among the least likely to result in callbacks for black testers, irrespective of criminal condition. This difference is large and statistically significant, with the size of the race effect more than doubling for restaurant jobs.[24]

The story among restaurant jobs has much more to do with race than criminal background. In fact, the results presented here likely overstate the impact of a criminal record in these jobs. Recall that testers presented résumés with information about their criminal history in all cases, even when the information was not explicitly solicited by employers. This

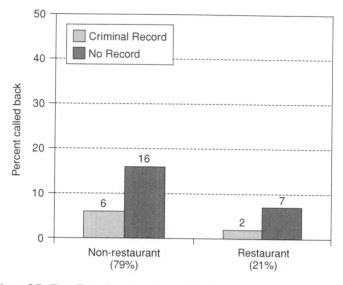

Figure 6.7 The effect of a criminal record for black applicants in restaurant and nonrestaurant jobs. The main effect of a criminal record is statistically significant ($p < .001$) whereas the main effect of restaurant occupation and the interaction between the two are not statistically significant.

approach ensures uniformity across the employer audits and provides information about how employers view criminal history information, whether or not they explicitly request it. Indeed, this information grows increasingly relevant given the rapid adoption of criminal background screens as part of standard hiring procedures. Nevertheless, because restaurant employers are the least likely of all employers to request information about criminal histories, it is worth considering how the results may have turned out had no unsolicited information been presented. Under some simple assumptions, we can recalculate callback rates to generate this estimate. Assume that in all cases where employers did not ask about criminal history, testers in the criminal record condition would have received callbacks if their nonoffender partner received a callback. This assumption imposes a condition of equal treatment in cases where the employer would not have otherwise known about the criminal record, ignoring any random variation in tester outcomes that can also produce differential treatment at the level of individual tests. Under this set of assumptions, 35 percent of white testers with a criminal record would have received callbacks in restaurant jobs (compared to the actual callback rate of 23 percent). This accounts for roughly 70 percent of the difference in treatment among whites with and without criminal records in restaurant jobs.

Likewise, the callback rate for black ex-offenders would have been close to 5 percent in the absence of unsolicited criminal background information, accounting for 50 percent of the difference in treatment among blacks with and without criminal backgrounds in restaurant jobs. Though the effects of a criminal record remain significant in all cases, restaurant jobs appear far more open to ex-offenders, particularly for whites. In stark contrast, however, the effects of race dominate the patterns of hiring outcomes in this job sector. Employment prospects for blacks in restaurant jobs are less than half that for other jobs types, and the hiring rates for black ex-offenders (without correction) drop close to zero.

It is surprising that such a low-wage, high-turnover job would demonstrate such strong signs of discrimination. On the other hand, the high level of customer contact required in restaurant jobs makes some forms of discrimination more likely. Other research on customer service positions has emphasized the relevance of "customer discrimination," or the idea that customers prefer to be waited on by members of a particular race or gender.[25] Following this reasoning, if employers believe that diners prefer white waiters to black ones, this creates an incentive to discriminate against black applicants. Though the rationale behind employers' decisions is difficult to investigate directly, the consequences are readily apparent in restaurants throughout the country. More often than not, we see whites heavily represented in positions at the "front of the house"—hosts and waitstaff—while minorities are concentrated at the back, among busboys, dishwashers, and cooks.[26] Unfortunately, with waitstaff positions representing the highest proportion of entry-level job openings in the Milwaukee labor market (making up nearly one-quarter of job openings in this sample), the effects of this racial coding of jobs are likely to be seriously debilitating for the employment prospects of black workers.

Compounding Stigma: Concluding Remarks

Exploring the interaction between race and criminal record across different contexts, we detect the ways in which black ex-offenders face an intensification of stigma, above and beyond the simple additive effects of either characteristic alone. Given the small sample sizes available for these comparisons, these findings can be considered only preliminary hypotheses in need of further investigation. The consistency of effects across domains, however, provides some assurance that this phenomenon is not merely artifactual. Compounding employers' general aversion to hiring blacks—shown most vividly in the context of restaurant jobs—the combination of blackness and a criminal record is met with stark resistance.

Even in cases where demand for workers is high, such as in the suburbs, employers appear unwilling to overlook the two strikes against black ex-offenders. Moreover, if these findings hold true among applicants with effective interpersonal skills, high levels of motivation, and reliable transportation, one can only wonder what the outcomes may be for black ex-offenders with additional disadvantages. Indeed, if representative of larger trends, these results suggest some troubling conclusions for the growing numbers of blacks with criminal records. Already burdened by their disproportionate representation in prison, blacks carry the added weight of compounding stigma. The combination of blackness and criminal record creates barriers to employment that in many contexts appear virtually impossible to overcome.

7

But What If...?:
Variations on the Experimental Design

Following any experiment, observers are likely to ask, "But what if the experimental condition had been constructed differently?" or "What if the experiment had been administered in a different time or place?" The beauty of the experiment is its clean execution of targeted mechanisms; its main limitation, however, is the inability to accommodate more than a few experimental conditions, and thus the difficulty in generalizing the findings to other contexts. Recognizing the limitations to the experimental approach, I decided to supplement my data collection by conducting a telephone survey of the employers as well. The audit study let things play out in one way; talking with employers, I was able to pursue the possibility of many others.

Following the completion of the audit study, each employer was asked to participate in a telephone survey about his/her priorities and concerns with respect to hiring entry-level workers.[1] In the survey, employers were asked a variety of questions about their attitudes towards applicants with criminal records, probing both general and specific dimensions of their reactions. The results of the survey allow us to follow up on a number of questions left unanswered by the audit study, providing a more complete understanding of how and why employers make the hiring decisions they do. For example, the survey allows us to ask: How do the attitudes of Milwaukee employers compare to those of employers in other metropolitan areas? How do employers' reactions to applicants with criminal records

117

compare to their reactions to other groups of marginalized workers? How do employers view drug offenders as opposed to individuals convicted of other kinds of crimes? How do employers respond to information about various criminal sanctions? Pursuing answers to these questions in the context of the audit methodology would require enormous amounts of time and resources. Each new condition added to an experiment requires a doubling of the sample size, with associated increases in logistical complications and cost. Incorporating each of these variations at once would be virtually impossible. In the context of a telephone survey, by contrast, multiple scenarios can be readily assessed.

In this chapter, I draw on employers' perspectives for an understanding of the ways things might have played out differently in the audit. At the same time, these responses can help us to better understand why things turned out the way they did. Probing employers' views on hiring entry-level workers, and in particular their views on applicants with criminal records, we can gain a deeper perspective as to when and how a criminal record becomes a determining factor in hiring decisions.[2]

It should be acknowledged from the outset that survey data have their own weaknesses. Surveys rely on respondents to provide accurate accountings of their attitudes and behaviors, a condition that is not always realized.[3] Nevertheless, survey data do provide a useful window into employers' perspectives. While not all survey answers can allow us to predict employers' behavior in any given hiring situation, they can shed light on how employers think about the hiring process and how they experience the various kinds of applicants they are confronted with in the search for low-wage workers.

How Do Milwaukee Employers Compare to Those in Other Cities?

One key limitation of the audit study design is its concentration on a single metropolitan area. Studies of this kind are time-consuming and costly, and thus multi-city designs are rare. Because levels of discrimination can be heavily influenced by regional and cultural forces, it is difficult to know how well the findings from one city can be generalized to others. In the present study, Milwaukee was chosen for having a profile common to many major American cities with respect to population size, racial composition, and unemployment rate. There are, however, certain features unique to Milwaukee that limit its representativeness. In particular, recent trends in incarceration in the state of Wisconsin, though low in an absolute sense, indicated rapid movement toward more a punitive approach toward crime control. Between 1991 and 1998, Wisconsin had the third largest

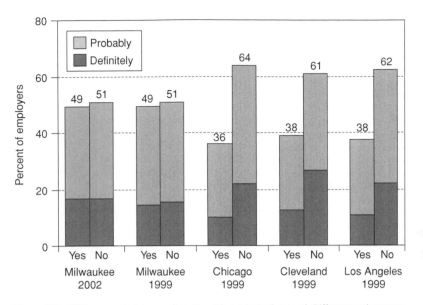

Figure 7.1 Willingness to hire applicants with a criminal record. Differences between Milwaukee and other cities, based on two-sample tests of proportions, are statistically significant ($p < .05$). Source for 1999 data: Harry J. Holzer and Michael Stoll, *Employers and Welfare Recipients: The Effects of Welfare Reform in the Workplace* (San Francisco: Public Policy Institute of California, 2001).

growth in incarceration rates and, at the time of the study, the highest rate of incarceration for blacks in the country.[4] If statewide incarceration trends are reflective of an especially punitive approach to crime, this could also affect the degree to which a criminal record is condemned by employers, particularly among black applicants.

In considering the distinctiveness of Milwaukee as a site for this study, we can look to existing survey research to gain some leverage on this issue.[5] One of the survey questions assessing employer attitudes about hiring ex-offenders was drawn from a previous survey administered in Milwaukee and several other cities in 1999. It is thus possible to directly compare the responses of Milwaukee employers in this sample to those of employers in other metropolitan areas. In both surveys, employers were asked: "Next, I am going to list several types of applicants. Please tell me if you would accept each type for [your most recent noncollege] position. . . . An applicant who has a criminal record?" The four response categories included "definitely will," "probably will," "probably not," and "definitely not." Figure 7.1 compares the distribution of response categories among employers in the four cities. Note that the distribution of responses for the earlier Milwaukee survey and the present study are identical, providing strong reassurance of the comparability of these samples. These findings demonstrate that Milwaukee employers, in fact, report a significantly greater openness to considering applicants with criminal records than employers in Chicago, Cleveland, and Los Angeles. Whereas in the other three cities nearly two-thirds of employers reported that they would definitely not or probably not accept an applicant with a criminal record, in Milwaukee only half of employers expressed negative reactions.[6] Far from expressing extreme negative responses, therefore, employers in Milwaukee demonstrate a surprising level of openness compared to employers in other metropolitan areas. If these patterns are indicative of actual hiring practices among employers in each of these cities, the employment prospects for ex-offenders elsewhere may be far worse than those documented here. It is rather surprising that Milwaukee represents such an outlier in this respect. There have been few regional comparisons of attitudes toward ex-offenders and therefore there is little prior research to draw from in forming an explanation. It may be the case that because of Wisconsin's tight labor market since the mid to late 1990s, employers have grown more tolerant of less desirable workers. Certainly, Milwaukee has had a substantially lower unemployment rate throughout the period of observation than any of the other cities listed here.[7] And yet, we do not see the same patterns in response to applicants with other undesirable characteristics. In fact, Milwaukee employers are less likely to consider hiring applicants with unstable work histories or those who have been unemployed for more than a year than employers in Chicago, Cleveland, and Los Angeles.[8] So worker shortages have not led Milwaukee employers to show more tolerance on all dimensions.

Alternatively, the greater openness of Milwaukee employers may have to do with the legal protection afforded to ex-offenders in Wisconsin, under expanded fair employment regulations. While very few cases have come to court, these laws may set a precedent for (or, alternatively, reflect a culture of) greater openness toward individuals with prior convictions.[9] The legal environment establishes a set of prescriptive norms about fair and appropriate hiring practices. To the extent that employers respond to these norms, hiring decisions may be modified as a result.[10] (See below for a discussion of an additional set of legal constraints.)

Whatever the reason, it seems that Milwaukee does not stand out for its negative views towards ex-offenders; if anything, the city is an outlier in its tolerance of applicants with criminal records. The results reported in this study, therefore, may represent a best-case scenario in portraying the views of employers in other metropolitan areas.

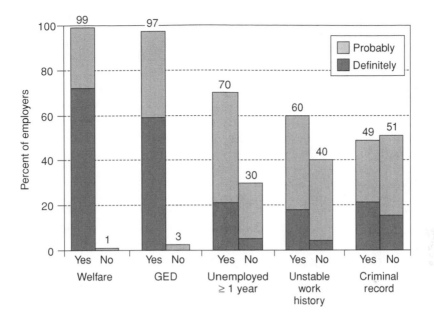

Figure 7.2   Willingness to hire applicants from various marginalized groups (Milwaukee employers, 2002). All comparisons with the criminal record category are statistically significant ($p < .05$), based on a one-sample test of proportions with repeated measures.

How Do Ex-Offenders Fare Compared to Other Groups of Low-Wage Workers?

Though Milwaukee employers may be more open to ex-offenders than are employers in other cities, it would be misleading to conclude that they were indifferent to the issue. Recall that at least half of employers would probably or definitely *not* accept an applicant with a criminal record. Thus without any additional information about the candidate, a criminal record forms a fairly strong basis for employment decisions.

The salience of a criminal record in the evaluations of employers can be better understood when compared to considerations of other marginalized workers. Figure 7.2 compares the distribution of responses concerning an applicant with a criminal record to those of an applicant on welfare, an applicant with a GED (instead of a high school diploma), an applicant who has been unemployed for a year or more, and an applicant with only short-term or part-time work experience.[11] These results demonstrate that virtually all Milwaukee employers are "probably" or "definitely" willing to accept applicants on welfare or with GEDs; roughly 70 percent are willing to accept applicants with long histories of unemployment, 60 percent are willing to accept applicants with only short-term or part-time work experience, while just under 50 percent are willing to accept applicants with criminal records. A criminal record, therefore, stands out as the most damaging characteristic in this array. Even characteristics directly related to worker quality (e.g., the work history variables) are less consequential than are the character traits or behavioral patterns associated with a criminal record. Ex-offenders remain at the bottom of the hiring queue, facing closed doors to employment from roughly half of all employers.

How Do Employers Respond to the Type of Conviction?

A logical question to ask about the results from the audit study has to do with how things might have been different given a different choice of offense. Perhaps employers are particularly wary of drug offenders because of their potential problems with addiction and the many complications that go along with drug abuse. Maybe if another crime had been chosen, the results would have turned out differently. Again, where adding several new variables to the experiment would have been unrealistic, the survey results allow us to directly probe employers' views about different classes of ex-offenders. Here we can see whether employers are sensitive to the type of conviction rather than the simple fact of law breaking and, if so, what crime types cause the greatest concern.

In order to explore the ways employers think about and react to various kinds of applicants with criminal records, respondents were read a vignette describing a hypothetical applicant with a prior felony drug conviction. A series of follow-up questions then measured responses to applicants with prior convictions for property or violent crimes. The applicant described in the vignette was designed to closely match the profile of the testers in the audit study in terms of age, education, and work experience. Employers who had been audited by white testers were read a vignette in which the hypothetical applicant was white; employers who had been audited by black testers were read a vignette in which the applicant was black. The hypothetical applicant was introduced with the following description:

> Chad is a twenty-three-year-old [black/white] male. He finished high school and has steady work experience in entry-level jobs. He has good references and interacts well with people. About a year ago, Chad was convicted of a drug felony and served twelve months in prison. Chad was released last month and is now looking for a job. How likely would you be to hire Chad for an entry-level opening in your company?

Overall, employers were fairly open to considering someone like Chad: fully 62 percent reported being "somewhat likely" or "very likely" to hire him.[12] Recall that, earlier in the survey, only 49 percent of employers indicated that they would "probably" or "definitely" hire a generic "applicant with a criminal record." Employers appear sensitive to the specifics of Chad's profile, which presents a more appealing candidate than the generic (stereotypical) image of an ex-offender, both in terms of personal qualifications and type of offense.[13]

Following the initial vignette, employers were asked to report the likelihood of hiring Chad if, instead of having been convicted of a drug crime, he had been convicted of a property crime such as burglary. Here we see a dramatic change in receptivity. Only 30 percent of employers reported being somewhat or very likely to hire this applicant–half the number who were willing to consider a drug offender (see figure 7.3). Presumably, employers are concerned about the common problem of employee theft, with a property crime conviction sending a red light that the applicant cannot be trusted. Indeed, a separate analysis of the association between job requirements and the likelihood of hiring various types of offenders confirms this intuition: employers hiring for jobs that require handling cash are significantly less likely to report a willingness to hire a property offender. By contrast, there is no significant relationship between the requirement of handling cash and employers' willingness to hire a drug offender (see table 7B.1). This reinforces the impression that employers are at least somewhat sensitive to the direct relationship between offense type and job requirements, apart from the general wariness of applicants with criminal backgrounds. In part because many entry-level positions require workers to handle money on the job, the number of employers willing to hire a property offender is quite low. The final conviction type employers were asked to consider was that of "a violent crime, such as assault." Here employers expressed even more serious reservations, with less than a quarter indicating that they would be somewhat or very likely to hire the applicant, and roughly half saying they were "very unlikely" to hire him. By contrast, only 20 percent of those considering a drug offender and 37 percent of those considering a property offender were "very unlikely" to make the hire because of the conviction. Not surprisingly, a history of violent crime is of greater concern to employers than the other crime types. In discussing their concerns about applicants with criminal records (at another point in the survey), several employers emphasized concerns over the "vulnerability of people we serve" or the "threat to the other workers." Introducing an ex-offender into the workplace leaves open the potential for threatening altercations. For these employers, a

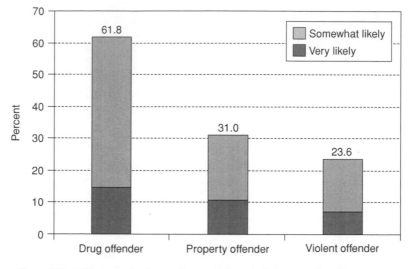

Figure 7.3 Willingness to hire applicants with a criminal record, by offense type. Percentages have been averaged across employers in both vignette conditions (i.e., black and white). Differences between the drug offender category and other crime types are statistically significant ($p < .01$).

primary concern was what the conviction might signal about the likelihood of future violence in the workplace. Irrespective of how accurate this expectation may be, the employment prospects for violent ex-offenders are likely to be minimal.

In interpreting these results, we should note that certain aspects of the survey design may inadvertently inflate contrasts among crime categories. Because employers are asked to respond to a series of items in which only one characteristic varies, their attention is fully focused on the particular variable in question (e.g., the difference between drug offender and property offender). In the real world, by contrast, employers' attention is rarely drawn to such specific dimensions of a criminal record, and thus the degree to which they distinguish among these characteristics may be more muted than the contrasts shown here.[14] If, however, these results do reflect the true preference ordering of employers (even if the absolute contrast is not as large), we would conclude that the audit study represents a fairly conservative estimate of the effect of a criminal record, given stronger negative reactions to other classes of offenders. If the audit study had included a property crime such as burglary or a violent crime such as assault instead of the drug crime, the penalty associated with a criminal record might well have been substantially larger that that reported earlier.

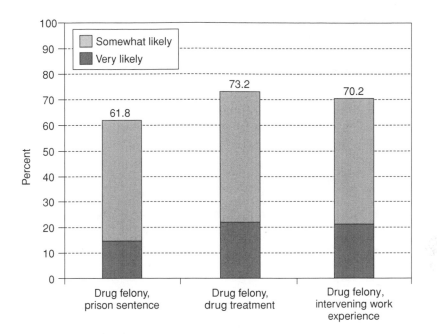

Figure 7.4 Willingness to hire applicants with a criminal record, by context of sanction. Percentages have been averaged across employers in both vignette conditions (i.e., black and white). Differences between the "prison sentence" category and others are statistically significant ($p < .05$).

How Do Employers Respond to the Type of Sanction?

One of the central questions of this book concerns how the increasing criminalization of young men affects labor market outcomes. The relevant policy implications encourage a rethinking of our system of punishment, or at least some careful attention to our choices of punishment. Are there alternative sanctions or interventions that may be less consequential for subsequent employment? This section takes a look at a few realistic sentencing alternatives in order to see whether employers may respond differently to applicants depending on the context of their conviction.

In the initial vignette (as in the audit study), Chad had recently been released from prison, having served time for a felony drug conviction. Employers were later asked to consider their reaction to Chad had he been through a drug treatment program instead of going to prison. Employers were indeed substantially more likely to consider this applicant, with roughly 73 percent of employers expressing a willingness to hire such a candidate compared to the 62 percent willing to hire the drug offender coming straight from prison (see figure 7.4).

Presumably, employers view treatment as an indicator of the likelihood of rehabilitation. An obvious concern to employers in considering a drug offender is the possibility that he might continue to be a user. Indeed, in open-ended portions of the survey, several employers explicitly stated this concern as their primary objection to hiring an applicant with a drug felony conviction (see Table 7B.2 for a summary of employers' open-ended responses). More than a dozen employers mentioned concerns about drug use, and half of those emphasized that hiring would be conditional on passing a drug test. "The only problem is if he's still a user," explained one employer. "I'm afraid of repeat behavior." Certainly drug use in the workplace is a major concern among employers, given the consequences for productivity and possible injury. Employers wanted evidence that the applicant had gone straight, with several employers mentioning that they would be much more likely consider Chad if he had participated in some type of rehabilitation program. An employer for a mechanical parts plant said he would hire Chad only "if he has gone through some type of rehab and is able to stay off the drugs." This employer, along with a number of others, sought tangible evidence that drug use would not continue to be a problem in the lives of these workers. As illustrated by the positive responses to the vignette item, knowledge that the individual has undergone treatment provides greater reassurance that he will be able to stay clean from drugs in the future.

Employers may also evaluate the seriousness of the offense according to the severity of the sanctions. Prison represents a more serious—and therefore more stigmatizing—form of punishment than does community-based treatment, even though there can be substantial overlap in the types of offenders placed in either setting. Employers may assume that drug offenders who are placed in treatment programs tend to be less serious offenders than are those who receive prison sentences. The choice of sanction can thus send an important signal to employers about who's okay and who is not.

Whether employers view treatment as an indicator of the seriousness of the offense or of the likelihood of recovery, it is clear that employers are more wary of individuals coming out of prison than of those who have received rehabilitative intervention. The context of the sanction can therefore matter for the outcomes of ex-offenders, apart from any impact on their own physical and psychological well-being, simply by signaling to employers differential levels of risk. Completion of a drug treatment program can provide its own sort of credential, partially offsetting the negative connotations of an individual's criminal status.

We also asked employers to consider a third scenario. In this item, instead of coming straight from prison, Chad had been released six months earlier and had been working at a car wash since that time. Once again, employers responded more favorably, with roughly 70 percent expressing a willingness to hire. We can infer from this increase in responsiveness that employers worry that individuals coming straight from prison are more likely to reengage in crime. Indeed, employers' concerns are largely supported by existing data. A recent report on recidivism demonstrates that 44 percent of inmates released in 1994 were rearrested for a felony or serious misdemeanor within one year of release. Recidivism within the first year accounts for nearly two-thirds of all recidivism in the first three years.[15] Evidence of intervening work experience, by contrast, can vouch for the applicant's ability to show up consistently and stay out of trouble.

The importance of this issue was reflected in a number of employers' comments. Several employers explicitly stated that the primary factor in their decision to hire Chad was how long ago the conviction had taken place. "How long ago it was would be important," said one employer. "How long they have been in circulation." "I wouldn't hire him if he just got out of prison," said another. Employers seemed concerned that recent releasees would be more likely to wind up back in prison, even if gainfully employed. Time out provides a testing ground to assess whether the applicant has gone straight.

The substantial variation in employer responses depending on the context of the sanction has strong implications for crime policy. Current crime policy emphasizes a strong punitive approach to dealing with offenders; treatment programs in prison reach only a fraction of inmates who report substance abuse problems.[16] The present results suggest that a greater emphasis on drug treatment programs, in concert with or in place of incarceration, could have a beneficial impact on the employability of these individuals after release. Several states have, in fact, recently reversed mandatory sentencing laws for drug offenders, moving instead to a system of drug courts with a primary emphasis on treatment (see chapter 8). Aside from the benefits these programs can have for the problems of addiction, they may further improve the long-term outcomes of ex-offenders by increasing the trust of those employers considering them for jobs.

A second set of policy recommendations can be drawn from the scenario of intervening work experience. Here again we see that employers respond to signals that an ex-offender has gone straight, with steady work experience following release from prison providing one such cue. These results suggest that a stronger emphasis on transitional supported work programs would likewise benefit ex-offenders in search of longer-term employment. The initial transition into the workforce is often the most difficult time, and one in which the lure of illicit activity can be the great-est. Assisting ex-offenders in their initial job placement could have lasting benefits for their economic stability and desistance from crime.[17]

The range of responses employers have to applicants depending on the specifics of their criminal history or the context of the criminal sanction demonstrates a fairly high level of sensitivity to the particulars of an ap-plicant's background. Though the actual magnitude of contrasts may be somewhat inflated by the survey design, employers do appear to differen-tially evaluate profiles of ex-offenders on the basis of the severity of their offense and the signs of their rehabilitation, presumably reflecting an internal calculus of continued risk.

Does the Race of the Employer Make a Difference?

Much of the discussion about discrimination takes as its baseline the de-cision making of white employers. Indeed, the empirical reality affirms that this is largely the case: more than 90 percent of the employers in-cluded in this study were white. Do minority employers make different assumptions about black applicants or applicants with criminal records?

Some ethnographic work suggests that black employers are every bit as wary of applicants from marginalized groups as white employers are. William Julius Wilson finds that black employers are just as likely (if not more) to endorse negative stereotypes about young black male employ-ees.[18] The same may be true with respect to the issue of criminal records. On the other hand, the high incidence of arrest, conviction, and incarcer-ation within the black community may mean that many black employers will have more familiarity with individuals who have had contact with the criminal justice system. Indeed, a survey of the general population indicates that being nonwhite is the strongest demographic predictor of knowing someone who is currently in state or federal prison.[19] As a result of this increased likelihood of personal contact, these employers may have a better understanding of the complex set of factors that lead someone into trouble with the law. Minority employers may thus be more likely to take a chance on an ex-offender applicant, at least for the purposes of acquiring additional information about his individual qualifications and disposition.

It would be ideal to analyze the outcomes of the audits according to the race of employers in order to assess whether white and minority employers do in fact use information about applicant characteristics dif-ferently in making their hiring decisions. Unfortunately, the extremely small number of minority employers in Milwaukee, combined with the extremely small number of callbacks received by black testers and those presenting criminal records, leaves an insufficient number of cases for adequate comparisons. Of the twenty-eight cases in which a tester visited a known minority-owned business, two black applicants and one white applicant received callbacks. Likewise, three applicants without criminal records and zero with criminal records received callbacks. Clearly, there are not enough callbacks from the audit study to adequately address the issue.

The survey data do provide one possible means of investigation, however. Relying on employers' statements concerning their willingness to hire applicants with criminal records, we can assess the relationship between the race of the employer and their stated hiring preferences. Indeed, analysis of the survey data indicates that employers in minority-owned businesses are roughly four times as likely to express willingness to hire an ex-offender.[20]

Comments by minority employers in response to probes about their expressed willingness to hire ex-offenders reinforce the impression of greater openness in viewing applicants with criminal histories. One African American employer emphasized the desire to give Chad "a second chance." Another minority employer elaborated, "I'd have to talk to him, check his references, and evaluate him, but not hold something like that against him. In this day and age it's easy to get a felony, and there are a lot of good people sitting around who are excellent workers." Rather than assuming a criminal record represented the mark of a bad apple, this sympathetic employer recognized that felony convictions have become common, and young men of all types may have had prior brushes with the law. The conviction is viewed in this context as an unfortunate handicap, one for which the applicant would benefit from special consideration.

Expressing similar sentiments, some minority employers emphasized the candidate's work-related qualifications independent of the criminal record. One such employer suggested that he would have no problem hiring Chad provided he was an "otherwise suitable candidate," suggesting that the conviction was insufficient to disqualify him. Another employer expressed a similar point of view: "As long as they can do the job." These employers seemed able to bracket consideration of the conviction in their review of the applicant, treating it as a largely irrelevant or inconsequential factor. Though such sentiments were not universal among this group, minority employers were significantly more likely to see beyond the conviction to consider a wider range of factors in assessing the applicant's suitability.

Why is it that minority employers appear more open to ex-offender applicants? It would be hard to answer this question definitively, but surely personal experiences come into play. As suggested above, it is much more likely that black employers have some personal familiarity with the criminal justice system, based on friends, family members, or neighbors who have had trouble with the law. In fact, one of the audit experiences illustrates this point. Russell, one of the black testers, was interviewing for a position at a pizza chain. The interviewer, a black woman in her thirties, was interested to see that his parole officer was listed as a reference. "So you get along with your parole officer, do you?" She asked, and then continued, "Yeah, me and my parole officer become pretty close after I did time back in Georgia. That was a good thing." The two of them had a long conversation about the job, and the employer made a number of encouraging remarks about Russell's prospects for a better future. The personal experiences of employers may thus represent an important influence on their evaluations, helping to personalize the applicant's experiences and encouraging a more individualized assessment. Though few black employers overall are likely to have had such personal experience with the criminal justice system, many are likely to know someone else who has. Other research using large-scale survey data has similarly found African American employers more likely to hire African American workers.[21] A related kind of empathy or understanding may likewise be at work.

How Much Do Prior Experiences Affect Employer Attitudes?

Discrimination against ex-offenders may be entirely rational if ex-offenders really do represent more problematic employees. Prior experiences with ex-offender employees may well have taught some employers a lesson. Nearly half of the employers in this study reported having hired one or more ex-offenders within the past year, and presumably the number of employers who have *ever* hired an ex-offender is larger still. The survey results indicate that employers who have hired ex-offenders in the past do indeed differ significantly in their current openness to hiring applicants with criminal records. But the difference is in a positive direction. In fact, employers who have hired an applicant with a criminal record in the past year are nearly three times more likely to report favorable attitudes towards hiring the applicant in question (with a felony drug conviction). Further, among those who reported having hired one or more ex-offenders over the past year, more than 80 percent reported having had a somewhat or very positive experience. While it is of course likely that employers who have hired ex-offenders in the past had more favorable attitudes to begin with, these experiences appear to have been sufficiently positive as to maintain their support.[22]

Are Employers Concerned about Liability?

In the post–September 11 world of security concerns, the responsibility of employers to thoroughly screen prospective employees has become more widely discussed. In addition to the commotion caused by the discovery that a number of ex-offenders had been employed as security personnel in airports across the country, hundreds of cases have been filed in which employers have been held responsible for the ill-deeds of their employees, some of whom have had histories of criminal activity.[23] Indeed, the legal precedent established under negligent hiring laws explicitly states that employers must demonstrate "reasonable care" in the selection of employees or else the employer may be held liable for acts of violence or loss of property caused by an employee against a customer or fellow employee. Unfortunately, the law does not provide explicit or consistent guidelines as to how an employer can demonstrate reasonable care. Particularly in states like Wisconsin, where fair employment law prohibits discrimination against individuals on the basis of a criminal record, employers face a difficult challenge in demonstrating compliance when existing laws impose confusing—and even contradictory—expectations. Several rulings, for example, have made it clear that employers are not required to conduct background checks on employees, because of the undue burden this requirement would place on employers. On the other hand, other cases assert that employers can be held liable for the employment of individuals with "known propensities or propensities which could have been discovered through a reasonable investigation."[24] Again, the reasonableness of the investigation is a vague condition, clarified on a case-by-case basis only after the fact.[25]

Very little is known about the impact of negligent hiring laws on the employment of ex-offenders. Despite active discussions within the field of labor law, it is unclear to what extent employers are aware of or concerned by the possible risks posed by negligent hiring legislation. In the open-ended portion of the survey, only one employer explicitly mentioned the issue of liability as a reason for not wanting to hire an ex-offender. Likewise, in a separate series of in-person interviews with employers, apart from a few very large firms with extensive human resources bureaucracies, very few had heard of negligent hiring laws or expressed any concern over the possible legal consequences of hiring ex-offenders (though many other concerns were raised). At present, then, it is unclear that negligent hiring laws have much direct impact on employers' willingness to hire ex-offenders. At the same time, this is an issue that will likely become more salient to employers over time, as the number of ex-offenders grows and the potential for lawsuits builds. With even a few high-profile cases of employers being sued for harm caused by an ex-offender employee, employers will quickly grow concerned about their own risks of lawsuits. It will be important, then, to monitor how negligent hiring laws affect efforts to promote employment among ex-offenders. Once again, if employers alone bear the risks of hiring ex-offenders, the employment opportunities available to this population will likely remain minimal.

Concerns over liability are fairly easy to understand given the specific provisions under negligent hiring laws. A more surprising finding emerged regarding employers' concerns about possible legal risks posed in hiring African Americans. After an initial paper from this study was published, I had the rare opportunity to hear interpretations of the results from a group of employers. The *Wall Street Journal* featured the results from this study in a column, generating a large response from readers. These readers, many of whom are involved in the hiring process at various levels in their firms, were eager to have their say in accounting for the results (particularly those results showing evidence of racial discrimination). One common theme emerged in a surprising number of the responses: employers are afraid of being sued. The argument, featured one week later in a second *Wall Street Journal* column, goes something like this: Employers face a great number of risks in taking on new employees, and in a nontrivial proportion of cases their new hires don't work out. Some of these individuals will be fired, others left to languish in dead-end positions with no chance of promotion. In the case of black employees, however, these employers feel their hands are tied. With the threat of public and legal allegations of racial discrimination, employers become wary of hiring black employees because, in the event these employees don't work out, the employer will be at risk of an unfair lawsuit for wrongful termination. Ironically, then, out of fear of being charged with discrimination, employers discriminate all the more.[26]

Here are illustrative comments from four different readers:

If it was as easy to replace poor hires when they are black as white, this differential would likely vanish. Given the prevalence of legal hassles when blacks are fired, an employer must make doubly sure a good hiring decision is made. In other words, why take a chance and regret it?

I know a few managers and business owners who have said they will not hire a black job applicant but it has nothing to do with racial hatred, it is all about fear. After hearing about or being held "hostage" by a black employee that threatens to play the race card in a performance issue, they fear being labeled a racist or having their authority undermined.

Given the choice between a potential hire who will respond reasonably if disciplined or dismissed (for cause or layoff) and one who will sue or drag in the government resulting in exorbitant legal fees and penalties even if you prove your actions justified, which would you hire?

I have hired about 50 or so people during my career. I have watched co-managers hire many more. . . . Your article is specifically about low-wage, entry-level jobs. . . . These jobs, by definition, are given to people with a limited track record. Employers want to be able to try these new hires out on a, more or less, probationary basis. If the new hire does not "work out", whether due to attendance, effort, reliability, ability, taking direction, or whatever, managers want to be able to dismiss that employee easily. Whether right or wrong, there is a perception that non-whites may make a legal issue out of a dismissal more often than whites. . . . This is not necessarily racism but a pre-emptive defense against being accused of racism. My gut tells me that this calculus causes most or all of the discrepancy revealed in your study.

Based on the scenarios described above, employers appear to be wrestling with the constant threat of being pulled into court by disgruntled or dismissed black workers.[27] For most employers, however, the actual risks of discrimination lawsuits remain very small. Analysis of the volume of discrimination claims over time suggests that at least 95 percent of employers have never been sued for discrimination, and, within any given year, only one half of one percent of firms covered by Title VII can expect to be sued.[28] The risks posed by any given employee are smaller still. While roughly 30 percent of black employees feel that they have experienced workplace discrimination in the past year, fewer than 1 percent actually file claims with the EEOC. Of those who file, only a small proportion prevail.[29] When we focus specifically on low-wage workers, those with little education and poor access to legal resources, the rate of filing discrimination claims drops even further.[30] Thus, while employers may fear that their decisions will be scrutinized under the spotlight of the EEOC, in fact very few will ever be held accountable for their hiring and firing decisions. Why then are these employers so concerned about liability in hiring black workers?

For one thing, employers are likely to have largely distorted impressions of their risk of being sued. Media accounts of discrimination suits boast jury awards of outrageous sums, leaving the impression that such cases are easy to win, and to win big. What the media do not often report, however, are the vast majority of discrimination suits that do not result in awards, or that result in relatively minor settlements. Sociologists Laura Beth Nielsen and Aaron Beim compared discrimination cases reported in the media to all those brought before U.S. District Courts over a ten-year period. They found that media accounts nearly triple the true win rate of plaintiffs (85 percent vs. 32 percent) and more than double the average award size ($2.6 million vs. $1.1 million).[31] If much of employers' information about legal risks comes from media accounts of discrimination suits, their fear of being sued will be largely overblown.

In addition to the influence of media, actual changes in employment discrimination litigation may further contribute to the calculus of employers in their avoidance of black workers. While in the mid-1960s charges of discrimination in hiring outnumbered charges of wrongful termination, by the mid 1980s there were more than six times the number of cases concerning fires than hires.[32] Declining rates of discrimination cases focusing on the point of hire lower the risk to employers who discriminate at this stage; the simultaneous increases in the rate of claims against wrongful termination increases the risks associated with firing minority workers.[33] Thus, despite the fact that claims of employment discrimination at any stage are rare, their relative distribution implies a greater vulnerability for employers over decisions made after the point of initial hire. It may be the case, then, that even if overall levels of racial discrimination have declined, the relative importance of hiring discrimination (compared to discrimination at later stages) may be increasing in importance.

Keep in mind that the small nonrandom sample of employers who commented on the initial *Wall Street Journal* article is not necessarily representative of employers more generally. In addition to any distinctive characteristics of the readership for this newspaper, it is possible that these particular employers had had negative experiences in the past, leading them to be overly cautious. At the same time, these responses do point to some of the possible unintended consequences of our employment laws. On the one hand, the perceived risks of frivolous lawsuits may have the unfortunate consequence of increasing the level of hiring discrimination against African Americans. The threat of discrimination charges adds one more to the long list of perceived risks already associated with black applicants. At the same time, the virtual absence of enforcement at the initial stages of the employment process makes possible the active avoidance of African American applicants. Antidiscrimination law may have helped to reduce employment discrimination overall, but its uneven enforcement leaves pockets of employment activity subject to hardly any form of oversight.

Employment law can and does influence the decisions employers make.[34] Unfortunately, even laws intended to offer protection—for customers, in the case of negligent hiring law, and for minority workers, in the case of antidiscrimination law—can create perverse incentives for employers, increasing discrimination against ex-offenders and/or racial minorities. While this analysis cannot reveal to what extent, if at all, legal concerns affected employers' decisions in the audit study, it does suggest an additional layer of concerns that must be taken into account in developing policies to support the employment of minorities and ex-offenders.

Conclusion

This chapter aimed to explore variations on the experimental design, drawing on the perspectives of employers for insights into how and why they make the decisions they do. Confirming the audit study results, interviews with employers indicate a strong reluctance to hire ex-offenders, even compared to applicants with limited educational attainment or unstable work histories. And yet Milwaukee employers are not uniquely punitive in this respect; compared to employers in other metropolitan areas, those in Milwaukee demonstrate a substantially greater openness to hiring ex-offenders. If these expressed attitudes are indicative of hiring behaviors, then the opportunities available to ex-offenders in other cities may be substantially worse.

The survey results further indicate substantial heterogeneity within the aggregate category of "criminal record." Employers are far more reluctant to hire individuals who have been convicted of property or violent crimes than of drug offenses. Given the already substantial effects of a criminal record demonstrated in the audit study (testing a drug felony), we can expect that the effects could have only been stronger had another type of crime been chosen.

Looking at the range of responses employers have to applicants depending on the specifics of their criminal history or the context of the criminal sanction is helpful in thinking about the ways in which we might facilitate prisoner reentry into the workforce. While for violent offenders alternatives to incarceration are unlikely to become a plausible strategy, for drug offenders such programs have shown potential to be both highly cost-effective and associated with significant reductions in recidivism.[35] If well-designed criminal sanctions can help not only to assist offenders in overcoming addictions but also to make them more employable following their release (by imposing less stigma than prison), their long-term effectiveness (with respect to an ex-offender's economic self-sufficiency and desistance from crime) could be substantially enhanced. Likewise, for all offenders, assistance in the transition to first-work after release may have lasting effects for subsequent employment opportunities. Helping offenders make it through their first year out of prison is of critical importance; and yet current parole systems are poorly equipped to offer meaningful assistance or supervision during this time.[36] A shift in resources from incapacitation to assistance with reentry has the potential to be a very worthwhile investment indeed.

And finally, it is important to keep in mind that the transition to employment can be successful only if employers are willing to hire individuals with criminal backgrounds. Evidence of largely positive experiences with recently hired ex-offenders bodes well for continued openness among these employers. And yet many employers are reluctant to take that chance. Risks to person and property, as well as legal risks imposed through negligent hiring lawsuits, can be powerful deterrents. Any policy designed to promote the employment of ex-offenders will have to address the real and perceived risks facing employers who hire individuals with criminal records.

···   ···   ···

APPENDIX 7A.   TELEPHONE SURVEY METHODOLOGY AND SAMPLING FRAME

Drawing on the sample of 350 employers selected for the audit study, respondents were asked to participate in a telephone survey focused on employers' concerns and considerations in hiring entry-level workers. Following a stipulation made by the University of Wisconsin Human Subjects Committee, no mention was made of the audit study that had taken place. The committee feared that disclosing the occurrence of the audit study could place subjects at greater risk, given that managers or human resource employees might be sanctioned if the study revealed discriminatory practices within individual establishments. Subjects who asked were told that they were selected on the basis of an entry-level job opening they had advertised within the past six months (the selection criterion for the audit study).

Calls were made to each establishment, asking to speak with the person in charge of hiring. In companies where more than one person was responsible for hiring decisions, it is possible that the individual participating in the telephone survey was different from the individual who reviewed the testers' applications in the audit study.[37] It is assumed that general hiring policies are shared among company representatives and, therefore, there should be a fairly high level of consistency in responses among individuals within firms; any individual differences should appear as random error.

The baseline survey instrument was developed by Harry Holzer and his colleagues.[38] It includes questions about the company, such as size, industry, employee turnover, and racial composition; questions about hiring procedures, such as the use of interviews, personality or aptitude tests, and background checks; questions about the last worker hired for a position not requiring a college degree, including age, race, and sex of the worker, recruitment method, wage, and promotion opportunities; and questions about the employer's attitudes about various kinds of applicants, including welfare recipients, applicants with long spells out of the labor market, unstable work histories, or criminal records. In addition, several survey items were added to more closely mirror the audit study (see chapter text). Additionally, an open-ended question was added to probe employers' reasons for being willing or unwilling to hire the applicant described in the original vignette. This question offers a view of employers' concerns in their own words, highlighting the issues most salient to employers about applicants with criminal records.

The survey was administered by the Michigan State Survey Center. The final survey sample included 199 respondents, representing a 58 percent response rate. Response rates were calculated according to the basic formula:

$$\sqrt{I + P/(I + P + R)}$$

where I equals the number of completed interviews, P equals the number of partial interviews, and R represents the number of refused eligible numbers.[39] Between the time of the audit and the survey, two companies had declared bankruptcy and an additional two had nonfunctioning numbers. These firms were dropped from the survey sample and are excluded from the denominator for calculations of response rates.[40]

In order to assess the possible bias that may result from selective participation, two comparison tests were made.[41] The first test compared basic characteristics of employers who responded to the survey to those who were eligible for participation but refused (see tables in appendix 7B). Based on industry, location, and callback rates, the two groups were very similar, though some differences in occupational distribution were apparent: employers for restaurant jobs were most likely to respond to the survey, while those for laborer or service positions were least likely. This difference probably has to do with the greater accessibility of employers in locally run restaurants compared to those in decentralized factories, warehouses, or companies. The overrepresentation of restaurant employers in this sample is cause for some concern, given that these employers tend to be more open to applicants with criminal records. In an effort to account for this overrepresentation, key outcomes were recalculated using weights to achieve the sample distribution of the audit study (not shown here).

Even without these adjustments, however, the distribution of responses on key attitude items closely matches those of a previous sample of Milwaukee employers. Indeed, in a second test of sample bias, basic employer characteristics from the present sample were compared to an identical set of questions asked of a more representative sample of Milwaukee employers conducted in 1999 (see table 7B.3). Though the earlier Milwaukee survey included a broader geographic area, oversampled large firms, and included industries that impose legal restrictions on hiring ex-offenders (health care, child care, etc.), the general attitudes expressed by employers in the two samples were strikingly similar. Most relevant, in both samples 49 percent of employers indicated a willingness to accept an applicant with a criminal record and 51 percent who would not. Distributions of responses concerning other applicant types also corresponded closely across surveys. Though the present sample differs in key respects from Holzer and Stoll's stratified random sample of employers in the Milwaukee metropolitan area, the consistency across key items of interest provides some reassurance concerning the generalizability of these findings.

APPENDIX 7B. TABLES

Table 7B.1. Logistic regression predicting willingness to hire applicant with drug felony.

Variable blocks (entered separately)	Coef.	Std. Err.
Location and occupation		
City	0.28	0.33
Restaurant	0.74	0.38*
Composition of workplace		
Percentage black	0.24	0.81
Percentage Hispanic	0.99	1.19
Number of employees	0.00	0.00
Experience with hiring ex-offenders		
Hired ex-offender in past year	0.95	0.55*
Positive experience with ex-offender employees	0.67	0.61
Received tax credit for hiring ex-offenders	−0.37	0.76
Demographics of supervision		
Minority-owned company	1.41	.79*
Black manager	1.67	1.07
Female manager	0.03	0.36
Hiring screens		
Official criminal background check	−0.79	0.38**
Drug test	−0.41	0.38
Aptitude/personality test	0.04	0.40
Job requirements		
Handling cash	0.06	0.41
Customer service	−0.35	0.47
Handling expensive merchandise	0.13	0.37

$^{*}p < .10, ^{**}p < .05, ^{***}p < .01$

Table 7B.2. Stated reason for hiring decision.

Percentage	Frequency	Reason
19.5	**29**	*Concerns over behavior*
4.7	7	Concerns over drug use
4.7	7	Drug test would be required
3.4	5	Signs of rehabilitation
6.7	10	Others would be influenced or harmed
7.4	**11**	*Concerns over character*
4.0	6	Trust, honesty
3.4	5	Reliability
12.8	**19**	*Against regulations*
7.4	11	Against: company policy
5.4	8	Conviction job relevant
8.1	**12**	*Conviction itself*
34.9	**52**	*Depends on other factors*
8.7	13	Depends on references and/or work experience
14.1	21	Depends on appearance, presentation, attitute, personality
4.7	7	Depends on nature of conviction
2.7	4	Depends on position
4.7	7	Depends on timing of conviction
12.7	**19**	*Not concerned about criminal record*
6.7	10	Otherwise suitable candidate
6.0	9	Second chance
4.7	**7**	*Other*
100%	N = 149	Total

Note: Following responses to the vignette item describing an applicant with a drug felony conviction, employers were asked the open-ended question, "Could you tell me your main consideration in deciding whether or not to hire someone with a felony drug conviction?"

Table 7B.3. Comparisons across two Milwaukee surveys.

Variable	2002	1999
Number of employees	66.95	180.47
Number of vacancies	4.48	7.79
% Minority owned	8.40	8.41
% Unionized	9.30	15.19
Industry		
% Manufacturing	12.43	20.00
% Retail trade	49.72	21.00
% Services	21.47	39.00
% Other industry	16.38	20.00
Hire welfare recipient		
% Definitely/probably would	97.40	96.62
% Definitely/probably not	2.60	3.37
Hire applicant with GED		
% Definitely/probably would	98.80	97.23
% Definitely/probably not	1.20	2.77
Hire applicant with criminal record		
% Definitely/probably would	49.20	49.20
% Definitely/probably not	50.80	50.80
Hire applicant unemployed >1 year		
% Definitely/probably would	70.90	80.15
% Definitely/probably not	29.00	19.86
Hire applicant with unstable work history		
% Definitely/probably would	60.50	67.49
% Definitely/probably not	39.50	32.51

Note: The 2002 data are those collected for the present study. The 1999 data were collected for a survey administered by Harry J. Holzer and Michael Stoll.

Table 7B.4. Distribution of industries by response category.

	Percentage of nonrespondents	Percentage of respondents	Total
Construction	0.72	1.13	0.95
Manufacturing	15.83	12.43	13.92
Transportation, communication	4.32	5.08	4.75
Wholesale trade	7.91	8.47	8.23
Retail trade	46.76	49.72	48.42
Finance, insurance, real estate	5.04	1.69	3.16
Services	19.42	21.47	20.57
Total	$n = 139$	$n = 177$	$n = 316$

Note: Whenever possible, representatives of employers who refused participation were asked to describe the main product or service of their company for the purpose of coding industry among nonrespondents.

Table 7B.5. Distribution of occupations by response category.

	Percentage of nonrespondents	Percentage of respondents	Total
Restaurant	17.26	29.94	23.77
Laborer/warehouse/driver	32.74	19.77	26.09
Production/operators	11.90	11.86	11.88
Sales	16.07	20.90	18.55
Service	11.90	9.60	10.72
Clerical/managerial	10.12	7.91	8.99
Total	$n = 173$	$n = 177$	$n = 350$

Table 7B.6. Distribution across locations by response category.

	Percentage of nonrespondents	Percentage of respondents	Total
City	65.70	56.50	61.03
Suburb	34.30	43.50	38.97
Total	$n = 173$	$n = 177$	$n = 350$

Table 7B.7. Distribution of callbacks by response category.

	Percentage of nonrespondents	Percentage of respondents	Total
Callback	24.28	24.29	24.29
No callback	75.72	75.71	75.71
Total	$n = 173$	$n = 177$	$n = 350$

Table 7B.8. Descriptive statistics of Milwaukee employers.

Employer characteristics	Mean	Std. Dev.
Number of employees	66.66	90.35
Use temporary employees	21.50	
Unionized employees (1 = yes)	9.30	
Minority owned	8.40	
Distance from public transportation (tenths of miles)	9.62	23.93
Minutes to work using public transportation	27.35	19.87
Turnover rate (# employees who left in past yr/ # current employees)	0.46	0.64
Employee composition		
% White	67.66	29.12
% Black	17.70	23.40
% Hispanic	12.07	16.73
Applicant composition		
% White	56.25	28.13
% Black	26.43	28.62
% Hispanic	13.99	13.92
Customer composition		
% White	70.88	23.98
% Black	18.69	18.24
% Hispanic	7.82	7.71
Recruiting and Screening Practices		
Recruitment time (weeks)	2.15	4.36
Recruitment method		
# applicants for last position	25.93	38.32
# applicants interviewed for last position	8.20	12.65
Require tests (1 = yes)	0.28	
% Verify references		
Always	60.80	
Sometimes	31.30	
Never	8.00	
% Drug test		
Always	32.90	
Sometimes	7.50	
Never	59.50	
% Applicants testing positive for drugs	7.27	16.22
% Asking criminal background question on application	79.40	
% Applicants self-reporting criminal record	11.60	20.98
% Performing criminal background check		
Always	36.30	
Sometimes	26.30	
Never	37.40	
% applicants found to have criminal background	14.37	23.38
N	177	

8 Conclusion: Missing the Mark

Dostoevsky once remarked that "the degree of civilization in a society can be judged by entering its prisons." In an era of mass incarceration, an equally relevant measure may be the success rate of those returning home. As the revolving door of the prison continues to turn, questions of prisoner reentry and, in particular, labor market reintegration have become of central concern. No longer a peripheral institution, the criminal justice system has become a dominant presence in the lives of young disadvantaged men, reducing opportunities for the attainment of economic self-sufficiency and deepening longstanding inequalities.

The Mark of a Criminal Record

The primary goal of this book has been to assess the consequences of incarceration for the employment prospects of black and white job seekers. Adopting an experimental audit methodology allowed us to bracket the complicated web of characteristics that affect an applicant's chances in real job searches in order to focus on the specific causal impact of a criminal record. The results of the study provide clear evidence for the significant effect of a criminal record, with employers using the information as a screening mechanism, weeding out ex-offenders at the very start of the hiring process. As a result, ex-offenders are one-half to one-third as likely to receive initial consideration from employers as equivalent applicants without criminal records. Mere contact with the criminal justice system—in the absence of any transformative or selective effects—severely limits subsequent job prospects. The mark of a criminal record indeed represents a powerful barrier to employment.

In observing employers' responses, we see powerful evidence of the negative credentialing process that operates through the criminal justice system. The status of "ex-offender" is formalized and legitimated by the imposition and dissemination of criminal records, which are in turn used by employers and other gatekeepers in ways that restrict access to valuable social resources. The magnitude of the effects demonstrated by this study indicate that employers view this credential as conveying important information centrally relevant to their hiring decisions.

At the same time, there are several reasons to believe the estimates from this study understate the full consequences of incarceration for employment outcomes. First, many features of the present study design represent a best-case scenario for ex-offenders: testers were bright, articulate college students with effective styles of self-presentation. Much of the ex-offender population, by contrast, suffers from multiple overlapping disadvantages, including low educational attainment, unstable work histories, and poor interpersonal skills, in addition to the burden of criminal stigma. The job prospects for these individuals, in the absence of serious job training and placement assistance, are likely to be far worse than what has been reported here.

Second, this study focuses on only one mechanism by which incarceration affects subsequent employment outcomes; namely, the credentialing effects of incarceration. Incarceration can also result in substantial decay in human capital or decline in psychological and physical well-being through time out of the labor market and prolonged exposure to a potentially harmful institutional environment. Though some inmates are able to use their time in prison to acquire a GED or participate in job training programs, a majority of inmates spend much of their time idle or involved in activities that have little relevance to building job skills. Add to this an institutional culture of brutal violence and psychological degradation; add further a weakening of ties to family and community members through prolonged periods of incarceration, and the development of new ties to fellow inmates with historically weak attachments to the formal labor market; add further an environment rife with infectious disease in which the spread of HIV, tuberculosis, and hepatitis is rampant.[1] In addition to the credentialing effects of criminal sanctions, therefore, a true estimate of the consequences of incarceration must also take into account the transformative effects of prisons and their subsequent impact on the employment prospects of those coming out.

The Mark of Race

The issue of incarceration in the United States cannot be fully addressed without a discussion of race. The disproportionate representation of blacks in prison means that any negative effects of incarceration will be felt most strongly by the black community. But the extraordinary overrepresentation of blacks in the criminal justice system has far more insidious effects than the mere numbers would predict. A wealth of social psychological research demonstrates the degree to which race and criminality have become powerfully enmeshed in the American consciousness, in no small part due to the frequency with which we see images of young black men in handcuffs, on wanted posters, and behind bars. Young black men trigger feelings of fear, anxiety, and discomfort and are often viewed with suspicion from the outset.[2] The consequences of contemporary crime policies, therefore, may extend well beyond those who directly experience incarceration. Indeed, an entire segment of the population has become suspect as a result of their embodiment of those physical characteristics we associate with crime. In this context, it is little wonder that race remains such a salient feature in the eyes of employers. In the present study, black job seekers presenting identical credentials to their white counterparts received callbacks from employers at less than half the rate of whites. Even more striking, the results show that even a black applicant *with no criminal background* fares no better—and perhaps worse—than does a white applicant with a felony conviction. That the impact of race could be as large or larger than that of a criminal record is shocking to those who see direct racial discrimination as a force in decline. But for the millions of young black men who notice the tense expressions or clutched purses in their daily interactions with whites, this finding is of little surprise.

Beyond the main effects of race, there is also some indication that blacks with criminal records face an added disadvantage, a finding that becomes stronger and statistically significant when analyzed separately among suburban employers or those with whom testers had extensive personal contact. These results are suggestive of a "two strikes and you're out" mentality among employers, who appear to view the combination of blackness and criminal record as an indicator of serious trouble. Black men already appear to be risky prospects for employment; those with known criminal pasts, however, are officially certified bad news. Where for whites a criminal background represents one serious strike against them, for blacks it appears to represent almost total disqualification.

The Cycle of Stigma

Beyond the visible forms of disadvantage to blacks and ex-offenders documented by this study, there is a pernicious epilogue to this story. The audit study measures the first round of what, in the course of real-life job searches, is an iterative process. As job seekers attempt to secure employment, they receive explicit and implicit feedback about their suitability for various kinds of jobs and their desirability to various kinds of employers. The information gathered during these initial searches is likely to guide subsequent search behavior and to influence expectations of the returns to investments in work-related capital.

Other research points to a powerful feedback effect created when the evaluations of others are internalized or imposed. A self-fulfilling prophecy can be generated as expectations become reality, regardless of how inaccurate the initial evaluations may have been.[3] To extrapolate from the findings of the present audit study, for example, consider the longer-term impact of discrimination at the point of hiring. The fact that blacks and ex-offenders were each one-half to one-third as likely to be considered for entry-level job openings implies that their search process will on average take two to three times the amount of time spent by whites or those without criminal records. While eventually these individuals are likely to wind up with job offers, the time to employment can have serious consequences in itself. The first potential consequence is its impact on an individual's psychic disposition, resulting from the frustration and disappointment from nearly continuous rejection. "Expecting and fearing rejection, people who have been [incarcerated] may act less confidently and more defensively, or they may simply avoid a potentially threatening contact altogether. The result may be strained and uncomfortable social interactions with potential stigmatizers, more constricted social networks, a compromised quality of life, low self-esteem, depressive symptoms, unemployment and income loss."[4] As stigmatized individuals come to expect disapproval or rejection, their internal defenses become activated. The tension caused by such interactions can be resolved either by dropping out of the labor market altogether, thereby preserving the congruence between one's aspirations and one's achievements, or by internalizing the negative attributions, with an associated lowering of expectations for success.[5] Elijah Anderson provides a vivid example of this sort of downward spiral in his account of John Turner, a young man whose initially minor contact with the criminal justice system triggers a sequence of adverse events. "After John had finished completing the successive weekends in jail, there was no job waiting for him. He then looked for a new job, without success, for many weeks. The places where he inquired told him they needed no help or that they would call him—which they never did. As his best efforts repeatedly proved unsuccessful, he became increasingly demoralized."[6]

The psychological toll this process can take on a job seeker was apparent even among the testers in this study, for whom these interactions were the substance of their paid employment. Testers in the criminal record condition reported feelings of frustration and demoralization as they witnessed the dismissive glances given to their applications. Fortunately, after gaining more experience with the project, the testers seemed to feel more secure in their interactions and better able to comfortably perform in their assigned roles. But it was clear from these initial reactions the degree to which such interactions can serve a serious blow to one's self-confidence and motivation. For job seekers actually in need of work (and not being paid to endure this ongoing humiliation), the process is likely to be far more discouraging. Watching the testers' daily experiences, it became more and more clear to me why increasing numbers of young disadvantaged men have exited the formal labor market altogether.[7]

Indeed, interviews I have conducted with real ex-offenders have raised similar issues, with certain individuals reporting feelings of heightened anxiety when approaching employers—not knowing what might be asked of them, not knowing whether or how to approach the topic of their criminal record, and not knowing how much it would be used against them. These anxieties can surely form their own self-fulfilling prophecies, as the unease of the applicant can translate into poor interactions with the employer. The psychic costs of stigma can thereby manifest themselves in very tangible ways, as the expectation of rejection leads to tense or defensive interactions. The cycle of stigma is thus reinforced as blacks or ex-offenders present the angry or shifty personality traits already associated with their group membership.

Beyond the possible psychic costs, a second potential long-term consequence of stigma (as experienced, in this case, through increased time to employment) is its impact on an individual's objective qualifications, as the job seeker spends more and more time out of work. Employers are reluctant to hire individuals who have large gaps in their employment histories.[8] For an ex-offender just released from prison, the weeks or months spent searching for employment accumulate as an objective basis on which to refuse consideration of the applicant. A job search, therefore, already two to three times more difficult from the outset, becomes increasingly problematic with the passage of time.[9] Racial and criminal stigmas trigger negative employment outcomes; negative employment outcomes then exacerbate the manifestation of stigma; the cumulative disadvantage that accrues to such individuals sets into motion a self-reinforcing cycle.

Perhaps even more damaging, the mechanisms producing these outcomes can remain entirely hidden. Employers mistakenly believe that the disadvantaged state of racial minorities or ex-offenders is due to some intrinsic property of the group, while in fact this association may be produced at least in part by faulty expectations imposed by the employers themselves.[10] Negative outcomes are seen as the confirmation of expectations rather than the consequence thereof, thereby perpetuating an unchallenged system of misattributions and faulty judgments.[11]

From Stigma to Stratification

The goal of an experimental audit study is to provide a rigorous examination of one specific domain: in this case, employment in entry-level jobs. Based on the results of a carefully designed experiment, we can begin to understand the ways in which singular status distinctions can have substantial impact on individual evaluations. But the localized nature of this research should not limit the scope of its insight. Rather, an emphasis on the formation and impact of individual-level perceptions should promote consideration of the broader consequences of these processes. In fact it is the collective impact of stigma—the sum of millions of micro-level interactions—that is of greatest concern. At the aggregate level we see how the sum of these micro-processes can result in the categorical exclusion of whole classes of individuals on the basis of their stigmatized group membership.

Consider further that the effects of stigma can be felt across multiple domains. While this discussion has focused primarily on employment opportunities, there are numerous additional contexts in which the stigmas of race and criminal record also result in significant disadvantage. In the case of racial discrimination, previous audit studies have documented substantial disparities in the context of housing searches, car sales, hailing taxis, applications for insurance, and home mortgages.[12] While the existing body of audit research investigates only a few of the nearly infinite domains of social life, it demonstrates the wide range of contexts in which race limits opportunity. Consider how these everyday interactions cumulate across the lifecourse to represent a form of sequential and additive disadvantage.[13] For blacks, everyday life achievements take longer, require more effort, and impose greater financial and psychic costs.

Similarly, the experience of incarceration can have serious consequences in a wide range of social domains, including the loss of civil liber-
ties, the disruption of family ties, the loss of work and permanent housing,
and an aggregate impact on neighborhoods and communities.[14] The magnitude of these effects, across the population and across domains of social
life, demonstrates the impact of this increasingly common criminal credential. As individuals come to be identified by some salient marking, their
identity, their opportunities, and their outcomes can be heavily influenced.
Likewise, as these patterns are produced and reproduced across the population, the group as a whole becomes increasingly relegated to subordi-
nate standing.

Certainly in many cases incarceration represents just one additional
burden among a broader constellation of disadvantage; but it is not clear
that this one additional state-imposed burden is sufficiently justified by
compensating benefits to society. The appropriate resolution of this trade-
off remains to be resolved in public and policy discussions; as the evidence
grows for the harmful consequences of incarceration, however, it will be
increasingly difficult to justify further expansion of the criminal justice
system.

Glimpsing into the Future of Crime and Punishment

Over much of the past three decades, the expansion of the criminal justice system received widespread support from politicians and the public,
with concern over crime consistently representing one of the major policy
issues of the 1970s and 1980s. The nearly universal call for stricter enforcement and harsher penalties largely muted consideration of viable alternatives to incarceration. In more recent years, however, there appears to be
some indication of a turning of tides. After a decade of falling crime rates
and an expanding economy, public sentiment appears more receptive to
alternatives, emphasizing longer-range solutions to the problems of crime
and delinquency.[15] Fully three-fourths of Americans surveyed in 2002, for
example, approved of sentencing nonviolent offenders to probation or
treatment instead of prison.[16] Likewise, over half of all Americans believe
that drug use should be treated as a disease rather than a crime.[17] Whereas
Americans were more evenly split in 1990 over the goals of prevention
versus punishment, more than two-thirds now believe that more money
should be spent "attacking the social and economic problems that lead
to crime through better education and training" as opposed to "deterring
crime by improving law enforcement with more prisons, police, and
judges." Further, the majority of Americans now favor the elimination

of mandatory sentencing laws and the return of discretion to judges.[18] These trends suggest a new willingness to rethink crime control strategies, focusing on more effective prevention and treatment rather than stricter enforcement. Despite the success of law and order rhetoric at the heart of political platforms for the past thirty years, the general public appears ready for a new approach to the crime problem.

At the same time, as the economy slows and states face tightening budgets, legislators are also looking for more cost-effective ways of managing crime. By 2003, more than a dozen states had made significant changes in their sentencing or corrections policy, including the repeal or reduction of mandatory sentencing laws for drug offenders, changes in approaches to technical violators of parole, increased investments in rehabilitative services, and the expansion of treatment alternatives to incarceration.[19]

If sustained, these changes could have long-term effects on the rate of incarceration and on the total number of individuals behind bars. Recall from the first chapter that changes in sentencing practices resulted in a more than a 50 percent increase in the likelihood of incarceration following an arrest and a 40 percent increase in the average length of sentences.[20] The reduction or elimination of these laws could have equally consequential effects in the opposite direction. There exists a glimmer of hope, then, that the rapid thirty-year expansion of the criminal justice system may at last be slowing its pace.

Avoiding the Mark

As states consider a move away from a strong reliance on imprisonment, there has been a renewed emphasis on finding alternatives to incarceration that contribute to public safety. Many states are experimenting with programs that place an emphasis on restorative justice, community service, treatment, or intensive community supervision. Evaluations of these programs have found that certain alternatives to incarceration can in fact have sustained positive effects. Indeed, despite the pessimistic reviews of prison rehabilitation from the early 1970s, there is more recent evidence to suggest that well-targeted programs can have lasting effects on drug abuse, employment, and recidivism.[21]

One model that has spread quickly in recent years is the drug court, involving a set of proceedings that runs parallel to, but independent of, the criminal court.[22] Drug courts recognize that users and first-time offenders are in need of treatment, mental health services, and close supervision rather than confinement. These diversion programs allow minor offenders the opportunity and assistance to go straight, before harsher sanctions kick in.

In some cases, those who successfully complete the drug-court-authorized treatment program avoid the formal markings of a criminal conviction altogether.

Preliminary research does suggest reduced rates of recidivism among drug court participants, and the savings compared to traditional court interventions are indisputable.[23] These results provide support for the notion that well-targeted, sustained interventions can complement, and in some cases replace, incarceration with more lasting positive results. If federal and state governments are willing to invest in the development and evaluation of prison alternatives, the long-term costs of crime and incarceration could be substantially reduced.[24]

Easing the Transition

A second strategy for easing the problems of prisoner reentry, and for reducing the extraordinarily high rates of recidivism, emphasizes assistance in the transition from prison to home. Chapter 1 discussed the weakening of parole and the retreat of government services in support of prisoner reentry. While the future of parole remains uncertain, a number of new models of service provision have developed as private nonprofit ventures, offering promising alternatives. One particular approach that has received less attention in the evaluation literature, despite its growing popularity in practice, involves the role of intermediaries in facilitating employment among returning inmates. Intermediaries function as liaisons between employers and ex-offenders, often making first contact with employers, discussing the employer's staffing needs and evaluating the possible fit between the employer and particular ex-offender job seekers. Intermediaries can help to reduce employers' concerns about hiring ex-offenders by vouching for the individual in question and by providing additional supervision capabilities to increase the likelihood that the new employee follows through. In this process, intermediaries also serve as staffing agents for employers, particularly those not large enough to have a human resources division and without the time to screen the large number of applicants from the open market. Further, intermediaries can address the job-readiness needs of ex-offenders, including straightforward issues such as attire and interview skills as well as larger concerns related to job skills and substance abuse. Several model programs in New York, Chicago, and Texas have been recognized for their success, each showing strong improvements in the employment outcomes of ex-offenders and significant reductions in recidivism.[25] For example, an independent evaluation of the Texas-based project RIO found that participants were nearly

twice as likely as a matched group of non-RIO parolees to have found employment (60 percent vs. 36 percent), and rates of rearrest and reimprisonment
were likewise significantly reduced.[26] These and other studies point to
promising developments in the field of prisoner reentry, and specifically
to the role that active interventions can play in promoting the employment of ex-offenders. Again, evaluations employing careful experimental
designs would strengthen our understanding of what works and point us
toward successful models for a national program of prisoner reentry.[27]

Supporting Employment by Supporting Employers

Intermediaries can ease employers' anxieties about hiring ex-offenders
by thoroughly screening and evaluating prospective employees. But no
amount of screening offers an infallible protection against risk. In the
event that an ex-offender employee does commit a crime in the workplace, it is the employer, not the intermediary, who may be held liable.
Given these risks, many employers will prefer to avoid individuals with
criminal backgrounds altogether. Although reentry policy has emphasized the critical importance of employment for keeping ex-offenders out
of crime, little has been done to safeguard those employers who stand at
the front lines of our reentry initiatives. Currently only one resource, the
Federal Bonding Program, provides some relief for employers who suffer
loss or damages caused by an employee. The bonding program will insure
ex-offender employees (at no cost to the employer) for between $5,000
and $25,000 for a six-month period.[28] This sum, however, is woefully in-
adequate given the size of negligent hiring lawsuits, which can reach a
hundred times that amount. We need to think more carefully about how
to put into place the necessary incentives to encourage employers to hire
ex-offenders. At a minimum, an effective policy would impose limits on
liability, or assume federal responsibility for a larger share of damages.[29]
If we believe that the employment of ex-offenders is an important step toward criminal desistance (and therefore relevant to public safety overall),
then employers should be encouraged, not punished, for providing this
population with a much-needed second chance.

Erasing the Mark

The criminal credential, this marker of graduation from the criminal
justice system, does not fade with time. With no mechanism for removal,
the information remains prominently displayed in background checks,
coloring the reception even of those most indisputably rehabilitated. The

testers in my study posed as job seekers who had been released from prison only a few weeks earlier. For someone in that situation, the prison experience would loom fresh in their minds and likewise in the minds of the employers who evaluate them. But more heartbreaking experiences come from the stories of real ex-offenders, whose last serious conviction may have been six, twelve, or twenty years ago, and yet their job searches are still plagued by the mark of their criminal record. A few months ago, for example, I received a letter from a forty-three-year-old man in Missouri. He had been laid off from his job as a carpenter/contractor about six months earlier, and had been searching for work ever since. A felony conviction from ten years earlier kept coming up in job interviews and, in the slow-growth economy, no employer seemed willing to take him on. He talked about his three young children and his deep frustration in not being able to provide for them. He said his heart broke each morning when his six-year-old daughter would leave for school and say to him, "Good luck in your job search, Daddy!" knowing that he would have to face her later that day with nothing more to offer.

As this study has emphasized, the criminal justice system inadvertently imposes barriers to successful reentry through the lingering mark of a criminal conviction. Individuals who come into contact with the criminal justice system are from that moment forward branded by the experience, with this official certification of criminal status triggering restricted access to a wide range of social goods. Trends in the dissemination of criminal records have been characterized by a uniform move toward greater access and wider distribution. It is implicit in this orientation that more information is always good, and that private citizens are equipped to make sense of a multitude of information available about the intimate details of each other's lives.[30] Currently, even those states prohibiting discrimination on the basis of criminal background continue to allow employers full access to information about criminal backgrounds, despite the fact that in most cases they are not supposed to use it. This policy is somewhat incongruous, especially given that other protected categories place corresponding restrictions on access to "incriminating" information: employers are not permitted to ask the age of applicants, nor their marital status; and information about the race of applicants, while often collected for EEOC reporting requirements, is always optional.

In my review of job applications during the course of this study, I noted that a few large national employers had modified the questions asked on their application forms to respond to specific state law. For example, one employer's application form asked about prior convictions for theft or embezzlement, but did not seek information about other types of criminal convictions. Another employer asked for criminal background information, but specified that the applicants in one of several states should not fill in the information (presumably responding to variation in state law concerning the use of criminal background information). These employers took it upon themselves to limit exposure to information that may taint their evaluation of candidates for reasons unrelated to the job or in ways prohibited by the state. While it is encouraging to see certain employers taking the initiative to regulate information about criminal backgrounds, it is unrealistic to expect all employers to adopt such sophisticated and variable screening procedures. Rather, state governments could far more effectively govern when and where criminal record information should be made available. In fact, the United States is unique in its privileging access to information over other social and political priorities.[31] Many other countries, by contrast, place significant restrictions on access to information about the private experiences of individual citizens with the law.[32] In France, for example, information about individual criminal backgrounds is carefully safeguarded within a single centralized government-controlled database (*le casier judiciare*). Certain employers have the right and/or are required to obtain criminal background information on prospective employees (e.g., those working in child care, in hospitals, etc.); the vast majority of employers, however, and other private citizens, have no grounds for accessing this information. Indeed it would scarcely occur to most French citizens to think of such information as relevant to the employment process. In the U.S. context, the twelve remaining closed-record states represent such a system, with criminal record information limited and regulated by centralized state agencies and provided to employers only when a reasonable case can be made for direct relevance.[33] There is a strong argument for mandating such a system throughout the country.[34]

A second approach, rather than focusing on specific types of crime for which (and/or employers to whom) information should be provided, would place time limits on access to information about an individual's criminal history. The risk of reoffending declines precipitously following the first three years after release, and after five years of arrest-free behavior, the rate of reoffending is extremely low.[35] The public safety rationale for identifying an individual's criminal history beyond this point thus becomes steadily less compelling. Simultaneously, the possibility of expungement (or the sealing of records) offers a tangible incentive for ex-offenders to stay out of crime. If an offender feels he will be relegated to dead-end jobs for the rest of his life as the result of a prior conviction, the lure of the illegal economy becomes all the more powerful. If, on the other hand, this individual knows that if he buckles down for just a few years he will eventually have the opportunity to escape his past and to try to build a better future, the incentives to stay clean increase. The case for imposing time limits on the distribution of incriminating information has direct precedence in the case of credit checks. Under the Fair Credit Reporting Act of 2002, reports of breaches of creditworthiness must be wiped clean after a period of seven years.[36] The law implicitly acknowledges that while lenders and financial agents must be aware of the credit risks of prospective clients, individuals must be granted an opportunity for a second chance at financial solvency. Time limits on credit blemishes allow individuals to move beyond past mistakes. The parallels to the case of criminal background checks are obvious. While public safety concerns mandate that employers and other members of the public retain the ability to identify those engaged in criminal activity, for individuals who have left their criminal past behind them (as the vast majority of young offenders eventually do), the opportunity for a fresh start should be granted.

In fact, the argument for the sealing or expungement of criminal records is not at all new. Idealistic reformers in the 1960s and '70s argued for the restoration of civil rights and removal of the impugning markers of criminal conviction.[37] As recently as 1981, the American Bar Association and the American Correctional Association jointly issued their Standards on the Legal Status of Prisoners, which called for the adoption of "a judicial procedure for expunging criminal convictions, the effect of which would be to mitigate or avoid collateral disabilities."[38] In the midst of the tough on crime movement of the 1980s and '90s, however, many states restricted or repealed their expungement provisions, limiting the circumstances under which records could be sealed or eliminated. Sealed records are not made available to the public (or to employers, landlords, etc.), but can typically be viewed by criminal justice agents and employers required by law to conduct criminal background checks (such as school districts). At the time of this writing, seventeen states allow certain convictions to be expunged or sealed.[39] Many of these laws limit expungements (or sealing) to first-time offenses or grant them after an individual has remained crime-free for a specified amount of time. As recently as 2004, Illinois passed legislation that allows ex-offenders with certain minor felonies, such as drug possession or prostitution convictions, to seal their records if they pass a drug test three years from the date of their last conviction. Other states limit expungements to misdemeanors only, impose longer waiting periods, or require specific efforts toward rehabilitation.[40] At least for the lower-level offenders, then, there are signs of renewed interest in the potential of expungements to assist ex-offenders in the process of starting over.

As a final note on this issue, one must acknowledge the problems of information dissemination. In order to make the sealing or expungement of records effective, some oversight of the public and private providers of criminal justice information is needed. At present, even when state records have been officially sealed or expunged, credit reporting agencies and criminal background services often continue to distribute incriminating information. Indeed, the regulation of information—provided by both public and private entities—should be a priority if rehabilitated ex-offenders are to be given a serious shot at a second chance.

Confronting Race

Eliminating information about certain prior convictions, either for first-time nonviolent offenders or for those who have remained crime free for a sustained period of time, solves one problem while potentially creating another. The suppression of criminal history information can give rehabilitated offenders a fresh start and provide an incentive for recently released offenders to stay clean. At the same time, however, employers with less information may be more likely to rely on other cues about job applicants to proxy their likelihood of criminal involvement. Indeed, some scholars argue that employers without access to criminal background information are less likely to hire blacks, implying that these employers, in the absence of direct information, may instead rely on race as a proxy for criminality.[41] As a policy implication for reducing racial bias in employment, this line of research implies that official criminal record information should be made widely available to employers, so that direct information about offenders rather than racial proxies can be used to screen applicants.

Unfortunately, as the criminal justice system continues to expand, this approach is unlikely to substantially reduce racial disparities in employment. If the criminal population represented only a tiny fraction of each group, sacrificing these individuals' employment prospects might represent a worthwhile trade-off for the greater good. But under the current incarceration regime, those affected are no longer a small minority. Uggen and colleagues estimate that, by 2004, 33 percent of adult black males had felony convictions on their records.[42] Add to this the hundreds of thousands of misdemeanor convictions imposed each year, and many times that number of arrests, and the proportion of black men with a criminal record easily reaches 50 percent.[43] With half or more of the black population at risk of rejection from employment as a result of their criminal histories, policies that enhance access to criminal record information are unlikely to ameliorate the employment problems of black men.

Rather than wringing our hands with concern that employers might respond to reduced access to information about criminal sanctions by increasing their discrimination against blacks, why not tackle the problem head on? The now common view that racial discrimination is no longer a problem dominates discussions of racial policy and enforcement efforts. And yet the basic assumption is simply wrong. The results of this research clearly demonstrate that employers continue to use race as an easy way to screen out applicants at the first stage of review. Even among those with no reported history of criminal activity, employers continue to view young black men with suspicion.

It's not enough, then, simply to tag those who have come into contact with the criminal justice system, hoping that employers will then open their doors to the rest. Instead, we need more active intervention—whether through better enforcement of antidiscrimination law, increased support for affirmative action, tax incentives to promote diversity, or all of the above—race must not disappear from our discussions of public policy, or our conversations about the problems of prisoner reentry. For the millions of black men who have been directly affected by our crime control efforts, and the millions more who have been implicated by association, the problem of racial discrimination will not disappear on its own. It is insufficient to assume that competitive markets will themselves drive out discriminatory employers. In order to ensure equal opportunity for job seekers, more active protections must be in place.

In 1997, the Equal Employment Opportunity Commission (EEOC) announced a plan to launch a series of pilot employment audits across the country to support a more proactive model of enforcement of antidiscrimination law.[44] Congressional leadership, at that time controlled by conservative house speaker Newt Gingrich, objected vehemently to this strategy of enforcement. According to Gingrich, "The use of employment testers, frankly, undermines the credibility of the EEOC. The government should not sanction applicants' misrepresentation of their credentials to prospective employers. The use of testers not only causes innocent businesses to waste resources (interviewing candidates not interested in actual employment), but also puts a government agency in the business of entrapment. It assumes guilt where there has been no indication of discriminatory behavior."[45] That year's budget appropriations bill provided funding for the EEOC conditional on its eliminating the use of testing. Unlike the arena of housing discrimination, in which dozens of federally sponsored testing studies have taken place, the use of the audit methodology for both research and litigation in the area of employment discrimination has thus remained negligible. The ethical concerns raised by Gingrich are important and should not be dismissed out of hand (see appendix 4A for a more extensive discussion of ethical issues related to audit research). At the same time, in the absence of some form of proactive investigation, hiring discrimination remains extremely difficult to identify or address. Job applicants typically have too little information at their disposal to make credible claims, and employers can easily come up with reasonable post hoc justifications for hiring decisions in individual cases. It is only through repeated observation of systematic hiring bias that discrimination at the early stages of the hiring process can be reliably identified and remedied. Recently the EEOC has shown signs of renewed interest in pursuing a testing program. It remains to be seen whether, within the prevailing political climate, this preliminary agenda can be realized.

The adequate enforcement of antidiscrimination laws represents a vital priority. At the same time, it is important to remember that the problems of discrimination cannot be eliminated through enforcement alone. Racial stereotypes, though often exaggerated distortions of reality, are fueled in part by real associations between race, crime, and incarceration. Tackling these social problems at their root—including a lack of quality child care for working mothers, inadequate schools, neighborhood instability, and a lack of employment opportunities—is likely to represent among the most far-reaching interventions. Long-term investments in the social and human capital development of minority youth could help both to reduce racial inequality and to eliminate the bleak social realities that fuel contemporary racial stereotypes.

Of course, the complicated problems of prisoner reentry and racial discrimination cannot be solved by any silver bullet. This book represents one effort to identify and empirically measure some of the core consequences of an expanding criminal justice system and their implications for ex-offender employment and racial inequality. While the appropriate policy responses remain a matter of public and political consensus, my hope is that the findings presented in this study will contribute to this important ongoing conversation.

Conclusion

The findings presented in this book provide strong evidence of the damaging effects of incarceration. Across a wide range of occupations and industries, ex-offenders are systematically excluded from entry-level job openings on the basis of their criminal record. And while this study has focused on the consequences for ex-offenders themselves, there are also substantial social costs implied by these results. Finding steady, quality employment is one of the strongest predictors of desistence from crime, and yet incarceration itself reduces the opportunities for ex-offenders to find work. This vicious cycle suggests that current "crime control" policies may in fact exacerbate the very conditions that lead to crime in the first place.[46]

These findings further point to the damaging indirect costs of our crime policies. As the numbers of young black men in custody has skyrocketed, blackness has come to embody criminality in the minds of many Americans. In some very real respects, all young black men are punished for the punishment of some.

Recent trends in public opinion and crime policy suggest a hopeful direction for the future. With the public favoring investments in prevention and rehabilitation and state officials seeking ways of reducing costs, there may well be sufficient momentum for gradual decarceration. And yet this is by no means a clear path to the future. During the next period of sustained economic recession, we can expect to see crime rates begin to rise. Once again, therefore, we may return to a scenario in which the immediate containment of crime becomes a top policy priority, while discussions of alternatives, treatment, and prevention efforts are pushed aside.

At this point in history, it is impossible to tell whether the massive presence of incarceration in today's stratification system is a unique anomaly of the late twentieth century, or part of a larger movement toward a system of stratification based on the official certification of individual character and competence. In many people's eyes, the criminal justice system represents an effective tool for identifying and segregating the objectionable elements of society. Whether this process will continue to form the basis of emerging social cleavages remains to be seen.

Notes

Preface

1. Bureau of Justice Statistics, "Key Facts at a Glance: Correctional Populations" (2004), available from http://www.ojp.usdoj.gov/bjs/glance.htm#corpop; Jeff Manza and Chris Uggen, *Locked Out: Felon Disenfranchisement and American Democracy* (New York: Oxford University Press, 2006), chap. 3.

Introduction

1. President's Commission on Law Enforcement and Administration of Justice, *The Problem of Crime in a Free Society* (Washington, DC: U.S. Government Printing Office, 1967), 159, 171.

2. National Advisory Commission on Criminal Justice Standards and Goals, *Corrections* (Washington, DC: U.S. Government Printing Office, 1973), 597, 358. This independent commission, composed of prosecutors, police chiefs, judges, and corrections leaders, was appointed by the Nixon administration's director of the Law Enforcement Assistance Agency with the task of formulating "national criminal justice standards and goals for crime reduction and prevention" (ii).

3. David Rothman, *The Discovery of the Asylum: Social Order and Disorder in the Republic* (Boston: Little, Brown, and Co., 1971), 295.

4. Between 1972 and 2002, the number of prison inmates increased from 192,092 to 1,380,516 (Bureau of Justice Statistics, *Sourcebook of Criminal Justice Statistics* [Washington, DC: U.S. Department of Justice, 2003]). Likewise, jail incarceration rates have been rising at a steady rate. In fact, where the state and federal prison population rose by 1.6 percent in 2005, the jail population rose by close to 5 percent (Bureau of Justice Statistics, 2006, "Jail and Prison Inmates at Midyear 2005").

5. U.S. Department of Justice, 1992, *The Case for More Incarceration* (Washington, DC: U.S. Government Printing Office, 1992), ii.

6. See Christopher Uggen, Jeff Manza, and Melissa Thompson, "Citizenship and Reintegration: The Socioeconomic, Familial, and Civic Lives of Criminal Offenders," *Annals of the American Academy of Social and Political Science* 605 (2006): 281–310, table 2. The estimated number of "ex-felons" includes only those who have completed their sentence of probation, prison, or parole. An additional 4.4 million felons are currently under some form of criminal justice supervision.

7. In 2004, 308,482 immigrants arrived in the United States from Mexico, Central America, and South America (Office of Immigration Statistics, 2004, http://uscis.gov/graphics/shared/statistics/yearbook/2004/table3.xls). These figures do not include illegal immigrants.

8. Bureau of Justice Statistics 2002, "Recidivism of Prisoners Released in 1994."

9. In 2004, 219,033 of the 644,084 individuals admitted to state prison were on parole at the time of their arrest (Bureau of Justice Statistics, 2006, "Prison and Jail Inmates at Midyear 2005," NCJ 213133). Supporters of the current incarceration regime argue that high recidivism rates simply indicate the need for longer sentences and more imprisonment (see, e.g., U.S. Department of Justice, *The Case for More Incarceration* [Washington, DC: U.S. Government Printing Office, 1992]; William J. Bennett, John J. DiIulio Jr., and John P. Walters, *Body Count: Moral Poverty and How to Win America's War against Crime and Drugs* (New York: Simon and Schuster, 1996). Others, by contrast, argue that high levels of recidivism reflect a failure of the criminal justice system to address the basic barriers to successful prisoner reentry. Richard B. Freeman, "Can We Close the Revolving Door?: Recidivism vs. Employment of Ex-Offenders in the U.S.," in *Urban Institute Reentry Roundtable*, 2003; Joan Petersilia, *When Prisoners Come Home: Parole and Prisoner Reentry* (New York: Oxford University Press, 2003), chaps. 6, 7; Jeremy Travis, *But They All Come Back: Facing the Challenges of Prisoner Reentry* (Washington, DC: Urban Institute Press, 2005), 87–117, 309–52.

10. Robert Sampson and John H. Laub, *Crime in the Making: Pathways and Turning Points through Life* (Cambridge, MA: Harvard University Press, 1993), esp. 244–45; William Julius Wilson, *When Work Disappears: The World of the New Urban Poor* (New York: Vintage Books, 1996), chap. 2.

11. Richard B. Freeman, "The Relation of Criminal Activity to Black Youth Employment," *Review of Black Political Economy* 16, no. 1–2 (1987): 99–107; Sampson and Laub, *Crime in the Making*; Neil Shover, *Great Pretenders: Pursuits and Careers of Persistent Thieves* (Boulder, CO: Westview, 1996); Chris Uggen, "Work as a Turning Point in the Life Course of Criminals: A Duration Model of Age, Employment, and Recidivism," *American Sociological Review* 65, no. 4 (2000): 529–46; Bruce Western, "The Impact of Incarceration on Earning," *American Sociological Review* 67, no. 4 (2002): 526–46.

12. Bureau of Justice Statistics, 2006, "Prison and Jail Inmates at Midyear 2005"; Bureau of Justice Statistics, 2000, "Correctional Populations in the United States, 1997," NCJ 177613, table 1.29. To be sure, these disparities reflect to some large degree differences in the level of criminal activity between groups. Particularly for violent crimes such as homicide, for example, blacks are represented in roughly equal proportion among those arrested and those imprisoned. In the case of drug crimes, by contrast, which have been a major source of prison growth since 1980, there is evidence to suggest that whites outnumber blacks in both consumption and distribution, despite enforcement trends in the opposite direction (see chap. 1). Robert J. Sampson and Janet L. Lauritsen, "Racial and ethnic disparities in crime and criminal justice in the United States," *Crime and Justice: Ethnicity, Crime and Immigration: Comparative and Cross-National Perspectives* 21 (1997):311–74; Alfred Blumstein, "On the Racial Disproportionality of

United States Prison Populations," *Journal of Criminal Law and Criminology* 73 (1982): 1259–81; Alfred Blumstein, "Racial Disproportionality Revisited," *University of Colorado Law Review* 64 (1993): 743–60; Michael Tonry, *Malign Neglect: Race, Crime, and Punishment in America* (New York: Oxford University Press, 1995).

13. Bureau of Justice Statistics 1997, "Lifetime Likelihood of Going to State or Federal Prison"; Becky Pettit and Bruce Western, "Mass Imprisonment and the Life Course: Race and Class Inequality in U.S. Incarceration," *American Sociological Review* 69 (2004): 151–69.

14. Paul M. Sneiderman and Thomas Piazza, *The Scar of Race* (Cambridge, MA: Harvard University Press, 1993), 45; see also Tom W. Smith, *Ethnic Images*, General Social Survey technical report 19 (Chicago: National Opinion Research Center, University of Chicago, 1991).

15. Patricia Devine and Andrew Elliot, "Are Racial Stereotypes Really Fading? The Princeton Trilogy Revisited," *Personality and Social Psychology Bulletin* 21 (1995): 1139–50; Jennifer L. Eberhardt, Phillip Atiba Goff, Valerie J. Purdie, and Paul G. Davies, "Seeing Black: Race, Crime, and Visual Processing" *Journal of Personality and Social Psychology* 87 (2004): 876–93; Sandra Graham and Brian S. Lowery, "Priming Unconscious Racial Stereotypes about Adolescent Offenders," *Law and Human Behavior* 28 (2004): 483–504.

16. Franklin D. Gilliam and Shanto Iyengar, "Prime Suspects: The Influence of Local Television News on the Viewing Public," *American Journal of Political Science* 44, no. 3 (2000): 560–73; Franklin D. Gilliam Jr., Shanto Iyengar, Adam Simon, and Oliver Wright, "Crime in Black and White: The Violent, Scary World of Local News," *Harvard International Journal of Press/Politics* 1, no. 6 (1996): 6–23; Robert M. Entman, "Modern Racism and the Images of Blacks in Local Television News," *Critical Studies in Mass Communication* 7 (1990): 332–45.

17. Loic Wacquant, "Deadly Symbiosis: When Ghetto and Prison Meet the Mesh," *Punishment and Society* 3-1 (Winter 2000): 95–134, addresses the interdependent and reciprocal nature of racial disproportionality in punishment. In what he speaks of as a "deadly symbiosis" between prison and ghetto, Wacquant's argument suggests a reinforcement of repression and social marginality driven by these twin institutions. The management and containment of poor black men become the dominant objective, with both prison and ghetto isolating this problematic population from the distant mainstream. As increasing numbers of blacks churn from poor neighborhoods to prison and back again, the functional equivalence of these institutions—in the eyes of residents, employers, and the general public—is powerfully reinforced.

18. More than seventy-one million criminal history records were maintained in state criminal history repositories by the end of 2003. Bureau of Justice Statistics, 2006, "Survey of State Criminal History Systems," NCJ 210297. As of 2004, thirty-eight states provided public access to their criminal record repositories, and twenty-eight made some or all of this information available on-line. Legal Action Center, "After Prison: Roadblocks to Reentry. A Report on State Legal Barriers Facing People with Criminal Records," ed. Paul Samuels and Debbie Mukamal (New York: Legal Action Center, 2004).

19. Harry J. Holzer, *What Employers Want: Job Prospects for Less-Educated Workers* (New York: Russell Sage Foundation, 1996), 60. Note, however, that in answer to a question about willingness to hire an applicant with a criminal record, roughly a quarter of employers responded "it depends." This suggests that, at least for some employers, the type of crime, or the circumstances of the conviction, provides relevant information above and beyond the simple fact of conviction (see chapter 7).

20. The literature on labeling provides a parallel approach to viewing the impact of formal negative markers (e.g., juvenile delinquent, mentally ill, homosexual, drug user, etc.). See Howard Becker, *Outsiders: Studies in the Sociology of Deviance* (New York: Free Press, 1963); Irving Goffman, *Stigma: Notes on the Management of a Spoiled Identity* (New York: Prentice Hall, 1963); and Harold Garfinkel, "Conditions of Successful Degradation Ceremonies," *American Journal of Sociology* 61 (1956): 420–24.

21. Members of the academic and policy communities in the 1960s and '70s were concerned about the problems of prisoner rehabilitation and reintegration, with the barriers to employment viewed as a central concern; see, e.g., Richard Schwartz and Jerome Skolnick, "Two Studies of Legal Stigma," *Social Problems* 10 (Autumn 1962): 133–42; Aidan R. Gough, "The Expungement of Adjudication Records of Juvenile and Adult Offenders," *Washington University Law Quarterly* 147 (1966): 148. After the mid-1970s, however, just as the rate of incarceration began its rapid growth, criminologists and policy makers largely turned their attention away from the problems of prisoner rehabilitation and reentry (see chapter 1).

Chapter 1

1. To be sure, earlier presidential administrations demonstrated considerable concern for the problems of crime, dating back to the Wickersham Commission in the 1930s (appointed by President Hoover) through the federal crime prevention initiative spearheaded by the Johnson administration in 1967. Nevertheless, the formal responsibilities of crime control rested with states and local governments. See Katherine Beckett and Theodore Sasson, *The Politics of Injustice: Crime and Punishment in America* (Thousand Oaks, CA: Pine Forge Press, 2000), chap. 4; for a broad historical perspective on the politics of punishment, see Marie Gottschalk, *The Prison and the Gallows: The Politics of Mass Incarceration in America* (New York: Cambridge University Press, 2006).

2. The origins of the "tough on crime" movement are generally credited to the 1964 presidential campaign of Barry Goldwater, who aggressively advocated stronger sanctions against criminal offenders. Although routed by the incumbent Lyndon Johnson, Goldwater's campaign gambit focused the national spotlight on the problem of crime in a new way. Richard Nixon's 1968 campaign furthered the Goldwater agenda, crafting a political message stressing the importance of escalated crime control at the national level. For more extensive discussions, see Bruce Western, *Punishment and Inequality in America* (New York: Russell Sage Foundation, 2006), 59–62; and Beckett and Sasson, *The Politics of Injustice*, 47–74.

3. Indeed, crime rates had increased substantially in the previous decade, with the rate of index crimes doubling between 1960 and 1970. The following decade showed a 50 percent increase in index crimes, after which crime rates remained stable (1980-90) or decreased (1990-2000). FBI Uniform Crime Reports, 1960-2000. Widespread social protests and several high-profile assassinations (esp. of Martin Luther King Jr. and John F. Kennedy) contributed to pervasive feelings of insecurity and social unrest.

4. In fact, incarceration rates did rise from 1925 until the start of World War II, increasing by more than 60 percent over that fifteen-year period, then falling quickly before resuming a fairly steady rate. Though these fluctuations were certainly meaningful at the time, in the context of recent incarceration trends this variation appears trivial.

5. Overall, between 1972 and 2004, the number of prison inmates increased from 192,092 to 1,433,793. Bureau of Justice Statistics, *Sourcebook of Criminal Justice Statistics*, 31st ed. (Washington, DC: U.S. Department of Justice, 2003), accessed 8/31/06). In the year 2005, the incarceration rate including jail inmates (not included in figures 1.1

and 1.2) was 738 per 100,000 residents. Of all inmates in the year 2005, 57 percent were in state prison facilities, 8 percent were in federal prisons, and 34 percent were in local jails. See Bureau of Justice Statistics, *Prison and Jail Inmates at Midyear 2005*, ed. Paige M. Harrison and Allen J. Beck (Washington, DC: U.S. Department of Justice, 2002). For statistics on probation and parole, see Bureau of Justice Statistics, *Probation and Parole in the United States, 2004* (Washington, DC: U.S. Department of Justice, 2005).

6. U.S. Department of Justice, *The Case for More Incarceration* (Washington, DC: Government Printing Office, 1992), v (emphasis in original). This report was originally written as an internal document by the Office of Policy and Communications, and then released to the public by then–attorney general William P. Barr (ii).

7. J. H. Lipschultz and M. L. Hilt, *Crime and Local Television News: Dramatic, Breaking, and Live from the Scene* (Mahwah, NJ: Lawrence Erlbaum Associates, 2002). Coverage of violent crime, in particular, is often sharply disconnected from actual crime trends. As the murder rate fell by roughly 40 percent during the 1990s, for example, the number of murder stories on NBC, ABC, and CBS evening news shows increased by more than 600 percent. This increase does not include stories related to the O. J. Simpson case. Author's calculations based on data from the Center for Media and Public Affairs; see also Joseph F. Sheley and Cindy D. Ashkins, "Crime, Crime News, and Crime Views," *Public Opinion Quarterly* 45, no. 4 (1981): 492–506; and D. A. Graber, *Crime News and the Public* (New York: Praeger, 1980). Media distortions notwithstanding, trends in public opinion did respond to falling crime rates. The percentage of Americans who ranked crime/violence as the number-one problem facing the country peaked in 1994 and then declined during the late 1990s. Likewise, between 1992 and 1999, a decreasing proportion of Americans believed that there had been more crime in the United States that year than in the year before. Nevertheless, the percentage ranking crime/violence as the number-one problem facing the country in 1999 (17 percent), after a decade of falling crime rates, was far higher than it had been at the start of the decade (1 percent), and more than half of all Americans in 1999 continued to believe that there had been more crime in the United States that year than in the year before. Bureau of Justice Statistics, *Sourcebook of Criminal Justice Statistics* (2003), tables 2.1, 2.33; see also Katherine Beckett, *Making Crime Pay: Law and Order in Contemporary American Politics* (New York: Oxford University Press,1997), 17–20, for a striking analysis of public opinion about crime and drugs during the preceding decades.

8. The two major sources of crime statistics in the United States are the FBI's Uniform Crime Report (UCR) and the National Crime Victimization Survey (NCVS). The UCR, based on crimes reported to the police, uses seven "index crimes" to proxy overall crime rates. These are murder and nonnegligent manslaughter, forcible rape, robbery, aggravated assault, burglary, larceny theft, and motor vehicle theft. The NCVS, based on a national survey of victimization, includes data on burglary, motor vehicle theft, theft, rape, sexual assault, robbery, and aggravated and simple assault, but does not include homicide rates. Neither crime measure includes data on drug offenses. Both indicators show a general decline in crime rates through the 1990s. See Bureau of Justice Statistics, *The Nation's Two Crime Measures* (Washington, DC: U.S. Department of Justice, 2003).

9. For an overview, see Alfred Blumstein and Joel Wallman, eds., *The Crime Drop in America*. (New York: Cambridge University Press, 2000); Alfred Blumstein and Richard Rosenfeld, "Explaining Recent Trends in U.S. Homicide Rates," *Journal of Criminal Law and Criminology* 88, no. 4 (1998): 1175–217; Jeffrey Fagan, Franklin E. Zimring, and June Kim, "Declining Homicide in New York City: A Tale of Two Trends," *Journal of Criminal Law and Criminology* 88, no. 4 (1998): 1277–306; Steven D. Levitt, "Understanding Why

Crime Fell in the 1990s: Four Factors That Explain the Decline and Six That Do Not," *Journal of Economic Perspectives* 18, no. 1 (2004): 163–90. Two main sources of information can be used to assess the association between crime and incarceration. The first comes from self-reported offending rates of current inmates. Extrapolating from inmate surveys recording the number of self-reported crimes an inmate committed in the year before incarceration, some scholars have estimated the number of crimes potentially averted as a result of the offender's confinement. Using this method, DiIulio and Piehl, for example, estimate that each newly imprisoned offender results in the reduction of an average of 141 crimes per year, suggesting that incarceration has indeed been highly effective in reducing crime. John DiIulio and Anne Morrison Piehl, "Does Prison Pay? The Stormy National Debate over the Cost Effectiveness of Imprisonment," *Brookings Review* 9 (Autumn 1991): 28–35. Critics of this approach argue that, since offenders reliably decrease rates of offending with age, this method of projection (assuming a constant rate of offending) overstates the impact of incarceration.

A second approach to studying the relationship between incarceration and crime is to statistically estimate patterns of incarceration over time or across states and their association with subsequent rates of crime. Efforts at such analyses have produced variable estimates, with the majority ranging between 5 and 25 percent (suggesting that the rise in incarceration can explain between 5 to 25 percent of the drop in crime). Differing assumptions about the appropriate specification for the statistical model produce estimates that can vary widely. In contrast to the majority of estimates suggesting a small to moderate effect of incarceration on crime, economist Steven Levitt argues that crime rates would have been 50–70 percent higher by 1993 had incarceration rates not tripled in the two preceding decades. Levitt's analysis attempts to correct for the reciprocal effects of crime and incarceration (e.g., crime leads to incarceration, incarceration reduces crime) by using prison overcrowding legislation as an instrument to capture exogenous variation in prison populations. This analysis leads to estimates of the effects of incarceration on crime rates that are roughly four times larger than conventional estimates. See Steven Levitt, "The Effect of Prison Population Size on Crime Rates: Evidence from Prison Overcrowding Litigation," *Quarterly Journal of Economics* 111, no.2 (1996): 319–51. For a critique of this approach, see Western, *Punishment and Inequality in America*, 179–88.

10. DiIulio and Piehl, "Does Prison Pay?"; Levitt, "The Effect of Prison Population Size on Crime Rates"; Edwin Zedlewski, *Making Confinement Decisions: The Economics of Deincarceration* (Washington, DC: U.S. Department of Justice, 1987); Anne Morrison Piehl and John J. DiIulio Jr., "'Does Prison Pay?' Revisited: Returning to the Crime Scene," *Brookings Review* 13 (1995): 21–25.

11. For an example of the time-out effect, see Kathryn Edin, Timothy Nelson, and Rochelle Parnal, "Fatherhood and Incarceration as Potential Turning Points in the Criminal Careers of Unskilled Men," in M. Pattillo, D. Weiman, and B. Western, *Imprisoning America: The Social Effects of Mass Incarceration* (New York: Russell Sage, 2003), 46–75. Of the three primary mechanisms through which incarceration might reduce crime—incapacitation, rehabilitation, and deterrence—incapacitation is thought to represent the dominant effect.

12. Robert J. Sampson and John H. Laub, "A Life-Course View of the Development of Crime," *Annals of the American Academy of Political and Social Science* 602 (2005): 12–45, figs. 2, 4.

13. Jacqueline Cohen and Jose Canela-Cacho, "Incapacitation and Violent Crime," in *Understanding and Preventing Violence*, ed. Albert Reiss and Jeffrey Roth (Washington, DC: National Academy of Sciences, 1994), 296–338; Edwin Zedlewski, *Making Confinement*

Decisions: The Economics of Deincarceration (Washington, DC: U.S. Department of Justice, 1987); D. Jacobs and R. E. Helms, "Towards a Political Model of Incarceration," *American Journal of Sociology* 102, no. 2 (1996): 323–57; W. A. Taggart and R. G. Winn, "Imprisonment in the American States," *Social Science Quarterly* 74 (1993): 736–49; William Spelman, "The Limited Importance of Prison Expansion," in *The Crime Drop in America*, ed. Alfred Blumstein and Joel Wallman (New York: Cambridge University Press, 2000), 97–129; R. Rosenfeld, "Patterns in Adult Homicide, 1980-1995," in *The Crime Drop in America*, ed. Alfred Blumstein and Joel Wallman (New York: Cambridge University Press, 2000), 130–63; Albert J. Reiss Jr. and Jeffrey A. Roth, eds., *Understanding and Preventing Violence* (Washington, DC: National Academy of Sciences, 1993); Western, *Punishment and Inequality in America*. Analyses at the state level demonstrate that the rate of growth in incarceration is virtually uncorrelated with state-level changes in crime rates. Jenni Gainsborough and Marc Mauer, "Diminishing Returns: Crime and Incarceration in the 1990s," policy report from the Sentencing Project, 2000.

14. Increasing incarceration may have diminishing returns for two reasons: First, as the net of incarceration widens, less serious offenders are more likely to be included, with a lower corresponding impact on crime rates. Second, the deterrent value of punishment (e.g., the stigma of incarceration) may be weakened as it becomes more common, particularly within those communities where incarceration has become an anticipated life event. Critics of the current system argue that alternatives to incarceration—including drug treatment and community supervision—can be equally effective in reducing crime at far lower costs to taxpayers. RAND, *Controlling Cocaine: Supply versus Demand Programs*, ed. C. Peter Rydell and Susan S. Everingham RAND publications MR-331-ONDCP/A/DPRC, 1994; James Austin, "Using Early Release to Relieve Prison Crowding: A Dilemma in Public Policy," *Crime and Delinquency* 32 (1986): 404–502.

15. Robert Sampson and John H. Laub, *Crime in the Making: Pathways and Turning Points through Life* (Cambridge, MA: Harvard University Press, 1993), chaps. 7, 9.

16. Official decennial crime rates (UCR index crimes per 100,000 residents) from 1970 to 2000 were 3,985, 5,950, 5,802, and 4,125. Incarceration rates for the same time points were 96, 139, 297, and 469. Note that trends in crime rates were not altogether linear within decades. In particular, the stable crime rate from 1980 to 1990 masks a 15 percent drop in crime from 1980 to 1984, followed by a 17 percent increase in crime from 1984 to 1991. Corresponding changes in incarceration during those periods were increases of 35 percent and 66 percent. Incarceration rates thus did escalate during the period of more steeply rising crime rates, but at no point did incarceration rates fall alongside periods of decreasing crime. Bureau of Justice Statistics, *Sourcebook of Criminal Justice Statistics*, 2003, tables 3.106.2004 and 6.28.2004. Bruce Western notes that states with the largest increases in crime in the 1960s and '70s demonstrate the largest growth in incarceration twenty years later. Western concludes, "Crime rates themselves may not have driven the prison boom, but long-standing fears about crime and other social anxieties may form the backdrop for the growth in imprisonment." Western, *Punishment and Inequality*, 48.

17. Excluding drug offenses from this decomposition, the growth in incarceration attributable to increases in crime is negligible, with more than 99 percent of the upward trend associated with changes in crime policy, including the increasing likelihood of incarceration (42 percent) and increases in the length of time served (58 percent). See Alfred Blumstein and Allen J. Beck, "Population Growth in U.S. Prisons, 1980-1996," in *Prisons*, ed. Michael Tonry and Joan Petersilia (Chicago: University of Chicago Press, 1999), 17–61.

18. Bureau of Justice Statistics, *Recidivism of Prisoners Released in 1994*, ed. Patrick Langan and David Levin (Washington, DC: U.S. Department of Justice, 2002). Technical violations of parole include failing a drug test, failing to maintain employment, moving without permission, associating with other felons, violating curfew, and missing a parole appointment. See Jeremy Travis, *But They All Come Back: Facing the Challenges of Prisoner Reentry* (Washington, DC: Urban Institute Press, 2005), 49. The percentage of parole violators among admissions to state prison increased from 29 percent in 1990 to 36 percent in 2001. In four states (California, Hawaii, Louisiana, and Utah), more than 50 percent of prison admissions were parole violators; in California this number reached fully 70 percent. Nearly 30 percent of all parole readmissions (and nearly 60 percent of those in California) are the result of technical violations. See Michael Jacobson, *Downsizing Prisons: How to Reduce Crime and End Mass Incarceration* (New York: New York University Press, 2005), 141–45. Petersilia, however, cautions that even technical violations often also have an underlying criminal charge. See Joan Petersilia, "Parole and Prisoner Reentry in the United States," in *Prisons*, ed. Michael Tonry and Joan Petersilia (Chicago: University of Chicago Press, 1999), 484, citing James Austin and Robert Lawson, *Assessment of California Parole Violations and Recommended Intermediate Programs and Policies* (San Francisco: National Council on Crime and Delinquency, 1998).

19. David Garland, *Punishment in Modern Society: A Study in Social Theory* (Chicago: University of Chicago Press, 1990), 20.

20. David Garland, *The Culture of Control: Crime and Social Order in Contemporary Society* (Chicago: University of Chicago Press, 2001), 34–37; Erik Olin Wright, *The Politics of Punishment: A Critical Analysis of Prisons in America* (New York: Harper Torchbooks, 1973), chap. 3.

21. Robert Martinson, "What Works? Questions and Answers about Prison Reform," *Public Interest* 35 (1974): 22–54. See also Francis Allen, *The Decline of the Rehabilitative Ideal: Penal Policy and Social Purpose* (New Haven: Yale University Press, 1981). Subsequent studies of program effectiveness have questioned whether this early pessimism was warranted. Martinson himself later softened his stance, acknowledging the diversity of findings, with a nontrivial number of studies finding positive effects. Robert Martinson, "New Views: A Note of Caution Regarding Sentencing Reform," *Hofstra Law Review* 7 (1979): 242–58. Since then, several well-designed studies have shown significant rehabilitation effects for certain groups of offenders. See, e.g., David P. Farrington and Brandon C. Welsh, "Randomized Experiments in Criminology: What Have We Learned in the Last Two Decades?" *Journal of Experimental Criminology* 1 (2005): 9–38; Francis T. Cullen and Paul Gendreau, "Assessing Correctional Rehabilitation: Policy, Practice, and Prospects," *Criminal Justice* 3 (2000): 109–42; Francis T. Cullen, "The Twelve People Who Saved Rehabilitation: How the Science of Criminology Made a Difference," *Criminology* 43, no. 1 (2005): 1–42; J. McGuire, *What Works? Reducing Reoffending* (New York: Wiley, 1995); Ted Palmer, "Martinson Revisited," *Journal of Research in Crime and Delinquency* 12, no. 2 (1975): 133–52.

22. James Q. Wilson, *Thinking about Crime*, rev. ed. (New York: Vintage, 1985), 260. Wilson writes elsewhere in the same volume, "Instead [of an emphasis on rehabilitation] we could view the correctional system as having a very different function—to isolate and to punish. That statement may strike many readers as cruel, even barbaric. It is not. It is merely the recognition that society must be able to protect itself from dangerous offenders. . . . It is also a frank admission that society really does not know how to do much else" (193).

23. Public opinion largely followed this shift in emphasis from rehabilitation to retribution. A 1995 survey found that fully 85 percent of Americans believed that

the enactment of "tougher anticrime legislation" should be a top or high priority of Congress. See L. C. McAneny, ed., "Gallup Poll on Crime," *Gallup Poll Monthly* 352, no. 3 (1995): 7.

24. See Marc Mauer, *Race to Incarcerate* (New York: New Press, 1999), 46.

25. See Allen, *The Decline of the Rehabilitative Ideal*; and Travis, *But They All Come Back*, 17–20.

26. This position was clearly articulated in an influential book by the Working Party of the American Friends Service Committee, an antiwar Quaker organization: "Beyond the special problems of effecting 'treatment' in prisons, is it possible to co-erce people into 'treatment' in any setting? Is the necessary therapeutic relationship between helper and the helped possible if the person to be helped is forced into the re-lationship?" See American Friends Service Committee, *Struggle for Justice* (New York: Hill and Wang, 1971), 97. See also Allen, *The Decline of the Rehabilitative Ideal*, for a detailed account of this emerging critique.

27. The federal Violent Crime Control and Law Enforcement Act of 1994 (and amended in 1996) provided $2.7 billion in federal grants to assist in the expansion of state prison capacity provided that state legislation was in place increasing the incarceration of violent offenders. The Violent Offender Incarceration and Truth-in-Sentencing (VOI/TIS) grant programs required that states either adopt laws mandating that convicted violent offenders serve at least 85 percent of their imposed sentence or that they demonstrate an increase in the severity of punishment for violent offenders, and that they have laws requiring that repeat violent offenders and drug offenders serve at least 85 percent of their imposed sentence. For comprehensive reviews, see William J. Sabol, Katherine Rosich, Kamala Mallik Kane, David Kirk, and Glenn Dubin, "The Influences of Truth-in-Sentencing Reforms on Changes in States' Sentencing Prac-tices and Prison Populations" (Research Report, Urban Institute, 2002); and Bureau of Justice Statistics, *Truth in Sentencing in State Prisons* (Washington, DC: U.S. Department of Justice, 1999).

28. Blumstein and Beck, "Population Growth in U.S. Prisons, 1980-1996."

29. For a more complete account of the political demise of the New Deal/Great Society Democratic Party order after the late 1960s, see Kevin Phillips, *The Emerging Republican Majority* (New Rochelle, NY: Arlington House, 1969).

30. Ronald Reagan, "Remarks at the Annual Convention of the Texas State Bar Asso-ciation in San Antonio," in *Public Papers of the Presidents, 1984* (Washington, DC: U.S. Gov-ernment Printing Office, 1985), 2, cited in Beckett and Sasson, *The Politics of Injustice*, 61.

31. William J. Bennett, John J. DiIulio Jr., and John P. Walters, *Body Count: Moral Poverty and How to Win America's War against Crime and Drugs* (New York: Simon and Schuster, 1996), 82. To be sure, Bennett and his coauthors acknowledge a strong social component to the rise of moral poverty through its purported association with the breakdown of the family, urban poverty and segregation, and widespread neglect of urban/poor youth (see chapter 2). Despite its attention to social causes, however, the approach locates the core responsibility for crime in deeply entrenched internal and individual dispositions of criminal offenders. See also Charles Murray, *Losing Ground: American Social Policy, 1950-1980* (New York: Basic Books, 1984), 178–91.

32. Quoted in Bennett, DiIulio, and Walters, *Body Count*, 141.

33. Kevin Reitz, "Sentencing," in *The Handbook of Crime and Punishment*, ed. Michael Tonry (New York: Oxford University Press, 1998), 545.

34. For broader discussions of the framing of poverty in individual and moral terms, see Herbert J. Gans, *The War against the Poor: The Underclass and Antipoverty Policy*

(New York: Basic Books, 1995); and Jeffrey Reiman, *The Rich Get Richer and the Poor Get Prison: Ideology Class, and Criminal Justice*, 7th ed. (Boston: Allyn and Bacon, 2004).

35. Garland, *The Culture of Control*, 102.

36. Although Richard Nixon had attempted to attack drug use during his first term (including appointing a "drug czar"), it was Reagan's determination to place drugs on the national agenda in the mid-1980s that truly codified the new moral order.

37. The number of offenders admitted to state prison grew from 8,800 in 1980 to 102,400 in 1990. Of those inmates in state prison at any given time (as opposed to those admitted each year), the proportion convicted of drug offenses grew from 1 in 16 in 1980 to 1 in 5 by 1990, remaining at this level through the time of this writing. Bureau of Justice Statistics, 1995, "Prisoners in 1994."

38. After increasing sharply between 1985 and 1991, the homicide rate stabilized and then dropped rapidly through the remainder of the decade. Blumstein and Rosenfeld, "Explaining Recent Trends in U.S. Homicide Rates"; Blumstein and Wallman, *The Crime Drop in America*.

39. U.S. Department of Health and Human Services, *National Household Survey on Drug Abuse: Population Estimates 1998* (Washington, DC: Substance Abuse and Mental Health Services Administration, 1999).

40. Although rising prosecution of drug offenses may have had a deterrent effect on drug use, most researchers believe that the direct effect of incarceration on drug markets is minimal. Drug kingpins are rarely arrested, and small-time dealers are easily replaced. Even those researchers who argue that incarceration substantially reduces crime overall consider drug crimes a notable exception. See DiIulio and Piehl, "Does Prison Pay?"; Piehl and DiIulio, "'Does Prison Pay?' Revisited"; and Cohen and Canela-Cacho, "Incapacitation and Violent Crime"; for an opposing view, see Ilyana Kuziemko and Steven Levitt, "An Empirical Analysis of Imprisoning Drug Offenders," *Journal of Public Economics* 88 (2004): 2043–66.

41. Blumstein and Beck, "Population Growth in U.S. Prisons, 1980–1996"; T. Caplow and J. Simon, "Understanding Prison Policy and Population Trends," in *Prisons*, ed. Michael Tonry and Joan Petersilia (Chicago: University of Chicago Press, 1999), 63–120.

42. On the emerging use of drug courts, see Greg Berman and John Feinblatt, "Problem-Solving Courts: A Brief Primer," *Law and Policy* 23, no. 2 (2001): 125–40; and James Nolan, *Reinventing Justice: The American Drug Court Movement* (Princeton, NJ: Princeton University Press, 2001).

43. Between 1985 and 1995, the increase in black inmates outpaced the increase in white inmates (including all offense categories) by 32,800 overall. But this aggregate trend masks substantial variation by crime type: for drug crimes, specifically, the increase in black inmates far outpaced whites (by 52,500), while the rise in violent and property offenders, by contrast, disproportionately affected whites. Bureau of Justice Statistics, *Prisoners in 1996* (Washington, DC: U.S. Department of Justice, 1997), table 13, posted on-line at http://www.ojp.usdoj.gov/bjs/pub/pdf/p96.pdf).

44. Bureau of Justice Statistics, *Prisoners in 2002* (Washington, DC: U.S. Department of Justice, 2003). By 1999, more than one-quarter of all black state inmates were incarcerated for drug offenses, compared to less than half that proportion of whites. Bureau of Justice Statistics, *Prisoners in 2000* (Washington, DC: U.S. Department of Justice, 2001). For incidence of illicit drug use over time by race, see Joseph Gfroerer and Marc Brodsky, "The Incidence of Illicit Drug Use in the United States, 1962–1989," *British Journal of Addiction* 87 (1992): 1345–51. Estimates from household surveys suggest that African Americans represent 19 percent of those reporting drug sales,

but they account for nearly two-thirds of those arrested. See J. P. Caulkins and D. McCaffrey, *Drug Sellers in the Household Population* (Santa Monica: RAND, 1993); Alfred Blumstein, "Youth Violence, Guns, and the Illicit Drug Industry," *Journal of Criminal Law and Criminology* 86, no. 1 (1995): 10–86. Explanations for racial disparities in drug convictions are complex and multifaceted. In part, enforcement efforts of the late 1980s were responsive to escalating violence associated with the drug trade in poor, largely African American neighborhoods. Indeed, sharp increases in the incarceration of African American drug offenders took place at a time of steeply increasing homicide rates among young African American men (1987-91), violence largely associated with conflict between rival drug markets. See Bureau of Justice Statistics, "Homicide Trends in the U.S.: Trends by Race" (Washington, DC: U.S. Department of Justice, 2006), posted on-line at http://www.ojp.usdoj.gov/bjs/homicide/tables/oracetab.htm).

At the same time, other factors are also likely to have played a role. Part of the racial disparity in enforcement can be accounted for by the concentration of blacks in central cities, where police surveillance is likely to be more pervasive. And within cities, specific decisions by police officers about how and where to target drug enforcement further results in the disproportionate arrest of minority drug users and sellers relative to their presence in the population. Katherine Beckett, Kris Nyrop, Lori Pfingst, and Melissa Bowen, "Drug Use, Drug Arrests, and the Question of Race: Lessons from Seattle," *Social Problems* 52, no. 3 (2005): 419–41. Specific sentencing enhancements have likewise taken a disproportionate toll on African Americans. In certain jurisdictions, for example, harsher penalties are imposed on individuals who sell drugs within a specified distance of a school or public housing building, which, in poor urban areas, encompasses virtually the entire community. John Gould, "Zone Defense," *Washington Monthly*, June 2002, 33. And finally, the penalties associated with specific kinds of drugs have been linked to rising racial disparities in incarceration. Federal sentencing laws passed in 1986 and 1988 made sentences associated with crack one hundred times as long as those for the analogous offenses with the same amount of cocaine powder. Though only fourteen states adopted laws that distinguish between crack and powder cocaine in their penalty schemes, and only one (Iowa) uses the 100-to-1 ratio of the federal system, these sentencing differences have been implicated in growing racial disparities in the incarceration rates of drug offenders at both the state and federal levels. See Bureau of Justice Statistics, *Sentencing in the Federal Courts: Does Race Matter? Transition to Sentencing Guidelines, 1986-90*, by Douglas C. McDonald and Kenneth E. Carlson (Washington, DC: U.S. Department of Justice, 1993), chaps. 4, 5.

45. RAND, *Controlling Cocaine: Supply versus Demand Programs*, ed. C. Peter Rydell and Susan S. Everingham, RAND publications MR-331-ONDCP/A/DPRC (Santa Monica: RAND, 1994).

46. The proportion of prison *admissions* in each offense category does not correspond to the proportion of prison inmates at any given time. Because property and violent offenders often serve longer sentences, they make up larger fractions of total prison inmates (50 and 20 percent of state inmates, respectively). See Bureau of Justice Statistics, *Prisoners in 2004* (Washington, DC: U.S. Department of Justice, 2005).

47. Between 1977 and 2001, spending on corrections rose by 1,101 percent, compared to increases in spending on education (448 percent), hospitals and health care (482 percent), interest on debt (543 percent), and public welfare (617 percent). Bureau of Justice Statistics, *Justice Expenditure and Employment in the United States, 2001* (Washington, DC: U.S. Department of Justice, 2004). Regarding other social welfare spending, see Isaac Shapiro and Robert Greenstein, *Cuts to Low-Income Programs May Far Exceed the Contribution of These Programs to Deficit's Return* (Washington, DC: Center on

Budget and Policy Priorities, 2005). See also Garland, *The Culture of Control*, 100; Katherine Beckett and Bruce Western, "Governing Social Marginality: Welfare, Incarceration, and the Transformation of State Policy," *Punishment and Society* 3 (2001): 43–59.

48. The total number of state and federal prisoners released in 2003 was 656,320, compared to 80,043 in 1970. See Bureau of Justice Statistics, *Prison and Jail Inmates at Midyear 2004*; Margaret Werner Cahalan, *Historical Corrections Statistics in the United States, 1850-1984* (Washington, DC: U.S. Department of Justice, Bureau of Justice Statistics, 1986).

49. National Advisory Commission on Criminal Justice Standards and Goals, *Corrections* (Washington, DC: U.S. Government Printing Office, 1973), 431.

50. Jonathan Simon, *Poor Discipline: Parole and the Social Control of the Underclass, 1890-1990* (Chicago: University of Chicago Press, 1993), 98.

51. Ibid., 96–98.

52. Martin F. Horn, "Rethinking Sentencing," *Corrections Management Quarterly* 5, no. 3 (2000): 34–40; Reitz, "Sentencing."

53. Travis, *But They All Come Back*, 40.

54. National averages in parole spending mask starker trends at the state level. In California, for example, spending on parole services was cut by 44 percent in 1997, causing caseloads to nearly double (averaging eighty-two parolees for each parole officer). Petersilia, "Parole and Prisoner Reentry in the United States." Note, however, that parole success is not a simple function of the level of supervision. In fact, some attempts to provide intensive supervision have resulted in increased recidivism, in part because greater supervision offers more opportunity to catch violations. Changes in the quality as well as quantity of supervision and support for parolees (e.g., promoting links between ex-offenders and prosocial resources) has shown more promising results. Jeremy Travis, Amy Solomon, and Michelle Waul, *From Prison to Home: The Dimensions and Consequences of Prisoner Reentry* (Washington, DC: Urban Institute Press, 2001). In addition to diminishing resources, changes in sentencing laws have also affected the functioning of parole. As prisoners are now required to serve a higher proportion of their sentences behind bars, with the possibility of discretionary parole highly curtailed, increasing numbers of offenders are being released with no formal supervision whatsoever. Between 1977 and 2000, releases due to expiration of sentence rose from 5 to 18 percent. By 2000, roughly one in five inmates was leaving prison with no form of postrelease supervision. See Bureau of Justice Statistics, *Trends in State Parole, 1990-2000* (Washington, DC: U.S. Department of Justice, 2001); and Joan Petersilia, *When Prisoners Come Home: Parole and Prisoner Reentry* (New York: Oxford University Press, 2003), fig. 3.1.

55. Simon, *Poor Discipline*, 192–93.

56. Petersilia, "Parole and Prisoner Reentry in the United States," 482–483, 505; Mona Lynch, "Waste Managers? New Penology, Crime Fighting, and the Parole Agent Identity," *Law and Society Review* 32 (1999): 839–69.

57. J. Irwin and J. Austin, *It's About Time: America's Imprisonment Binge*, 3rd ed. (Belmont, CA: Wadsworth, 1994), 129.

58. Petersilia, "Parole and Prisoner Reentry in the United States," 513.

59. According to federal housing policies, all public housing authorities, Section 8 providers, and federally assisted housing programs are permitted, and in some cases required, to deny housing to individuals who have prior criminal convictions. Among the range of public resources off-limits to ex-offenders, certain restrictions on cash assistance and food stamps, public housing eligibility, and educational loans are

specifically targeted to individuals with drug convictions. Travis, Solomon, and Waul, "From Prison to Home."

60. Mercer L. Sullivan, *"Getting Paid": Youth Crime and Work in the Inner City* (Ithaca, NY: Cornell University Press, 1989), 103–5; Sampson and Laub, *Crime in the Making*, chaps. 7, 9.

61. Dina Rose and Todd Clear, "Incarceration, Social Capital, and Crime: Implications for Social Disorganization Theory," *Criminology* 36, no. 3 (1998): 441–79; see also James P. Lynch and William Sabol, "Prison Use and Social Control," in *Criminal Justice 2000: Policies, Processes, and Decisions of the Criminal Justice System*, ed. Julie Horney (Washington, DC: U.S. Department of Justice, 2000), 7–44.

62. California Department of Corrections, *Preventing Parolee Failure Program: An Evaluation* (Sacramento: California Department of Corrections, 1997).

63. Sampson and Laub, *Crime in the Making*, 162.

64. David B. Wilson, Catherine Gallagher, and Doris L. MacKenzie, "A Meta-Analysis of Corrections-Based Education, Vocation, and Work Programs for Adult Offenders," *Journal of Research in Crime and Delinquency* 37 (2000): 347–68. See also Chris Uggen, "Work as a Turning Point in the Life Course of Criminals: A Duration Model of Age, Employment, and Recidivism," *American Sociological Review* 65, no. 4 (2000): 529–46, which finds particularly strong effects for older ex-offenders; and Steven Raphael and David F. Weiman, "The Impact of Local Labor Market Conditions on the Likelihood That Parolees Are Returned to Custody" (working paper, University of California-Berkeley, 2005), which finds particularly strong effects for low-risk offenders. Note that Bushway and Reuter find only mixed evidence for employment interventions on the outcomes of ex-offenders. Shawn D. Bushway and Peter Reuter, "Labor Markets and Crime Risk Factors," in *Preventing Crime: What Works, What Doesn't, What's Promising*, a report to the United States Congress, prepared for the National Institute of Justice, 1997, chap. 6.

65. Petersilia, *When Prisoners Come Home*, 83.

66. Though information is limited, some research suggests that joblessness among ex-offenders has increased over time. Simon, *Poor Discipline*, reports that roughly 40 percent of ex-offenders in 1970 reported employment within a year after release, compared to more recent studies that estimate employment rates of only 15 to 25 percent. Petersilia, *When Prisoners Come Home*, 119; Marcia Festen and Sunny Fischer, *Navigating Reentry: The Experiences and Perceptions of Ex-Offenders Seeking Employment* (Chicago: Urban League, 2002); Marta Nelson, Perry Deess, and Charlotte Allen, *The First Month Out: Post-incarceration Experiences in New York City* (New York: Vera Institute of Justice, 1999). Looking further back in time, a 1935 report indicates that fully 82 percent of parolees in the state of New York were employed. See *Proceedings of the Governor's Conference on Crime, the Criminal, and Society*, September 30 to October 3, 1935, Albany, NY (Albany, NY: J. B. Lyon, 1935), 1137.

Chapter 2

1. Data from http://www.starbucks.com/aboutus/Company_Profile.pdf, last accessed 12/10/06; http://www.mcdonalds.com/corp/values/report.html, accessed 12/10/06; http://www.walmartfacts.com/FactSheets/10242006_Corporate_Facts.pdf, accessed 12/10/06; Bureau of Justice Statistics, *Prison and Jail Inmates at Midyear 2005* (Washington, DC: U.S. Department of Justice, 2006).

2. The Bureau of Labor Statistics produces estimates of the number of job openings by occupation, combining new job creation and replacement positions. The

projected number of job openings for "food preparation and serving workers, including fast food" for the period 2002 to 2012 is 1,317,000. Averaging this estimate over the ten-year time span suggests an annual 131,700 jobs opening per year. See http://www.bls.gov/opub/ooq/2003/winter/art02.pdf.

3. See Bruce Western, *Punishment and Inequality in America* (New York: Russell Sage Foundation, 2006), chap. 4; Bruce Western and Katherine Beckett, "How Unregulated Is the U.S. Labor Market? The Penal System as a Labor Market Institution," *American Journal of Sociology* 104, no. 4 (1999): 1030–60; Bruce Western and Becky Pettit, "Incarceration and Racial Inequality in Men's Employment," *Industrial and Labor Relations Review* 54 (2000): 3–16.

4. Excluded groups are those living in military barracks, student dormitories, mental institutions, and prisons.

5. Western and Beckett, "How Unregulated Is the U.S. Labor Market?" A focus on adjusted unemployment rates requires assumptions about the likelihood that current inmates would be unemployed if they were not in prison. Other work, focusing simply on the number of employed individuals relative to the total population (an employment-to-population ratio), requires no such assumptions. This more straightforward accounting exercise charts the overall rate of employment, taking into account all possible sources of joblessness (including incarceration). See, e.g., Bruce Western and Becky Pettit, "Black-White Wage Inequality, Employment Rates, and Incarceration," *American Journal of Sociology* 111 (2005): 553–78, which estimates the impact of incarceration on measures of black-white wage inequality.

6. Western and Pettit, "Black-White Wage Inequality, Employment Rates, and Incarceration"; quotation in text is from 553. Western and Beckett calculated adjusted unemployment rates that reveal a 40 percent larger black-white disparity than standard labor market estimates would predict. Western and Beckett, "How Unregulated Is the U.S. Labor Market?" Western and Pettit calculate employment-to-population ratios that show a 7 percent rise in the black-white gap among all working-age men and a 45 percent rise among young high school dropouts. See Western and Pettit, "Incarceration and Racial Inequality in Men's Employment." The increasing selectivity of blacks into the labor market likewise affects our estimates of black-white earning disparities: Western and Pettit calculate adjusted wage rates for black and white workers, correcting for the disproportionate number of low-wage earners among black men in prison or otherwise missing from standard labor force statistics. Including blacks in prison or out of the labor market in our earnings estimates leads to an increase in the black-white wage gap of between 7 to 20 percent; among young men (ages 22-30), this gap increases by up to 60 percent.

7. Interestingly, though removed from our official economic indicators, prison inmates are counted in local population estimates. Sarah Lawrence and Jeremy Travis report that in the ten states with the highest rates of prison growth, more than 20 percent of the "residents" in thirteen counties were actually imported prison inmates. These rural counties, in which prison growth has been fastest, benefit substantially from the reported population growth, becoming eligible for increases in certain federal financial aid and in the apportionment of political representation, each allocated on the basis of population counts. See Sarah Lawrence and Jeremy Travis, *The New Landscape of Imprisonment: Mapping America's Prison Expansion* (Washington, DC: Urban Institute, 2004).

8. In addition to the more than 650,000 state and federal inmates released from prison each year, there are over 750,000 individuals currently incarcerated in county

and local jails, the majority of whom will be released within the year. See Bureau of Justice Statistics, "Prison and Jail Inmates at Midyear 2005" (Washington, DC: U.S. Department of Justice).

9. Petersilia cites a study of California state parolees that found that 80 percent remained without full-time employment up to a year after release. See Joan Petersilia, *When Prisoners Come Home: Parole and Prisoner Reentry* (New York: Oxford University Press, 2003), 119. Festen and Fischer report findings from an in-depth study of seventy-two returning inmates, only a quarter of whom had found steady employment eighteen months after release. See Marcia Festen and Sunny Fischer, "Navigating Reentry: The Experiences and Perceptions of Ex-Offenders Seeking Employment" (Chicago: Urban League, 2002). Similar findings are reported in a study conducted by the Vera Institute of Justice, tracking forty-nine ex-offenders during their first month after release from prison. Of the forty-nine ex-offenders, thirty-one were unable to find jobs in the first month out. See Marta Nelson, Perry Deess, and Charlotte Allen, *The First Month Out: Post-incarceration Experiences in New York City* (New York: Vera Institute of Justice, 1999).

10. Robert Sampson and John H. Laub, *Crime in the Making: Pathways and Turning Points through Life* (Cambridge, MA: Harvard University Press, 1993), 162–78. These data were initially collected by Sheldon and Eleanor Glueck in 1950. Job stability is measured as a composite scale of employment status, stability of most recent employment (length of time on current or most recent job), and work habits (three-point scale of worker reliability and assets).

11. Other research has produced similar evidence of the negative effects of criminal sanctions on employment. See, e.g., Western and Beckett, "How Unregulated Is the U.S. Labor Market?"; Jeffrey Grogger, "Arrests, Persistent Youth Joblessness, and Black/White Employment Differentials," *Review of Economics and Statistics* 74 (1992): 100–06; John Bound and Richard B. Freeman, "What Went Wrong? The Erosion of Relative Earnings and Employment among Young Black Men in the 1980s," *Quarterly Journal of Economics* 107 (1992): 201–32; Shawn D. Bushway, "The Impact of an Arrest on the Job Stability of Young White American Men," *Journal of Research in Crime and Delinquency* 35, no. 4 (1998): 454–79. On earnings, see Joel Waldfogel, "Does Conviction Have a Persistent Effect on Income and Employment?," *International Review of Law and Economics* 14 (1994): 103–19; Richard B. Freeman, "Crime and the Employment of Disadvantaged Youths," National Bureau of Economic Research Inc., 1991; Daniel Nagin and Joel Waldfogel, "The Effect of Conviction on Income through the Life Cycle," *International Review of Law and Economics* 18, no. 1 (1998): 25–40. Note, however, that there are also several studies that report little or no lasting effect of incarceration on employment or earnings. Jeffrey Kling, "Incarceration Length, Employment, and Earnings," *American Economic Review* 96, no. 3 (2006): 863–76; Jeffrey Grogger, "The Effect of Arrests on the Employment and Earnings of Young Men," *Quarterly Journal of Economics* 110 (1995): 51–72; Karen E. Needels, "Go Directly to Jail and Do Not Collect? A Long-Term Study of Recidivism, Employment, and Earning Patterns among Prison Releases," *Journal of Crime and Delinquency* 33 (1996): 471–96.

12. Jeremy Travis, *But They All Come Back: Facing the Challenges of Prisoner Reentry* (Washington, DC: Urban Institute Press, 2005), 157–58; Bureau of Justice Statistics, "Comparing Federal and State Prison Inmates 1991," NCJ 145864, table 2 (1994).

13. This explanation could also be referred to as an argument about the treatment effects of incarceration. I refer to the "transformative effects" here as a means of differentiating this treatment effect from the one discussed below ("credentialing effects").

14. On the relationship between prison and social networks, see John Hagan, "The Social Embeddedness of Crime and Unemployment," *Criminology* 31, no. 4 (1993):

465–91; on violence in prisons, see Christian Parenti, *Lockdown America: Police and Prisons in the Age of Crisis* (New York: Verso, 1999); for an overview of some of the potentially debilitating effects of incarceration, see Jeremy Travis, Amy Solomon, and Michelle Waul, *From Prison to Home: The Dimensions and Consequences of Prisoner Reentry* (Washington, DC: Urban Institute Press, 2001).

15. Bureau of Justice Statistics, "Education and Correctional Populations."

16. In many respects, the credentialing process works similarly for all forms of criminal justice contact. Individuals who receive noncustodial sentences (e.g., probation or fines) are nevertheless marked by their conviction, with most legal penalties attaching to felony status irrespective of incarceration. (In fact, however, under today's sentencing regime it has become increasingly unusual to receive a felony conviction without a prison sentence. Indeed, roughly 70 percent of those convicted of felonies in 2002 were sentenced to a term in jail or prison. See Bureau of Justice Statistics, "Felony Sentences in State Courts, 2002" [Washington: U.S. Department of Justice, 2004]). Even arrests have been shown to have negative effects on employer evaluations, despite the fact that many states explicitly bar the use of arrest records in hiring decisions. See Richard Schwartz and Jerome Skolnick, "Two Studies of Legal Stigma," *Social Problems* 10 (Autumn 1962): 133–42; Shawn D. Bushway, "The Impact of an Arrest on the Job Stability of Young White American Men," *Journal of Research in Crime and Delinquency* 35, no. 4 (1998): 454–79. There is, however, evidence that incarceration is viewed by employers as an indicator of more serious trouble, an issue I will return to in chapter 7. Because of its particularly stigmatizing qualities, I place a strong emphasis on incarceration as a credentialing process. It should be kept in mind, however, that many forms of contact with the criminal justice system produce similar, if less severe, credentialing outcomes.

17. Six states categorically deny public employment to felons, with the remainder imposing varying degrees of legal restrictiveness. See Kathleen M. Olivares, Velmer S. Burton Jr., and Francis Cullen, "The Collateral Consequences of a Felony Conviction: A National Study of State Legal Codes 10 Years Later," *Federal Probation* 60 (1996): 10–17.

18. Mitchell Dale, "Barriers to the Rehabilitation of Ex-offenders," *Crime and Delinquency* 22 (1976): 322–37; Bruce E. May, "The Character Component of Occupational Licensing Laws: A Continuing Barrier to the Ex-Felon's Employment Opportunities," *North Dakota Law Review* 71 (1995): 187; Petersilia, *When Prisoners Come Home*, 113–15.

19. Elena Saxonhouse, "Unequal Protection: Comparing Former Felons' Challenges to Disenfranchisement and Employment Discrimination," *Stanford Law Review* 56 (2004): 1597–639; Joan Petersilia, *When Prisoners Come Home*, 113–15.

20. Industrial shifts have also affected the employment opportunities available to ex-offenders, blacks in particular, with the decline of manufacturing jobs in the central cities removing large numbers of jobs previously open to individuals with criminal backgrounds. See Mona Lynch, "Waste Managers? New Penology, Crime Fighting, and the Parole Agent Identity," *Law and Society Review* 32 (1999): 839–69; Jonathan Simon, *Poor Discipline: Parole and the Social Control of the Underclass, 1890–1990* (Chicago: University of Chicago Press, 1993), chap. 5.

21. *Green v. Missouri Pacific Railroad Co.*, 523 F.2d 1290, 1295 (8th Cir. 1975), quoted in Linda Lye, "Title VII's Tangled Tale: The Erosion and Confusion of Disparate Impact and the Business Necessity Defense," *Berkeley Journal of Employment and Labor Law* 19, no. 2 (1998): 315–61, quoting p. 337.

22. *EEOC v. Carolina Freight Carriers Corp.*, 723 F. Supp. 734 (S.D. Fla. 1989), quoted in Lye, "Title VII's Tangled Tale," 345; see also EEOC, Policy Guidance on Consideration

of Arrest Records in Employment Under Title VII of the Civl Rights Act of 1964, as Amended, II EEOC Compliance Manual § 604, N: 6005 (Sept. 7, 1990).

23. Bruce E. May, "The Character Component of Occupational Licensing Laws: A Continuing Barrier to the Ex-Felon's Employment Opportunities," *North Dakota Law Review* 71 (1995): 187–93.

24. Lonnie Freeman Husley, *Attitudes of Employers with Respect to Hiring Released Prisoners* (Ph.D. Dissertation, Mankato State University, 1990), 4.9. Employer attitudes are found to vary moderately by type of occupation, with sales, service, and clerical jobs placing somewhat greater restrictions on ex-offenders than do operative or laborer positions. In general, however, a criminal record appears to be a deterrent to employers for all job types, serving as a more general indicator of employability rather than providing specific information regarding particular job requirements. See especially Harry J. Holzer, *What Employers Want: Job Prospects for Less-Educated Workers* (New York: Russell Sage Foundation, 1996), 60; see also May, "The Character Component of Occupational Licensing Laws," 187.

25. *Parker v. Ellis,* 362 U.S. 574, 593–94; quoted in Margaret Colgate Love, "Starting over with a Clean Slate: In Praise of a Forgotten Section of the Model Penal Code," *Fordham Urban Law Journal* 30 (2003): 1705–41.

26. As one indication, more than half of all fingerprints submitted to the FBI for processing in 2001-2 were for non-criminal justice background checks, compared to only 9 percent in 1993. See Bureau of Justice Statistics, "Compendium of State Privacy and Security Legislation: 2002 Overview" (Washington, DC: U.S. Department of Justice, 2003), 9. Likewise, the number of providers of criminal record information has increased substantially. A proliferation of private services offer quick state or national background checks over the Internet for as little as $15 per person. Wal-Mart recently introduced a product called "Check-In-A-Box," which allows individuals or small businesses to conduct background checks more easily by using a CD-ROM that taps into national crime databases. There has been virtually no attention, however, to the quality of these data. Many background check services require only a name and birth date, with more careful services also requiring a Social Security number. For some services (or for certain states), information is derived primarily from court records (rather than corrections databases), which often do not contain disposition data for charges. One study found that between 20 and 40 percent of arrest records from within the past five years lack accurate disposition data. Bureau of Justice Statistics, "Survey of State Criminal History Information Systems, 2001." Another study reported that at least half of arrests in the FBI database have no final disposition information. Bureau of Justice Statistics, "Use and Management of Criminal History Record Information: A Comprehensive Report, 2001 Update" (Washington, DC: U.S. Department of Justice, 2002), 39. An arrest or court hearing may be recorded, therefore, without the information that the charges were ultimately dismissed or the individual found not guilty. As one striking example of the poor data quality implicated in these background checks, Shawn Bushway and colleagues compared records from an FBI database with those from several private services, finding an agreement rate of less than 50 percent on the criminal backgrounds of a sample of known offenders. Shawn Bushway, Shauna Briggs, Faye Taxman, Mischelle Van Brakle, and Meridith Thanner, "Private Providers of Criminal History Records: Do You Get What You Pay For?" in *The Impact of Incarceration on Labor Market Outcomes,* ed. Shawn Bushway, Michael Stoll, and David Weiman (New York: Russell Sage Foundation Press, forthcoming). See also SEARCH, "Report of the National Task Force on the Commercial Sale of Criminal Justice Record Information"

(Washington, DC: National Consortium for Justice Information and Statistics, 2005); and "Report of the National Task Force on the Commercial Sale of Criminal Justice Record Information."

27. Many professional organizations and licensing boards require members to submit to a common code of ethics, with the resulting credential thus certifying both a set of skills and a set of moral principles.

28. Max Weber, *Economy and Society: An Outline of Interpretive Sociology*, ed. Guenther Roth and Claus Wittich (New York: Bedminster Press, 1968), 302–7, introduced the distinction between "positive" and "negative" forms of stratification in a rough outline. Here he distinguishes between positively and negatively privileged property classes (e.g., land owners versus slaves) and between positively and negatively privileged commercial classes (e.g., entrepreneurs versus laborers).

29. For the purposes of this illustrative diagram, I exclude the category of achieved characteristics that are not characterized as credentials (e.g., occupation or income).

30. Current norms exert considerable pressure against racial distinctions. Whether or not these norms are internalized, and whether or not they affect actual behavior, they have direct influence on the legitimacy with which racial attitudes or behaviors are viewed. See Howard Schuman, Charlottee Steeh, Lawrence Bobo, and Maria Krysan, *Racial Attitudes in America: Trends and Interpretations* (Cambridge, MA: Harvard University Press, 1997), 2–8.

31. See Paul Samuels and Debbie Mukamal, *After Prison—Roadblocks to Reentry: A Report on State Legal Barriers Facing People with Criminal Records* (New York: Legal Action Center, 2004). Some have argued that legal restrictions on ex-offenders themselves legitimate and reinforce private forms of exclusions. The National Advisory Commission on Criminal Justice, for example, asserted in 1973 that "[r]estrictive government practices are a bad example to private employers who can ask properly why they should hire ex-offenders who are not 'safe bets' for governmental employment." See the commission's *Corrections* (Washington, DC: U.S. Government Printing Office, 1973), 47.

32. According to David Cole, "[W]hen the results of the criminal justice system are as racially disproportionate as they are today, the criminal stigma extends beyond the particular behaviors and individuals involved to reach all young black men, and to a lesser extent all black people. The criminal justice system contributes to a stereotyped and stigmatic view of African-Americans as potential criminals." David Cole, "The Paradox of Race and Crime: A Comment on Randall Kennedy's 'Politics of Distinction,'" *Georgetown Law Journal* 83 (1995): 2561.

33. According to John Dovidio, because most Americans today "consciously endorse egalitarian values, they will not discriminate directly and openly in ways that can be attributed to racism; however, because of their negative feelings they will discriminate, often unintentionally, when their behavior can be justified on the basis of some factor other than race." John F. Dovidio, "On the Nature of Contemporary Prejudice: The Third Wave," *Journal of Social Issues* 57, no. 4 (2001): 829–49, at 835.

34. Jennifer Leavitt, "Walking a Tightrope: Balancing Competing Public Interests in the Employment of Criminal Offenders," *Connecticut Law Review* 34 (2001): 1281–1315.

35. Among prisoners expected to be released to the community in 1999, 84 percent reported being involved in drugs or alcohol at the time of the offense; nearly 25 percent were determined to be alcohol dependent; 21 percent had committed the offense to obtain money for drugs; 15 percent were determined to be mentally ill; and 12 percent reported being homeless at the time of arrest. Bureau of Justice Statistics, "Trends in State Parole, 1990–2000" (Washington, DC: U.S. Department of Justice, 2001).

36. These statistics come from a variety of sources, depending on information available. Among those entering parole in 1997, 35% were between 35 and 54 years of age, compared with only 25% in 1985; during that same period, only 24% had been convicted of a violent offense in 1997, compared to 35% in 1985. Inmates in 1997 were more likely to be first-time offenders than those in 1979 (25% vs. 16%). Other trends show no change or movement toward higher risk offenders: There was no change in the proportion of inmates who report being under the influence of drugs at the time of their arrest (33% in 1997 vs. 34% in 1979); a lower likelihood of being employed prior to incarceration (67% in 1997 vs. 74% in 1979); and lower likelihood of being married (17% in 1997 vs. 26% in 1979). In addition, changes in crime policy have led to some worsening indicators: Inmates reentering society today are more likely to have failed at parole previously, not to have participated in educational and vocational programs in prison, and to have served longer sentences. See Margaret Werner Cahalan, *Historical Corrections Statistics in the United States, 1850–1984* (Washington, DC: U.S. Department of Justice, Bureau of Justice Statistics. NCJ 102529, 1986); Bureau of Justice Statistics, "Correctional Populations in the United States, 1997" (Washington, DC: U.S. Department of Justice, 2000); Bureau of Justice Statistics, "Reentry Trends in the U.S.: Releases from State Prison."

37. It is beyond the scope of this study to assess how great these risks are in reality. Very few data exist on the work performance of ex-offenders. Among the employers surveyed in this study who had hired one or more ex-offenders over the past year, more than 80 percent reported having had a somewhat or very positive experience with this employee (see chapter 7; see also Marvin A. Jolson, "Are Ex-Offenders Successful Employees?" *California Management Review* 17 (1975): 65–73). In a majority of cases, then, ex-offenders appear to pose little concern for employers. This survey does not, however, offer much information about the remainder of employers who reported somewhat (11.9 percent) or very (7.5 percent) negative experiences with ex-offender employees, nor whether the frequency of negative experiences was greater for ex-offenders than for nonoffender employees.

Chapter 3

1. For a complementary discussion of methodological approaches to the study of racial discrimination, see National Research Council, *Measuring Racial Discrimination: Panel on Methods for Assessing Discrimination*, ed. Rebecca M. Blank, Marilyn Dabady, and Constance F. Citro (Washington, DC: Committee on National Statistics, Division of Behavior and Social Sciences and Education, National Academies Press, 2004).

2. Harry Holzer and his colleagues have conducted some of the highest-quality survey research in this area to date, drawing from interviews with hundreds of employers in each of at least six metropolitan areas. See especially Harry J. Holzer, *What Employers Want: Job Prospects for Less-Educated Workers* (New York: Russell Sage Foundation, 1996), 59; and Holzer, Steven Raphael, and Michael Stoll, "The Labor Market for Ex-Offenders in Los Angeles: Problems, Challenges, and Public Policy," CSUP Working Paper, 2003 (available at http://www.sscnet.ucla.edu/issr/csup/pubs/papers/item.php?id=20). Other smaller surveys of employers have produced similar results. A survey of employers in seventeen metropolitan areas in Texas, for example, finds that 70 percent of employers were unwilling to hire individuals who have served time in prison. See Lonnie Freeman Husley, "Attitudes of Employers with Respect to Hiring Released Prisoners" (Ph.D. dissertation, Mankato State University, 1990), 40–41. In the late 1940s, one survey reported that 66 percent of employers said they would never hire a released offender; see Clem Wyle, "The Employment of Released Offenders,"

Probation 25 (1946): 9–20. Results of a survey of Milwaukee employers are presented in chapter 7.

3. Holzer, *What Employers Want,* 58–62; Husley, *Attitudes of Employers with Respect to Hiring Released Prisoners,* 43; see also chapter 7 below.

4. Richard T. LaPiere, "Attitudes vs. Actions," *Social Forces* 13 (1934): 230–37; Bernard Kutner, Carol Wilkins, and Penny Rechtman Yarrow, "Verbal Attitudes and Overt Behavior Involving Racial Prejudice," *Journal of Abnormal Social Psychology* 47 (1952): 649–52; Gerhart Saenger and Emily Gilbert, "Customer Reactions to the Integration of Negro Sales Personnel," *International Journal of Opinion and Attitude Research* 4 (1950): 57–76; Devah Pager and Lincoln Quillian, "Walking the Talk: What Employers Say versus What They Do," *American Sociological Review* 70, no. 3 (2005): 355–80. It is important to note that concerns about the validity of survey responses may increase as social pressures to hire ex-offenders, or at least to eliminate blanket restrictions on hiring ex-offenders, grow more salient over time.

5. Neal Miller, "Employer-Barriers to the Employment of Persons with Records of Arrest or Conviction: A Review and Analysis" (Washington, DC: U.S. Department of Labor, ASPER, report no. PUR-79-3204-A, 1979), 32–33. Likewise, David Downing finds that roughly 75 percent of Illinois employers sampled were willing to consider ex-offender applicants. David Downing, "Employer Biases toward the Hiring and Placement of Male Ex-Offenders" (Ph.D. dissertation, Southern Illinois University, 1982), 138.

6. Some research has, however, investigated how concerns about applicant criminality affect the hiring of African Americans. Holzer and colleagues, for example, find evidence that employers concerned about hiring ex-offenders may use race as a proxy for criminal background. See Harry J. Holzer, Steven Raphael, and Michael Stoll, "Perceived Criminality, Criminal Background Checks, and the Racial Hiring Practices of Employers," *Journal of Law and Economics* 49, no. 2 (2006): 451–80.

7. See Devah Pager and Lincoln Quillian, "Walking the Talk: What Employers Say versus What They Do," *American Sociological Review* 70, no. 3 (2005): 355–80; Devah Pager and Jeremy Freese, "Who Deserves a Helping Hand? Attitudes about Government Assistance for the Unemployed by Race, Cause of Unemployment, and Worker History," in *Annual Meetings of the American Sociological Association* (Montreal, 2006).

8. Mercer L. Sullivan, *"Getting Paid": Youth Crime and Work in the Inner City* (Ithaca, NY: Cornell University Press, 1989), 69.

9. Alford Young, *The Minds of Marginalized Black Men: Making Sense of Mobility, Opportunity, and Future Life Chances* (Princeton, NJ: Princeton University Press, 2003), 95.

10. Mitchell Duneier, *Sidewalk* (New York: Farrar, Straus and Giroux, 1999), 121–22. Other accounts tell similar stories of struggle and discouragement for individuals making the transition from prison to work. See Elijah Anderson, *Code of the Streets: Decency, Violence, and the Moral Life of the Inner City* (New York: W. W. Norton, 1999), 244; Jennifer Gonnerman, *Life on the Outside: The Prison Odyssey of Elaine Bartlett* (New York: Picador, 2004), chaps. 23, 25.

11. Sullivan, *"'Getting Paid,'"* 68, emphasis added.

12. Duneier, *Sidewalk,* 121–22.

13. Richard B. Freeman, "Crime and the Employment of Disadvantaged Youths," NBER Working Paper 3875, 1991.

14. Bruce Western and Katherine Beckett, "How Unregulated Is the U.S. Labor Market? The Penal System as a Labor Market Institution," *American Journal of Sociology* 104, no. 4 (1999): 1030–60; for further research on the employment consequences of in-

carceration using large-scale datasets, see especially Bruce Western, *Punishment and In-equality in America* (New York: Russell Sage Foundation, 2006); Jeffrey Grogger, "Arrests, Persistent Youth Joblessness, and Black/White Employment Differentials," *Review of Economics and Statistics* 74 (1992): 100–106; John Bound and Richard B. Freeman, "What Went Wrong? The Erosion of Relative Earnings and Employment among Young Black Men in the 1980s," *Quarterly Journal of Economics* 107, no. 1 (1992): 201–32; Shawn D. Bushway, "The Impact of an Arrest on the Job Stability of Young White American Men," *Journal of Research in Crime and Delinquency* 35, no. 4 (1998): 454–79; Joel Waldfogel, "Does Conviction Have a Persistent Effect on Income and Employment?," *International Review of Law and Economics* 14 (1994): 103–19; Richard B. Freeman, "Crime and the Employ-ment of Disadvantaged Youths" (National Bureau of Economic Research, 1991); Daniel Nagin and Joel Waldfogel, "The Effect of Conviction on Income through the Life Cycle," *International Review of Law and Economics* 18, no. 1 (1998): 25–40. For a review of the lit-erature, see Bruce Western, Jeffrey R. Kling, and David F. Weiman, "The Labor Market Consequences of Incarceration," *Crime and Delinquency* 47 (2001): 410–27.

15. Western and Beckett find a larger effect of youth incarceration on average weeks worked for blacks than whites; the effect of adult incarceration, by contrast, shows little difference in initial effects for blacks and whites, and appears to fade more quickly among blacks. Western and Beckett, "How Unregulated Is the U.S. Labor Mar-ket?" 1049. In a separate analysis, Western reports a larger earnings penalty associated with incarceration for blacks than for whites (47 percent vs. 29 percent), though the ag-gregate effect of incarceration on black-white earnings inequality remains quite small. Western, *Punishment and Inequality in America*, 116–28. Finally, Freeman finds small in-creases in the effects of jail and conviction on employment for African Americans, but these racial differences are not statistically significant. Freeman, "Crime and the Em-ployment of Disadvantaged Youths," table 4. The limited evidence on racial differences in the effects of incarceration thus remains inconclusive.

16. These studies find employment effects associated with incarceration that range in magnitude from 0 to 4 percent. Jeffrey Kling, "Incarceration Length, Employment, and Earnings," *American Economic Review* 96, no. 3 (2006): 863–76 (using data from fed-eral inmates in California and state inmates in Florida); Jeffrey Grogger, "The Effect of Arrests on the Employment and Earnings of Young Men," *Quarterly Journal of Economics* 110 (1995): 51–72 (using data from state inmates in California); Karen E. Needels, "Go Directly to Jail and Do Not Collect? A Long-Term Study of Recidivism, Employment, and Earning Patterns among Prison Releases," *Journal of Crime and Delinquency* 33 (1996): 471–96 (using data from state inmates in Georgia); Becky Pettit and Christopher Lyons, "The Consequences of Incarceration on Employment and Earnings: Evidence from Washington State" (working paper, Department of Sociology, University of Washing-ton) (using data from state inmates in Washington State). R. Curtis Brand and William L. Claiborn find no greater stigma for ex-offenders than for ex-tuberculosis patients or ex-mental patients. R. Curtis Brand and William L. Claiborn, "Two Studies of Compar-ative Stigma: Employer Attitudes and Practices toward Rehabilitated Convicts, Mental and Tuberculosis Patients," *Community Mental Health Journal* 12 (1976): 168–75.

17. Researchers have employed creative techniques for addressing these issues, such as looking at pre- and postincarceration outcomes for the same individuals (e.g., Richard B. Freeman, "On the Economic Analysis of Labor Market Institutions and In-stitutional Change," working paper, Harvard Institute of Economic Research, 1992; Grogger, "Arrests, Persistent Youth Joblessness, and Black/White Employment Differ-entials"); comparing ex-offenders to future offenders (e.g., Jeffrey Grogger, "The Effect

of Arrests on the Employment and Earnings of Young Men"; Waldfogel, "Does Conviction Have a Persistent Effect on Income and Employment?"); estimating fixed- and random-effects models (e.g., Bruce Western, "The Impact of Incarceration on Earnings," *American Sociological Review* 67, no. 4 [2002]: 526–46); and using instrumental variables approaches to correct for unmeasured heterogeneity (e.g., Freeman, "On the Economic Analysis of Labor Market Institutions and Institutional Change"). There remains little consensus, however, about the degree to which these techniques effectively account for the problems of selection endemic to this type of research.

18. On stigma, see Richard Schwartz and Jerome Skolnick, "Two Studies of Legal Stigma," *Social Problems* 10 (1962): 133–42; on social networks, see John Hagan, "The Social Embeddedness of Crime and Unemployment," *Criminology* 31, no. 4 (1993): 465–91; on human capital disruption, see Gary S. Becker, *Human Capital* (New York: Columbia University Press, 1975); on prison violence, see Christian Parenti, *Lockdown America: Police and Prisons in the Age of Crisis* (New York: Verso, 1999); on legal barriers to ex-offenders, see Mitchell Dale, "Barriers to the Rehabilitation of Ex-offenders," *Crime and Delinquency* 22 (1976): 322–37; on claims of spurious effects, see Kling, "Incarceration Length, Employment, and Earnings," Grogger, "The Effect of Arrests on the Employment and Earnings of Young Men," and Karen E. Needels, "Go Directly to Jail and Do Not Collect?" *Journal of Crime and Delinquency* 33 (1996): 471–96. Each of these mechanisms represents a subset of the primary mechanisms discussed in chapter 2: selection, transformation, and credentialing.

19. John Yinger, *Closed Doors, Opportunities Lost* (New York: Russell Sage Foundation, 1995); Ronald E. Wienk, Clifford E. Reid, John C. Simonson, and Frederick J. Eggers, *Measuring Discrimination in American Housing Markets: The Housing Market Practices Survey* (Washington, DC: U.S. Department of Housing and Urban Development, 1979); Jon Hakken, *Discrimination against Chicanos in the Dallas Rental Housing Market: An Experimental Extension of the Housing Market Practices Survey* (Washington, DC: U.S. Department of Housing and Urban Development, 1979).

20. Margery Turner and Felicity Skidmore, eds., *Mortgage Lending Discrimination: A Review of Existing Evidence* (Washington, DC: Urban Institute Press, 1999) (mortgage lending); Ian Ayres and Peter Siegelman, "Race and Gender Discrimination in Bargaining for a New Car," *American Economic Review* 85, no. 3 (1995): 304–21 (car dealership); Stanley Ridley, James A. Bayton, and Janice Hamilton Outtz, "Taxi Service in the District of Columbia: Is It Influenced by Patrons' Race and Destination?" (mimeographed) (Washington, DC: Washington Lawyers' Committee for Civil Rights under the Law, 1989) (hailing a taxi); Yinger, *Closed Doors, Opportunities Lost* (housing); Douglas Massey and Garvey Lundy, "Use of Black English and Racial Discrimination in Urban Housing Markets: New Methods and Findings," *Urban Affairs Review* 36 (2001): 452–69 (housing). There are also several preexisting audits of employment searches: Harry Cross, *Employer Hiring Practices: Differential Treatment of Hispanic and Anglo Job Seekers* (Washington, DC: Urban Institute Press, 1990); Margery Turner, Michael Fix, and Raymond Struyk, *Opportunities Denied, Opportunities Diminished: Racial Discrimination in Hiring* (Washington, DC: Urban Institute Press, 1991); Marc Bendick Jr., Charles Jackson, and Victor Reinoso, "Measuring Employment Discrimination through Controlled Experiments," *Review of Black Political Economy* 23 (1994): 25–48; David Neumark, "Sex Discrimination in Restaurant Hiring: An Audit Study," *Quarterly Journal of Economics* 111, no. 3 (1996): 915–41 (employment). For a review of field experiments in international contexts, see P. A. Riach and J. Rich, "Field Experiments of Discrimination in the Market Place," *Economic Journal* 112 (November 2002): 480–518.

21. Schwartz and Skolnick, "Two Studies of Legal Stigma"; quotation from p. 134. It is important to note that Schwartz and Skolnick's study differs from traditional correspondence tests in several respects. First, rather than sending applications by mail, a researcher posing as an employment agent approached employers with the prospective candidate files and asked whether the employer could use the man in question. Second, each employer was presented with only a single applicant file, with results based on contrasts across the sample of employers. The strength of the audit methodology, by contrast, is better exploited when each employer is presented with two or more applicants for consideration, so that observed differences in employers' responses can be directly attributed to characteristics of the applicant pairs without the possibility of confounding factors introduced by variation in the characteristics of employers. With random assignment and sufficient sample sizes, between-employer comparisons should provide valid results; nevertheless, within-pair comparisons offer more efficient estimates and are less vulnerable to flaws in randomization.

22. Dov Cohen and Richard E. Nisbett, "Field Experiments Examining the Culture of Honor: The Role of Institutions in Perpetuating Norms about Violence," *Personality and Social Psychology Bulletin* 23, no. 11 (1997): 1188–99; R. H. Finn and P. A. Fontaine, "The Association between Selected Characteristics and Perceived Employability of Offenders," *Criminal Justice and Behavior* 12 (1985): 353–65; R. Boshier and Derek Johnson, "Does Conviction Affect Employment Opportunities?" *British Journal of Criminology* 14 (1974): 264–68; W. Buikhuisen and F. P. H. Dijksterhuis, "Delinquency and Stigmatisation," *British Journal of Criminology* 11 (1971): 185–87; Theodore S. Palys, "An Assessment of Legal and Cultural Stigma Regarding Unskilled Workers," *Canadian Journal of Criminology and Corrections* 18 (1976): 247–57.

23. See Peter B. Riach and Judith Rich, "Measuring Discrimination by Direct Experimentation Methods: Seeking Gunsmoke," *Journal of Post-Keynesian Economics* 14, no. 2 (1991-92): 143–50; Joanna Lahey, "Age, Women, and Hiring: An Experimental Study," National Bureau of Economics Research Working Paper 11435, 2005.

24. Marc Bendick Jr., Lauren Brown, and Kennington Wall, "No Foot in the Door: An Experimental Study of Employment Discrimination," *Journal of Aging and Social Policy* 10, no. 4 (1999): 5–23; Lahey, "Age, Women, and Hiring."

25. Ronald G. Fryer Jr. and Steven D. Levitt, "The Causes and Consequences of Distinctively Black Names," *Quarterly Journal of Economics* 109, no. 3 (2004): 767–805, reports that "Blacker names are associated with lower income zip codes, lower levels of parental education, not having private insurance, and having a mother who herself has a Blacker name" (786). Note that the authors of the study, Marianne Bertrand and Sendhil Mullainathan, discuss the issue. Bertrand and Mullainathan, "Are Emily and Greg More Employable than Lakisha and Jamal? A Field Experiment on Labor Market Discrimination," *American Economic Review* 94, no. 4 (2004): 991–1013, see p. 1007–1009.

26. Other correspondence test studies have used the "extracurricular activities" or "voluntary memberships" section of the résumé to bolster the signal of the applicant's race. Membership in the student league of the NAACP, for example, would strongly signal an African American applicant. The matched white applicant would then be given a race-neutral activity (e.g., Student Democratic Alliance) that, in the absence of any racial identifiers, is typically (by default) associated with whites. For an example of this approach, see John F. Dovidio and Samuel L. Gaertner, "Aversive Racism and Selection Decisions," *Psychological Science* 11, no. 4 (2000): 315–19. Whatever strategy is used, it is important that résumés be pretested carefully before using them in the field. Names, extracurricular activities, neighborhoods, and high schools may each have

connotations that are not readily apparent to the researcher. Directly assessing these connotations is an important first step in developing appropriate materials for a study of this kind.

27. For an exception, see Theodore S. Palys, "An Assessment of Legal and Cultural Stigma Regarding Unskilled Workers," *Canadian Journal of Criminology and Corrections* 18 (1976): 247–57, which finds a stronger effect of a criminal background for Canadian Indians than for whites.

28. For an in-between approach using telephone contact (with voice signaling race, class, and gender), see Massey and Lundy, "Use of Black English and Racial Discrimination in Urban Housing Markets"; Thomas Purnell, William Idsardi, and John Baugh, "Perceptual and Phonetic Experiments on American English Dialect Identification," *Journal of Language and Social Psychology* 18, no. 1 (1999): 10–30.

29. This feature has certain desirable properties from the perspective of gaining approval from an institutional review board (e.g., a university ethics committee). Concerns about confidentiality and risks to employers are reduced when no single participant can be identified as a discriminator. See appendix 4A for a discussion of the ethics of audit research.

30. James J. Heckman, "Detecting Discrimination," *Journal of Economic Perspectives* 12, no. 2 (1998): 101–16, at 107–11; see also James Heckman and Peter Siegelman, "The Urban Institute Audit Studies: Their Methods and Findings," in *Clear and Convincing Evidence: Measurement of Discrimination in America*, ed. Michael Fix and Raymond J. Struyk (Washington, DC: Urban Institute Press, 1993), 187–258, which identifies five potential threats to the validity of results from audit studies: (1) problems in effective matching; (2) the use of "overqualified" testers; (3) limited sampling frame for the selection of firms and jobs to be audited; (4) experimenter effects; and (5) the ethics of audit research. Each of these issues is addressed in detail in appendix 4A, with specific reference to the strategies used in this particular study to address these concerns. Also, for a useful discussion of these concerns, see the essays published in Fix and Struyk, *Clear and Convincing Evidence*. In addition to the criticisms expressed by Heckman, audit studies are often costly and difficult to implement and can be used only for selective decision points (e.g., hiring decisions but not promotions).

31. Given these extensive demands, it is common for researchers to screen between fifty and one hundred applicants (already selected on age, race, and gender) before finding a single matched pair.

32. Heckman, "Detecting Discrimination," 111

33. See appendix 7C.

Chapter 4

1. In the real world, of course, one cannot fully disentangle correlated characteristics, and employers may be often confronted with applicants who have criminal backgrounds *and* other undesirable attributes. I do not question here the validity of employers' assumptions about ex-offenders (discussed further in chapter 7). Rather, this chapter seeks to investigate the consequences of these assumptions in the absence of any actual negative attributes (other than the criminal record itself).

2. The primary goal of this study was to measure the effect of a criminal record, and thus it was important for this characteristic to be measured as a within-pair effect. Although it would have been ideal for all four testers to visit the same employers, this would have likely aroused suspicion (particularly given that two testers were presenting evidence of identical felony convictions). The testers were thus divided

into separate teams by race. Over the course of the study, eight young men (twenty-three years of age) were hired as testers (with four testers active at any given time). The names of the testers have been changed to protect their privacy.

3. Employment services such as Jobnet have become a much more common method of finding employment in recent years, particularly for difficult-to-employ populations such as welfare recipients and ex-offenders. A survey conducted by Harry Holzer, Michael Stoll, and Steven Raphael found that nearly half of Milwaukee employers (46 percent) use Jobnet to advertise job vacancies in their companies (analysis of unpublished data provided to the author by Holzer).

4. When a tester was offered a job on the spot, he told the employer that he was still waiting to hear back about another job he had interviewed for earlier. The tester then called the employer back at the end of the same day to let him/her know that the other job had come through and he was therefore no longer available.

5. Marc Bendick Jr., Lauren Brown, and Kennington Wall, "No Foot in the Door: An Experimental Study of Employment Discrimination," *Journal of Aging and Social Policy* 10, no. 4 (1999): 5–23.

6. James Heckman, "Detecting Discrimination," *Journal of Economic Perspectives* 12, no. 2 (1998): 101–16, makes a similar argument in his critique of audit studies of racial discrimination (see discussion in chapter 3).

7. Specifically, testers reported having been convicted of "possession with intent to distribute" and having been released from prison in the past month.

8. See chapter 1 for an overview of recent changes in drug policy and their implications for racial disparities in incarceration. If anything, the emphasis on drug crimes is likely to produce conservative estimates of the effect of a criminal record: survey results indicate that employers are substantially more averse to applicants convicted of violent crimes or property crimes than to those convicted of drug crimes. Harry Holzer, Steven Raphael, and Michael Stoll, "Employer Demand for Ex-Offenders: Recent Evidence from Los Angeles," Urban Institute Working Paper, 2003; see also chapter 7 below.

9. See Harry Cross, Genevieve Kenney, Jane Mell, and Wendy Zimmerman, *Differential Treatment of Hispanic and Anglo Job Seekers: Hiring Practices in Two Cities* (Washington, DC: Urban Institute Press, 1989), appendix B.

10. In 1991, 49 percent of federal and 46.5 percent of state inmates had a high school degree (or equivalent). Bureau of Justice Statistics, "Comparing Federal and State Prison Inmates, 1991" (Washington, DC: U.S. Department of Justice, 1994).

11. Little information exists about the employment experiences of young men prior to incarceration. Longitudinal data from a cohort of young men indicate that, among those who wind up in prison, the distribution of jobs prior to incarceration includes: laborers (25%), craft workers (21 percent), operatives (20 percent), service workers (16 percent), clerical workers (5 percent), sales workers (3 percent), and professional, technical, and managerial workers (4 percent). Devah Pager, "Criminal Careers: The Consequences of Incarceration for Occupational Attainment," presented at the American Sociological Association Annual Meeting, Anaheim; see also Bureau of Justice Statistics, "Comparing Federal and State Prison Inmates, 1991."

12. Testers reported working either as an assistant manager at a national chain restaurant or as a supervisor at a national home retail store.

13. Although time out of the labor market is in fact one component of the total impact of incarceration, this study sought to isolate the credentialing effects of a criminal

record from other potential consequences of incarceration. Again, an estimate of the full effect of incarceration would also need to take account of employment difficulties resulting from a prolonged labor market absence.

14. To the extent that real ex-offenders lie about their criminal record on application forms, this approach may lead to an overestimate of the effect of a criminal record. See appendix 4A for a more thorough consideration of this issue.

15. This approach was developed in discussion with several Milwaukee employment counselors and parole officers and is based on a composite profile of résumés belonging to real ex-offenders. For one specific example, see Jennifer Gonnerman's description of ex-offender Elaine Bartlett's résumé, which listed "her GED, her associate's degree, and fourteen prison jobs" in her *Life on the Outside: The Prison Odyssey of Elaine Bartlett* (New York: Picador, 2004), 187.

16. At the time of this study Milwaukee was the nineteenth-largest city in the country, with a population of 1.84 million, nearly 25 percent of whom were African American. U.S. Census Bureau, "2001 Supplementary Survey Profile: Milwaukee-Waukesha, WI PMSA," Washington, DC: U.S. Census Bureau, 2002.

17. Monthly unemployment rates in Milwaukee fluctuated modestly over the duration of the study: June (5.2 percent), July (4.7 percent), August (4.9 percent), September (4.5 percent), October (4.7 percent), November (5.1 percent), December (4.9 percent). National unemployment rates were lower in June (4.6 percent), but rose above Milwaukee's unemployment rate to a high of 5.8 percent in December. Bureau of Labor Statistics, 2002, *Local Area Unemployment Statistics,* Online Public Data Query, 2002 (available from http://www.bls.gov/data).

18. Freeman and Rodgers find that the tight labor market of the 1990s was associated with substantial gains in both employment and earnings for young African American men. Richard B. Freeman and William M. Rodgers III, "Area Economic Conditions and the Labor Market Outcomes of Young Men in the 1990s Expansion," National Bureau of Economic Research working paper no. 7073, 1999. While this analysis does not measure discrimination directly, one implication is that in periods of extremely low unemployment, demand for labor overrides preferences for particular categories of workers. See also Hilary W. Hoynes, "The Employment, Earnings, and Income of Less Skilled Workers over the Business Cycle," in *Finding Jobs: Work and Welfare Reform*, ed. David Card and Rebecca M. Blank (New York: Russell Sage Foundation, 2000), 23–71.

19. The unemployment rate in Milwaukee had been as low as 2.7 percent in September 1999. Bureau of Labor Statistics, 2002, *Local Area Unemployment Statistics.*

20. John Pawasarat and Lois M. Quinn, *Survey of Job Openings in the Milwaukee Metropolitan Area: Week of May 15, 2000,* Employment and Training Institute, University Outreach, University of Wisconsin-Milwaukee, 2000.

21. Ibid.

22. As noted above, this sample excludes health care workers—which represented the largest category of entry-level employment—and other occupations with legal restrictions on ex-felons.

23. An overwhelming majority of employers used generic questions about criminal backgrounds (with the only major source of variation stemming from an emphasis on all prior convictions versus felonies only). A handful of large national companies, however, used questions that reflected a more nuanced understanding of the law. One company, for example, instructed applicants *not* to answer the question if they were residents of certain specified states; another asked only about prior convictions for theft and burglary, ignoring all other possible offenses. These questions presumably

reflect a nuanced interpretation of state and federal guidelines regulating the use of criminal record information in making hiring decisions.

24. The issue of official background checks raises some concern as to the validity of the experimental condition, given that the information provided by testers can be (dis)confirmed on the basis of other sources of information available to employers. In cases where employers in this study did perform background checks on testers, the check would come back clean (none of the testers in this study actually had a criminal record). It is my expectation that because employers would not expect someone to lie about *having* a criminal record; and because employers know that criminal history databases are fraught with errors, they would be inclined to believe the worst-case scenario—in this case, the self-report.

25. See appendix 4B for coefficients from the logistic regression model. Sensitivity analyses testing for possible tester or period effects found no significant differences (not reported here).

26. Patricia Devine and Scott Elliot, "Are Racial Stereotypes Really Fading? The Princeton Trilogy Revisited," *Personality and Social Psychology Bulletin* 21 (1995):1139–50; Tom W. Smith, *Ethnic Images*, General Social Survey technical report 19 (Chicago: National Opinion Research Center, University of Chicago, 1991); Paul M. Sneiderman and Thomas Piazza, *The Scar of Race* (Cambridge, MA: Harvard University Press, 1993).

27. J. M. Darley and P. H. Gross, "A Hypothesis-Confirming Bias in Labeling Effects," *Journal of Personality and Social Psychology* 44 (1983): 20–33; Lincoln Quillian and Devah Pager, "Black Neighbors, Higher Crime? The Role of Racial Stereotypes in Evaluations of Neighborhood Crime," *American Journal of Sociology* 107, no. 3 (2001): 717–67.

28. Previous audit studies, focusing on one comparison only, have often relied on net differences in percentages as the primary measure of discrimination. Extending this approach to the present design, it would likewise be possible to compare the percentage difference in treatment among whites (between nonoffenders and offenders) to that among blacks (a difference-in-differences approach). Given that the baseline rate of callbacks is substantially different for blacks and whites, however, this measure would be misleading. In an absolute sense, whites have greater opportunity overall and thus have more to lose. Taking into account this differential baseline, we see that the *relative* effect of a criminal record is in fact larger among blacks than it is among whites.

29. Sandra Graham and Brian S. Lowery, "Priming Unconscious Racial Stereotypes about Adolescent Offenders," *Law and Human Behavior* 28 (2004): 483–504.

30. Galen Bodenhausen, "Stereotypic Biases in Social Decision Making and Memory: Testing Process Models of Stereotype Use," *Journal of Personality and Social Psychology* 55 (1988): 726–37. See also Lawrence Bobo, "Racial Attitudes and Relations at the Close of the Twentieth Century," in *America Becoming: Racial Trends and Their Consequences*, ed. N. Smelser, W. J. Wilson, and F. Mitchell (Washington, DC: National Academy Press, 2001), 262–99, esp. 279.

31. The strong association between race and crime in the minds of employers provides some indication that the "true effect" of a criminal record for blacks may be even larger than what is measured here. If black nonoffenders receive fewer callbacks because of generalized concerns about black criminality, the contrast between blacks with and without criminal records may be suppressed. Evidence for this type of statistical discrimination can be found in Shawn D. Bushway, "Labor Market Effects of Permitting Employer Access to Criminal History Records," *Journal of Contemporary Criminal Justice* 20 (2004): 276–91, and Harry J. Holzer, Steven Raphael, and Michael Stoll,

"Perceived Criminality, Criminal Background Checks, and the Racial Hiring Practices of Employers," *Journal of Law and Economics* 49, no. 2 (2006). I discuss these further in the next chapter.

32. James Heckman and Peter Siegelman, "The Urban Institute Audit Studies: Their Methods and Findings," in *Clear and Convincing Evidence: Measurement of Discrimination in America*, ed. Michael Fix and Raymond J. Struyk (Washington, DC: Urban Institute Press, 1993), 187–258.

33. Note that even in cases where the experimental condition can be randomly assigned, it is nevertheless desirable to match testers as closely as possible, so as to minimize extraneous noise in the comparisons of tester outcomes.

34. Typically résumés are constructed to reflect a range of entry level work experience, including, for example, jobs in sales, restaurant work, and manual labor.

35. In these discrimination cases, testers serve as the plaintiffs. Despite the fact that the testers themselves were not in fact seeking housing (or employment) at the time their application was submitted, their treatment nevertheless represents an actionable claim. This issue has received close scrutiny by the courts, including rulings by the highest federal courts (see below). See Roderic Boggs, Joseph Sellers, and Marc Bendick Jr., "Use of Testing in Civil Rights Enforcement," in *Clear and Convincing Evidence: Measurement of Discrimination in America*, ed. Michael Fix and Raymond J. Struyk (Washington, DC: Urban Institute Press, 1993), 345–76.

36. As one classic example, see Stanley Milgram, *Obedience to Authority: An Experimental View* (New York: Harper and Row, 1974).

37. Department of Health and Human Services, Code of Federal Regulations, title 45, part 46: Protection of Human Subjects, section 46.116 (http://www.hhs.gov/ohrp/humansubjects/guidance/45cfr46.htm).

38. 56 Federal Register 117, 28017, June 18, 1991.

39. In the present research, I further limit imposition on employers by restricting audits to the first stage of the employment process. In most cases, then, I look only at whether or not an employer invites the tester for an interview, rather than including the interview and job offer stages as well. Limiting the research design to the initial process can thus further reduce the burden to subjects.

40. *Havens Realty Corp. v. Coleman*, 455 U.S. 363, 373 (1982).

41. From a press release issued on December 5, 1997, which can be found at http://www.eeoc.gov/press/12-5-97.html (last accessed 8/15/06).

42. This is particularly consequential for employees in states such as Wisconsin where employers are not allowed to fire someone for *having* a criminal record, but they are allowed to fire him for *lying* about his record.

43. Harry J. Holzer, "Search Methods Used by Unemployment Youth," *Journal of Labor Economics* 6 (1988): 1–20.

44. Michael Fix, George C. Galster, and Raymond Struyck, "An Overview of Auditing for Discrimination," in *Clear and Convincing Evidence: Measurement of Discrimination in America*, ed. Michael Fix and Raymond J. Struyk (Washington, DC: Urban Institute Press, 1993), 1–68, esp. 32; Harry J. Holzer, "Informal Job Search and Black Youth Unemployment," *American Economic Review* 77 (1987): 446–52.

45. Marc Bendick Jr., Charles Jackson, and Victor Reinoso, "Measuring Employment Discrimination through Controlled Experiments," *Review of Black Political Economy* 23 (1994): 25–48. Ethnographic evidence further suggests that white ex-offenders benefit more from personal networks in seeking employment than do blacks. Sullivan, for

example, finds that, among juvenile delinquents, whites and Hispanics were readily placed in employment by relatives or extended networks following release from incarceration; blacks, by contrast, benefited much less from social networks in finding work. Mercer L. Sullivan, *"Getting Paid": Youth Crime and Work in the Inner City* (Ithaca, NY: Cornell University Press, 1989). These informal methods of job search behavior, therefore, are likely to result in greater evidence of racial disparities in employment following incarceration than what is reported here.

46. Kevin D. Henson, *Just a Temp* (Philadelphia: Temple University Press, 1996); Jenny Bussey and John Trasviña, *Racial Preferences: The Treatment of White and African American Job Applicants by Temporary Employment Agencies in California* (Berkeley, CA: Discrimination Research Center of the Impact Fund, 2003; available at http://drcenter.org/studies/temp_applicants_03.pdf).

47. Center on Wisconsin Strategy, *Milwaukee Area Regional Economic Analysis*, Center on Wisconsin Strategy, University of Wisconsin-Madison, 1996.

Chapter 5

1. *EEOC v. Target Corporation*, case # 02-C-146. A preliminary ruling by the Eastern District Court dismissing all charges was later reversed upon appeal at the Seventh Circuit Court (case # 04-3559). As of this writing the case is awaiting resolution at the Eastern District Court.

2. Ward Connerly, *Creating Equal: My Fight against Racial Preferences* (San Francisco: Encounter Books, 2000), 20–21; see also Dinesh D'Souza, *The End of Racism: Principles for a Multiracial Society* (New York: Free Press, 1995).

3. Dovidio and Gaertner find support for the stability of discrimination in a study that measured racial attitudes and discrimination at two points in time (late 1980s and late 1990s). To test for discrimination, the researchers performed a simulated hiring experiment in which subjects were asked to evaluate the application materials for black and white job applicants of varying qualification levels. When applicants were either highly qualified or poorly qualified for the position, there was no evidence of discrimination. When applicants had acceptable but ambiguous qualifications, however, subjects were nearly 70 percent more likely to recommend the white applicant than the black applicant. This finding was consistent across the two time periods. Thus, although the authors find substantial declines in self-reported racial prejudice, evidence of discrimination remained stable. See John F. Dovidio and Samuel L. Gaertner, "Aversive Racism and Selection Decisions," *Psychological Science* 11, no. 4 (2000): 315–19.

4. William Julius Wilson, *The Declining Significance of Race: Blacks and Changing American Institutions* (Chicago: University of Chicago Press, 1978), chap. 5.

5. In 1942, only 32 percent of Americans believed that "white students and black students should go to the same schools"; by 1995, this proportion increased to 96 percent. In 1944, 45 percent believed that blacks "should have as good a chance as white people to get any kind of job"; by 1972, this proportion had increased to 97 percent. See Howard Schuman, Charlottee Steeh, Lawrence Bobo, and Maria Krysan, *Racial Attitudes in America: Trends and Interpretations* (Cambridge, MA: Harvard University Press, 1997), 104–5.

6. As one simple empirical measure of this trend, I calculated the number of articles included in *Sociological Abstracts* that have the words "race" or "racial" together with "discrimination" in their title and those that merely reference "race" or "racial," without "discrimination." Nearly 20 percent fewer articles in the period 1986-2002

reference the word "discrimination" in their title than in the period 1963-85; among those written in 2003-4, nearly 40 percent fewer articles about race directly indicate an emphasis on discrimination in their titles. In recent years, therefore, an explicit emphasis on discrimination seems increasingly uncommon in sociological research. Political resources devoted to the problems of racial discrimination have likewise declined. For example, the number and proportion of EEOC charges of racial discrimination declined from 29,548 in 1992 (representing 41 percent of all claims) to 28,819 in 1999 (representing 37 percent of all claims); during this period, claims focusing on discrimination by gender or disability increased. John J. Donahue III and Peter Siegelman, "The Evolution of Employment Discrimination Law in the 1990s: A Preliminary Empirical Investigation," in *Handbook of Employment Discrimination Research*, ed. L. B. Nielsen and R. L. Nelson (Dordrecht, Netherlands: Springer, 2005), 273. For a more extensive discussion of the retreat from issues of racism and discrimination, see Stephen Steinberg, *Turning Back: The Retreat from Racial Justice in American Thought and Policy* (Boston: Beacon Press, 1995), esp. chap. 5.

7. Robert M. Hauser, "Progress in Schooling: A Review," in *Social Inequality*, ed. Katherine Neckerman (New York: Russell Sage Foundation, 2004), chap. 7; Christopher Jencks and Meredith Phillips, eds., *The Black-White Test Score Gap* (Washington, DC: Brookings Institution Press, 1998). Note, however, that the black-white test score gap remains large and statistically significant.

8. Reynolds Farley, "The New American Reality: Who We Are, How We Got Here, and Where We Are Going" (New York: Russell Sage Foundation, 1996); Roderick J. Harrison and Claudette E. Bennett, "Racial and Ethnic Diversity," in *State of the Union: America in the 1990s, Social Trends*, ed. Reynolds Farley (New York: Russell Sage Foundation, 1995), 141–210.

9. Harry J. Holzer, Paul Offner, and Elaine Sorensen, "What Explains the Continuing Decline in Labor Force Activity among Young Black Men?" *Labor History* 46, no. 1 (2005): 37–55. Current Population Survey data show that in the early 1980s, only 14 percent of young white men (aged twenty to thirty-five) with a high school diploma were not working compared to 25 percent of their black counterparts. By 2000, the jobless rate for young high school—educated white men had dropped below 10 percent, but joblessness among black men of the same age and education was around 22 percent. Racial inequality in joblessness had thus increased (with the ratio of black to white nonemployment increasing from 1.79 to 2.20), and employment rates for young noncollege blacks at the height of the economic boom in 2000 were little better than during the recession of the early 1980s.

10. William Julius Wilson, *The Declining Significance of Race: Blacks and Changing American Institutions* (Chicago: University of Chicago Press, 1978); Richard B. Freeman and Harry J. Holzer, eds., *The Black Youth Employment Crisis* (Chicago: University of Chicago Press 1986); Richard Murnane, John Willett, and Frank Levy, "The Growing Importance of Cognitive Skills in Wage Determination," *Review of Economics and Statistics* 77 (1995): 251–66; Roger Waldinger, *Still the Promised City? African-Americans and New Immigrants in Postindustrial New York* (Cambridge, MA: Harvard University Press, 1999). Differences in intergenerational wealth accumulation by race have also been linked to racial differences in human capital development and economic stability. See Dalton Conley, *Being Black, Living in the Red: Race, Wealth, and Social Policy in America* (Berkeley: University of California Press, 1999).

11. More than 80 percent of white respondents indicate that blacks have "as good a chance as white people . . . to get any kind of job for which they are qualified," and

similar proportions believe that blacks are not discriminated against in access to housing or managerial jobs. Respondents are more evenly split when asked about whether blacks are treated fairly by the police (53 percent believe that they are). Schuman et al., *Racial Attitudes in America,* 159–60). The most common explanation for black disadvantage is "a lack of motivation or willpower," with over half of white respondents endorsing this view. By contrast, fully two-thirds of black respondents believe that discrimination is an important explanation, with "poor quality education" representing the second most common choice (author's calculations from the 2000 General Social Survey, http://gss.norc.org).

12. Susan T. Fiske, "Stereotyping, Prejudice, and Discrimination," in *The Handbook of Social Psychology,* ed. Daniel Gilbert, Susan T. Fiske, and Gardner Lindzey (Boston: McGraw-Hill, 1998), 357–411; Galen Bodenhausen, "Stereotypic Biases in Social Decision Making and Memory: Testing Process Models of Stereotype Use," *Journal of Personality and Social Psychology* 55, no. 5 (1988): 726–37; Yaacov Trope and Erik P. Thomson, "Looking for Truth in All the Wrong Places? Asymmetric Search of Individuating Information about Stereotyped Group Members," *Journal of Personality and Social Psychology* 73, no. 2 (1997): 229–41; M. R. Banaji, C. Hardin, and A. J. Rothman, "Implicit Stereotyping in Person Judgment," *Journal of Personality and Social Psychology* 65, no. 2 (1993): 272–81. Despite the progressive changes in racial attitudes generally, research indicates that the content of racial stereotypes has changed little over time; what has changed is the conscious effort on the part of nonprejudiced individuals to inhibit the activation of these stereotypes. See Patricia Devine and Scott Elliot, "Are Racial Stereotypes Really Fading? The Princeton Trilogy Revisited," *Personality and Social Psychology Bulletin* 21 (1995): 1139–50; Patricia Devine, "Stereotypes and Prejudice: Their Automatic and Controlled Components," *Journal of Personality and Social Psychology* 56 (1989): 5–18. While these conscious strategies have successfully resulted in a substantial reduction in the expression of racial bias, actions taken under pressure or in cognitively demanding situations remain vulnerable to the influence of implicit racial attitudes. See Daniel T. Gilbert and Gregory Hixon, "The Trouble with Thinking: Activation and Application of Stereotypic Beliefs," *Journal of Personality and Social Psychology* 60, no. 4 (1991): 509–17.

13. For discussions of the rising importance of skill, see George Farkas, "Cognitive Skills and Noncognitive Traits and Behaviors in Stratification Processes," *Annual Review of Sociology* 29 (2003): 541–62; Richard Murnane, John Willett, and Frank Levy, "The Growing Importance of Cognitive Skills in Wage Determination," *Review of Economics and Statistics* 77 (1995): 251–66. Derek Neal and William Johnson use data from the National Longitudinal Study of Youth to analyze the black-white gap for a cohort born between 1958 and 1963. They find that a measure of cognitive ability (AFQT) explains three-quarters of the wage gap for young men. See Derek Neal and William Johnson, "The Role of Premarket Factors in Black-White Wage Differences," *Journal of Political Economy* 104, no. 5 (1996): 869–95; see also George Farkas and Kevin Vicknair, "Appropriate Tests of Racial Wage Discrimination Require Controls for Cognitive Skill: Comment on Cancio, Evans, and Maume," *American Sociological Review* 61 (1996): 557–60; June O'Neill, "The Role of Human Capital in Earnings Differences between White and Black Men," *Journal of Economic Perspectives* 4, no. 4 (1990): 25–45. Subsequent analyses following up on the Neal and Johnson paper indicate that changes in model specification—for example, adjusting for the number of years of schooling completed at the time cognitive ability was measured, or measuring the wage gap in the years following labor force entry—leaves a larger proportion of the racial wage gap unexplained. Pedro Carneiro, James J. Heckman, and Dimitriy V. Masterov, "Labor Market

Discrimination and Racial Differences in Premarket Factors," *Journal of Law and Economics* 48 (2005): 1–39; Donald Tomaskovic-Devey, Melvin Thomas, and Kecia Johnson, "Race and the Accumulation of Human Capital across the Career: A Theoretical Model and Fixed-Effects Application," *American Journal of Sociology* 111, no. 1 (2005): 58–89; John Cawley, Karen Conneely, James Heckman, and Edward Vytlacil, "Cognitive Ability, Wages, and Meritocracy," in *Intelligence, Genes, and Success: Scientists Respond to the Bell Curve*, ed. Bernie Devlin, Stephen Fienberg, Daniel Resnick, and Kathryn Roeder (New York: Springer Verlag, 1997).

14. James Heckman, "Detecting Discrimination," *Journal of Economic Perspectives* 12, no. 2 (1998): 101–16, at 101.

15. In addition, the black and white testers in this study were carefully selected from the outset to match on key characteristics, such as height, weight, attractiveness, and verbosity. Testers then participated in a week-long training session designed to train testers to follow a well-specific protocol for how to approach employers, how to respond to standard interview questions, and how to present oneself in an interview setting in order to maximize similarity across testers.

16. The primary source of bias in a between-team design is incomplete or ineffective random assignment. If the composition of employers visited by black testers differs in some systematic and consequential way from those employers visited by white testers, our comparison of black-white outcomes will be distorted by this sample heterogeneity. I conducted sensitivity tests to assess the comparability of sample characteristics. No significant differences were found in occupational distribution, industry, or location (city vs. suburb).

17. The sound bite that has emerged from this study is somewhat misleading. The research has been cited among politicians and the media as demonstrating that "whites with a felony conviction have a better chance at getting a job than do blacks with clean criminal histories." This isn't quite right. The difference between a callback rate of 17 percent (for white felons) and 14 percent (for black nonoffenders) is small and not statistically significant. An accurate way to summarize these findings is to say that a white felon has about the same chance of getting a callback as a black man with no criminal background.

18. The magnitude of effects reported in previous audit studies of racial discrimination range from 12 percent to 31 percent. See LeAnn Lodder, Scott McFarland, and Diana White, *Racial Preferences and Suburban Employment Opportunities* (Chicago: Legal Assistance Foundation of Metropolitan Chicago, 2003) (12 percent); Margery Turner, Michael Fix, and Raymond Struyk, *Opportunities Denied, Opportunities Diminished: Racial Discrimination in Hiring* (Washington, DC: Urban Institute Press, 1991) (13 percent); Devah Pager and Bruce Western, "Discrimination in Low Wage Labor Markets," working paper, Princeton University, Department of Sociology, 2006; Marc Bendick Jr., Charles Jackson, and Victor Reinoso, "Measuring Employment Discrimination through Controlled Experiments," *Review of Black Political Economy* 23 (1994): 25–48 (24 percent); Jenny Bussey and John Trasviña, *Racial Preferences: The Treatment of White and African American Job Applicants by Temporary Employment Agencies in California* (Berkeley, CA: Discrimination Research Center of the Impact Fund, 2003; available at http://drcenter.org/studies/temp_applicants_03.pdf) (31 percent). In these comparisons I report percentage differences in order to compare equivalent measures across studies. As I discuss below, however, I find it useful to calculate relative differences (ratio tests) when comparing an effect across two groups with different baseline rates. Un-

fortunately, not all researchers include the raw numbers in their results, and it is thus not possible to calculate comparative ratios in this case.

19. Bendick, Jackson, and Reinoso, "Measuring Employment Discrimination through Controlled Experiments." Note that this study included an assessment of the full hiring process, from application to job offer. That the racial disparities reported here (at the first stage of the employment process) closely mirror those from more comprehensive studies provides further reassurance that this design is capturing a majority of the discrimination that takes place in the hiring process.

20. Marianne Bertrand and Sendhil Mullainathan, "Are Emily and Greg More Employable than Lakisha and Jamal? A Field Experiment on Labor Market Discrimination," *American Economic Review* 94 (2004): 991–1013. The lower overall callback rates in the Bertrand and Mullainathan study may reduce the observed contrasts between résumé pairs. If, for example, 5 percent of employers tend to call back *all* applicants as a matter of policy, the resulting contrast would be based on a very small number of employers who conduct any type of screening at the résumé submission stage.

21. See David Harris, "Factors for Reasonable Suspicion: When Black and Poor Means Stopped and Frisked," *Indiana Law Journal* 69 (1994): 659–93. A recent study by the National Institute of Justice found that while black and white drivers were stopped by the police at roughly equal rates, once stopped blacks were substantially more likely to have their cars and/or bodies searched. Contrary to arguments that the use of race is warranted by higher rates of illegal activity among blacks, searches of blacks produced significantly lower yield (evidence of contraband) compared to searches of whites (3.5 vs. 14.5 percent). See Bureau of Justice Statistics, "Contacts between Police and the Public: Findings from the 2002 National Survey," NCJ 207845, tables 9, 11).

22. Such predicaments have been discussed elsewhere in many contexts. Some middle-class blacks indicate that they sometimes dress up even to go grocery shopping or to the mall, as a necessary precaution for dealing with street wary whites. See Karyn R. Lacy, "Black Spaces, Black Places: Strategic Assimilation and Identity Construction in Middle-Class Suburbia," *Ethnic and Racial Studies* 27, no. 6 (2004): 908–30; Joe R. Feagin and Melvin P. Sikes, *Living with Racism: The Black Middle-Class Experience* (Boston: Beacon Press, 1994). Having the luxury of wearing sweatpants to the grocery store is not something most whites think of as among the privileges they enjoy as a function of their skin color. (The testers in this study dressed in "business casual"; typically a button-down shirt and slacks.)

23. The level of suspicion greeting black job applicants has been similarly documented in the work of Susan Gooden. Comparing the treatment of black and white welfare recipients, Gooden found that black job applicants were required to complete a preapplication twice as often as whites and were significantly more likely to be subjected to drug tests and criminal background checks than were their white counterparts. Interviews with black applicants that Gooden monitored were shorter and less thorough. In short, blacks faced additional hurdles in the application process, while simultaneously receiving fewer opportunities to demonstrate their qualifications. Susan T. Gooden, "The Hidden Third Party: Welfare Recipients' Experiences with Employers," *Journal of Public Management and Social Policy* 5 (1999): 69–83.

24. Elijah Anderson, *Streetwise: Race, Class, and Change in an Urban Community* (Chicago: University of Chicago Press, 1990), 190. Farmer and Terrell begin with the assumption that the higher rates of criminal activity among African Americans provide useful information in evaluating the criminal propensities of an unknown African American individual. Their estimates, however, suggest that such inferences alone (without

other mediating information) produce a rate of error whereby—at its logical extreme—an innocent African American would be almost five times more likely to be wrongfully convicted of a violent crime than an innocent white individual (eight times, in the case of murder). Amy Farmer and Dek Terrell, "Crime versus Justice: Is There a Trade-Off?" *Journal of Law and Economics* 44 (October 2001): 345–66.

25. Robert M. Entman, "Modern Racism and the Images of Blacks in Local Television News," *Critical Studies in Mass Communication* 7 (1990): 332–45. A similar overrepresentation of African American involvement in crime has been shown in Joseph F. Sheley and Cindy D. Ashkins, "Crime, Crime News, and Crime Views," *Public Opinion Quarterly* 45, no. 4 (1981): 492–506; P. Klite, R. A. Bardwell, and J. Salzman, "Local TV News: Getting Away with Murder," *Harvard International Journal of Press/Politics* 2 (1997): 102–12.

26. Travis L. Dixon and Daniel Linz, "Overrepresentation and Underrepresentation of African Americans and Latinos as Lawbreakers on Television News," *Journal of Communication* 50, no. 2 (2000): 131–54. Limiting attention to felonies yields identical results. Daniel Romer, Kathleen H. Jamieson, and Nicole J. deCouteau, "The Treatment of Persons of Color in Local Television News: Ethnic Blame Discourse or Realistic Group Conflict?" *Communication Research* 25, no. 3 (1998): 286–305, find a similar overrepresentation of blacks as violent perpetrators (and whites as victims) compared to official crime statistics in Philadelphia. Mary Beth Oliver, "Portrayals of Crime, Race, and Aggression in 'Reality-Based' Police Shows: A Content Analysis," *Journal of Broadcasting and Electronic Media* 38, no. 2 (1994): 179–92, does not find this overrepresentation in her analysis of "reality-based" police shows (e.g., *Cops*).

27. Robert M. Entman and Andrew Rojecki, *The Black Image in the White Mind: Media and Race in America* (Chicago: University of Chicago Press, 2000), 81–84, quoting p. 82.

28. William G. Mayer, "Poll Trends: Trends in Media Usage," *Public Opinion Quarterly* 57, no. 4 (1993): 593–611. See also Sheley and Ashkins, "Crime, Crime News, and Crime Views."

29. According to the FBI, approximately 45 percent of arrestees in 1990 were black. 1991 National Race and Politics Survey, http://sda.berkeley.edu:7502/archive .htm; "Uniform Crime Reports, 1990."

30. When the race of the perpetrator was not identified, 44 percent of respondents falsely recalled seeing a black perpetrator; 19 percent falsely recalled seeing a white perpetrator. In conditions in which the race of the suspect was identified, subjects were better able to recall the suspect's race when he was presented as black (70 percent) than when he was presented as white (64 percent). Franklin D. Gilliam and Shanto Iyengar, "Prime Suspects: The Influence of Local Television News on the Viewing Public," *American Journal of Political Science* 44, no. 3 (2000): 560–73, table 2.

31. The pervasive images of black offenders may have implications for perceptions of the "crime problem" as well. For example, Lincoln Quillian and I studied residents' perceptions of the crime problem in their own neighborhoods. We then compared these perceptions to actual neighborhood crime rates, as measured by police statistics and victimization reports. After taking into account a whole host of individual- and neighborhood-level factors that could influence perceptions of crime, including signs of physical and social disorder *and* official crime rates, we found racial composition to be one of the strongest determinants. As the percentage of young black men in a neighborhood increased, so too did residents' perceptions of crime, above and beyond any real increases in crime. The strong attributions of criminality to young black men result in race being readily invoked as a visible proxy for danger. While there may indeed be a statistical basis for associating young black men with crime (i.e., there is a

correlation between racial composition and neighborhood crime rates), this evidence suggests that residents significantly overestimate that correlation, assuming far more of an association between race and crime than actually exists. See Lincoln Quillian and Devah Pager, "Black Neighbors, Higher Crime? The Role of Racial Stereotypes in Evaluations of Neighborhood Crime," *American Journal of Sociology* 107, no. 3 (2001): 717–67.

32. Jennifer L. Eberhardt, Phillip Atiba Goff, Valerie J. Purdie, and Paul G. Davies, "Seeing Black: Race, Crime, and Visual Processing," *Journal of Personality and Social Psychology* 87 (2004): 876–93; Patricia Devine, "Stereotypes and Prejudice: Their Automatic and Controlled Components," *Journal of Personality and Social Psychology* 56 (1989): 5–18; H. A. Sagar and J. W. Schofield, "Racial and Behavioral Cues in Black and White Children's Perceptions of Ambiguously Aggressive Acts," *Journal of Personality and Social Psychology* 39 (1980): 590–98; B. Keith Payne, "Prejudice and Perception: The Role of Automatic and Controlled Processes in Misperceiving a Weapon," *Journal of Personality and Social Psychology* 81, no. 2 (2001): 181–92; Joshua Correll, Bernd Wittenbrink, and Charles M. Judd, "The Police Officer's Dilemma: Using Ethnicity to Disambiguate Potentially Threatening Individuals," *Journal of Personality and Social Psychology* 83, no. 6 (2002): 1314–29.

33. Birt L. Duncan, "Differential Social Perception and Attribution of Intergroup Violence: Testing the Lower Limits of Stereotyping of Blacks," *Journal of Personality and Social Psychology* 34, no. 4 (1976): 590–98, finds that mildly aggressive behavior is perceived as more threatening when the actor is African American than when the actor is white. Likewise, Sagar and Schofield presented subjects with verbal accounts of ambiguous interactions, and found that actors depicted as African American were viewed as more threatening than otherwise identical white actors. They find that this effect holds for both black and white subjects, suggesting that the underlying mechanism is likely a more generalized cultural stereotype rather than personal prejudice or racial animosity. See Sagar and Schofield, "Racial and Behavioral Cues in Black and White Children's Perceptions of Ambiguously Aggressive Acts."

34. Correll, Wittenbrink, and "The Police Officer's Dilemma: Using Ethnicity to Disambiguate Potentially Threatening Individuals."

35. The effects of media representations are unlikely to be independent of the broader influence of racial stereotypes. Images of groups are easier to assimilate and remember when they are consistent with stereotypes of that group. See, e.g., Galen Bodenhausen M. and Lichtenstein, "Social Stereotypes and Information Processing Strategies: The Impact of Task Complexity," *Journal of Personality and Social Psychology* 52 (1987): 871–80; Fiske, "Stereotyping, Prejudice, and Discrimination."

36. It is important to note that these dynamics can emerge even in the absence of conscious negative feelings or ill-will. Both race and criminal background are sensitive topics, which can lead to strained or uneasy interactions even among the most well-meaning individuals. Unfortunately, mere discomfort in interactions can produce some of the same consequences as intentional discrimination. For example, an experimental study in which subjects were asked to interview job applicants in a simulated hiring situation found that interviews with black applicants contained a greater number of pauses, speech errors, and were terminated more quickly. Job candidates (of any race) subjected to interviews characterized by these nonverbal disruptions were in turn evaluated as less qualified by external observers. C. O. Word, M. P. Zanna, and J. Cooper, "The Nonverbal Mediation of Self-Fulfilling Prophecies in Interracial Interactions," *Journal of Experimental Social Psychology* 10 (1974): 109–20. Anxiety or discomfort in interracial interactions and/or with ex-offenders can thus produce outcomes that

look very similar to outright discrimination. See Jennifer Crocker, Brenda Major, and Claude Steele, "Social Stigma," in *Handbook of Social Psychology*, ed. D. Gilbert, Susan Fiske, and G. Lindzey (Boston: McGraw Hill, 1998), 512–15.

37. Shawn Bushway and Harry Holzer and his colleagues have both argued that employers who have access to official criminal background information can replace generalized attributions and assumptions with objective information about actual criminal status, thereby reducing discrimination against blacks without criminal backgrounds. See Shawn D. Bushway, "Labor Market Effects of Permitting Employer Access to Criminal History Records," *Journal of Contemporary Criminal Justice* 20 (2004): 276–91; and Harry J. Holzer, Steven Raphael, and Michael Stoll, "Perceived Criminality, Criminal Background Checks, and the Racial Hiring Practices of Employers," *Journal of Law and Economics* 49, no. 2 (2006): 451–80. The audit data provide only limited support for this hypothesis: employers who conduct official background checks (identified by survey self-reports) were roughly 3 percent more likely to hire black nonoffenders than were employers who do not do checks. Furthermore, only 15 percent of employers reported conducting background checks at the initial stages of selection. A great deal of informal screening thus takes place before more objective background checks are administered.

38. In this discussion, I do not interrogate the validity of specifications used in existing studies of wage inequality, taking at face value the reliability of the analyses. It should be acknowledged, however, that within the survey literature there exist a wide range of estimates of the black-white wage gap, with numerous studies reporting a large and persistent racial gap (see, e.g., A. Silvia Cancio, T. David Evans, and David J. Maume, "Reconsidering the Declining Significance of Race: Racial Differences in Early Career Wages," *American Sociological Review* 61 (1996): 541–56; David Neumark, "Wage Differentials by Race and Sex: The Roles of Taste Discrimination and Labor Market Information," *Industrial Relations* 38, no. 3 (1999): 414–45). Likewise, analysis following the Neal and Johnson (1996) paper has found some evidence that the original results overstate the extent to which cognitive ability can account for racial disparities in wages. Carneiro and colleagues, for example, find that adjustments for the age at which the respondent's cognitive ability was measured lead to the reemergence of a substantial wage differential (Carneiro, Heckman, and Masterov, "Labor Market Discrimination and Racial Differences in Premarket Factors"). Tomaskovic-Devey and colleagues find that, while wages measured in early adulthood show little evidence of racial inequality (because there is little wage dispersion to begin with), the racial wage gap then grows across the life course, reaching 14 percent by the time these men reach 40 (controlling for cognitive ability and other person-specific characteristics) (Tomaskovic-Devey, Thomas, and Johnson, "Race and the Accumulation of Human Capital across the Career," 76.) It thus remains an open question exactly how much of the wage gap can be explained by individual attributes like cognitive ability. Nevertheless, this discussion takes as its starting point the argument that, after extensive controls, analyses of black-white wage disparities can be largely explained by observed individual characteristics. In contrast to evidence from audit studies, these survey results suggest little reason to be concerned with the problems of discrimination.

39. Aside from active assumptions about average productivity by race, mere uncertainty can likewise lead to bias. Generally individuals have access to greater and more reliable information about members of their own group (whether due to familiarity with their neighborhoods, schools, social networks, or simply due to a greater ability to recognize individuating information). See David A. Strauss, "The Law and Economics of Racial Discrimination in Employment: The Case for Numerical Standards," *George-*

town *Law Review* 79 (1991): 1619; Elijah Anderson, *Streetwise: Race, Class, and Change in an Urban Community* (Chicago: University of Chicago Press, 1990). If the information white employers have about black applicants is seen as less reliable (simply as a result of less familiarity), risk-averse employers will be less inclined to consider these workers. See Dennis J. Aigner and G. Glen G. Cain, "Statistical Theories of Discrimination in Labor Markets," *Industrial and Labor Relations Review* 30, no. 2 (1977): 175–87. Pervasive occupational and residential segregation by race may contribute to the preservation of inaccurate assumptions and/or the simple enhancement of uncertainty. See Kenneth J. Arrow, "What Has Economics to Say About Racial Discrimination?" *Journal of Economic Perspectives* 12, no. 2 (1998): 91–100; Donald Tomaskovic-Devey and Sheryl Skaggs, "An Establishment-Level Test of the Statistical Discrimination Hypothesis," *Work and Occupations* 26, no. 4 (1999): 420–43. Gerald S. Oettinger has developed an empirical model of how information uncertainty can lead to growing racial disparities over time. See Gerald S. Oettinger, "Statistical Discrimination and the Early Career Evolution of the Black-White Wage Gap," *Journal of Labor Economics* 14 (1996): 52–78.

40. See Joseph G. Altonji and Charles R. Pierret, "Employer Learning and Statistical Discrimination," *Quarterly Journal of Economics* 116, no. 1 (2001): 313–50. While there is evidence that on-the-job evaluations may continue to be affected by racially biased perceptions, these effects can be mediated to some degree by objective performance indicators. See Emilio Castilla, "Gender, Race, and Meritocracy in Organizational Careers," unpublished paper presented to the Culture and Inequality Workshop, Department of Sociology, Princeton University, 2005.

41. As part of his critique, Heckman warns us not to interpret the findings from audit studies as accurate measures of the prevalence of discrimination in everyday life. "The impact of market discrimination is not determined by the most discriminatory practices in the market, or even by the average level of discrimination among firms, but rather by the level of discrimination at the firms where ethnic minorities or women actually end up buying, working and borrowing. It is at the margin that economic values are set. . . . Purposive sorting within markets eliminates the worst forms of discrimination." James Heckman, "Detecting Discrimination," *Journal of Economic Perspectives* 12, no. 2 (1998): 101–16. Heckman's argument assumes that, in the presence of discrimination, blacks and whites can sort into different labor markets with little consequence. This assumption, however, is true only if those employers willing to hire blacks are no different (in compensation, security, number of vacancies, opportunities for promotion, etc.) from those employers who prefer to hire whites and if the additional search costs required to locate nondiscriminatory employers are trivial. By contrast, we know from previous research that occupational segregation (or crowding) within labor markets (whether due to discrimination or self-selection) is often associated with lower wages, less job security, longer search times, and/or reduced labor force participation. See, e.g., Toby L. Parcel and Charles W. Mueller, *Ascription and Labor Markets: Race and Sex Differences in Earnings* (New York: Academic Press, 1983). Assessing the possible indirect effects of discrimination, in addition to any direct effects on hiring decisions, would provide a more complete understanding of the role of discrimination in contemporary labor markets.

42. Current Population Survey data show that in 2000, joblessness among black men aged twenty to thirty-five with a high school diploma was around 22 percent while it was less than 10 percent for white men of the same age and education.

43. For example, Neal and Johnson, "The Role of Premarket Factors in Black-White Wage Differences," 881–85, includes a correction for labor force participation, using a median regression technique that assigns all nonparticipants a wage of zero. This cor-

rection produces a race coefficient nearly double the size of the original (.134 vs. 072) and reduces the amount of the race gap explained by cognitive ability from roughly 70 to 60 percent. When predicting annual earnings instead of hourly wages (thus incorporating "hours worked"), the racial gap not explained by cognitive skills is three times as large. William Johnson and Derek Neal, "Basic Skills and the Black-White Earnings Gap," in *The Black-White Test Score Gap*, ed. Christopher Jencks and Meredith Phillips (Washington, DC: Brookings Institution Press), 494; see also Richard Butler and James Heckman, "The Government's Impact on the Labor Market Status of Black Americans: A Critical Review," in *Equal Rights and Industrial Relations*, ed. Farrell Bloch and Leonard J. Hausman (Madison, WI: Industrial Relations Research Association, 1977), 235–81; Robert D. Mare and Christopher Winship, "The Paradox of Lessening Racial Inequality and Joblessness among Black Youth: Enrollment, Enlistment, and Employment, 1964–1981," *American Sociological Review* 49 (1984): 39–55; Bruce Western and Becky Pettit, "Black-White Wage Inequality, Employment Rates, and Incarceration," *American Journal of Sociology* 111 (2005): 553–78.

44. Western and Pettit, "Black-White Wage Inequality, Employment Rates, and Incarceration"; see also Amitabh Chandra, "Labor-Market Dropouts and the Racial Wage Gap: 1940–1990," *American Economic Review* 90, no. 2 (2000): 333–38; Robert W. Fairlie and William A. Sundstrom, "The Racial Unemployment Gap in Long-Run Perspective," *American Economic Review* 87, no. 2 (1997): 306–10. Note that Western and Pettit are concerned specifically with the effects of incarceration on estimates of black-white wage inequality. High rates of incarceration among young black men remove large segments of the low-wage population, thereby skewing labor market comparisons. Discrimination may produce similar effects, pushing those at the bottom of the distribution out of the labor market altogether.

45. This discussion focuses on discrimination against African Americans without a college education, as the majority of audit studies focus on the experiences of job candidates for low-skilled jobs. Patterns of discrimination would likely differ at higher levels of the occupational hierarchy, with college-educated blacks less likely to experience barriers to access and more likely to experience channeling or barriers to mobility within the organizational setting. See Joe R. Feagin and Melvin P. Sikes, *Living with Racism: The Black Middle-Class Experience* (Boston: Beacon Press, 1994); Sharon Collins, "The Marginalization of Black Executives," *Social Problems* 36 (1989): 317–31; Eric Grodsky and Devah Pager, "The Structure of Disadvantage: Individual and Occupational Determinants of the Black-White Wage Gap," *American Sociological Review* 66 (2001): 542–67.

Chapter 6

1. J. M. Darley and P. H. Gross, "A Hypothesis-Confirming Bias in Labeling Effects," *Journal of Personality and Social Psychology* 44 (1983): 20–33; Susan Fiske and S. L. Neuberg, "A Continuum Model of Impression Formation: From Category-Based to Individuating Processes: Influence of Information and Motivation on Attention and Interpretation," in *Advances in Experimental Psychology*, ed. M. P. Zanna (New York: Academic Press, 1990), 1–74. Note that this discussion does not address the question of stereotype accuracy, which will likewise vary across individuals and contexts.

2. Stereotypes work to facilitate the processing of consistent information, while evidence not confirming to stereotypes is more easily overlooked or discounted. See M. Rothbart, M. Evans, and S. Fulero, "Recall for Confirming Events: Memory Processes and the Maintenance of Social Stereotyping," *Journal of Experimental Social Psychology* 15

(1979): 343–55. James D. Johnson, Mike S. Adams, William Hall, and Leslie Ashburn, "Race, Media, and Violence: Differential Racial Effects of Exposure to Violent News Stories," *Basic and Applied Social Psychology* 19 (1997): 81–90, find that subjects interpret information about a black defendant as more dispositional (i.e., more indicative of internal attributes) than for equivalent white defendants; dispositional attributions are further activated for black defendants following exposure to media coverage of violent crime.

3. Fiske and Neuberg develop a model of impression formation in which stereotypes provide a resilient starting point for interpersonal assessments. See Fiske and Neuberg, "A Continuum Model of Impression Formation," 3–4.

4. Gordon Allport, *The Nature of Prejudice* (New York: Doubleday Anchor Books, 1954); Fiske and Neuberg, "A Continuum Model of Impression Formation."

5. Testers often had lengthy conversations with other employees while filling out their applications. In this analysis, only conversations with the person in charge of hiring were counted as personal contact. The initial tester response form did not include an explicit item regarding contact with the employer; rather, testers were asked to write about such interactions in the narrative section. As it became clear that this variable was salient for the audit outcomes, the response form was modified to include an explicit item measuring the extent of interaction with the person in charge of hiring: 1 (no contact); 2 (minimal); 3 (conversational); to 4 (formal interview). The changes in coding, affecting roughly 10 percent of the sample, could imply higher levels of measurement error in tests using the first version of the form.

6. This finding is consistent with social psychological research on stereotypes, which predicts that the presentation of individuating information will reduce the impact of categorical judgments. Of course, personal contact will not always serve in an individual's favor. For ex-offenders with poor interpersonal skills, employers' negative stereotypes will instead be reinforced. This comparison presents a best case scenario, demonstrating that appealing interpersonal characteristics can in part offset the stigma of a conviction, at least among whites.

7. Note that the rate of callbacks among black nonoffenders who had personal contact with the employer (36 percent) is higher than that among white nonoffenders who had had no personal contact (28 percent). It may be the case that the appealing interpersonal abilities of these testers weighed more favorably than the mean value of interpersonal ability assigned to white testers when no direct evidence was available. It is also possible, however, as mentioned above, that the employers available to conduct on-the-spot interviews may be different in some way (e.g., those most in need of new staff), in which case the higher rate of callbacks would imply differences in demand in addition to or in place of the effect of any supply-side characteristics.

8. In a logistic regression predicting callbacks, the interaction between personal contact and criminal status is statistically significant. Likewise, the interaction between race and criminal record among audits involving personal contact is statistically significant, $p < .05$.

9. Richard B. Freeman and Harry J. Holzer, eds., *The Black Youth Employment Crisis* (Chicago: University of Chicago Press, 1986); William Julius Wilson, *The Truly Disadvantaged: The Inner City, the Underclass, and Public Policy* (Chicago: University of Chicago Press, 1987), 100–101.

10. John Pawasarat and Lois M. Quinn, *Survey of Job Openings in the Milwaukee Metropolitan Area: Week of May 15, 2000* (Employment and Training Institute, University Outreach, University of Wisconsin-Milwaukee, 2000).

11. Employment and Training Institute, "Survey of Job Openings in the Milwaukee Metropolitan Area: Week of October 15, 2001," University of Wisconsin-Milwaukee, http://www.uwm.edu/Dept/ETI/openings/jobs2001.htm. The ratio of job seekers to full-time employment opportunities in the city of Milwaukee was 7.8 to 1, as opposed to a ratio of 3.4 to 1 for the county as a whole.

12. Harry J. Holzer, "The Spatial Mismatch Hypothesis: What Has the Evidence Shown?" *Urban Studies* 28, no. 1 (1991): 105–22; Christopher Jencks and Susan E. Mayer, "Residential Segregation, Job Proximity, and Black Job Opportunities," in *Inner-City Poverty in the United States*, ed. Laurence Jr. Lynn and Michael G. H. McGeary (Washington, DC: National Academy Press, 1990), 187–222; John F. Kain, "The Spatial Mismatch Hypothesis: Three Decades Later," *Housing Policy Debate* 2 (1992): 371–460; Keith R. Ihlanfeldt and David L. Sjoquist, "The Spatial Mismatch Hypothesis: A Review of Recent Studies and Their Implications for Welfare Reform," *Housing Policy Debate* 9, no. 4 (1998): 849–92; Roberto Fernandez and Celina Su, "Space and the Study of Labor Markets," *Annual Review of Sociology* 30 (2004): 545–69.

13. David Ellwood, "The Spatial Mismatch Hypothesis: Are There Teenage Jobs Missing in the Ghetto?" in *The Black Youth Employment Crisis*, ed. Richard B. Freeman and Harry J. Holzer (Chicago: University of Chicago Press, 1986), 147–85; Fernandez and Su, "Space and the Study of Labor Markets." For a test of the purely spatial consequences of employer relocation for minority employment, see Roberto Fernandez, "Race, Spatial Mismatch, and Job Accessibility: Evidence from a Plant Relocation," MIT Sloan School of Management, working paper, 2006.

14. Kain, "The Spatial Mismatch Hypothesis."

15. William Julius Wilson, *When Work Disappears: The World of the New Urban Poor* (New York: Vintage Books, 1996), 112, 118. Note, however, that interview studies often find greater expression of negative attitudes among inner city employers than suburban employers, despite the fact that inner-city employers are more likely to hire blacks. See Wilson, *When Work Disappears*, 119; see also Philip Moss and Chris Tilly, *Stories Employers Tell: Race, Skill, and Hiring in America* (New York: Russell Sage Foundation, 2001), 149–52.

16. Studies of this kind do not permit controls for the quality of applicants, leaving open the possibility that racial differences in hiring practices reflect differences in the relative human capital characteristics of black and white applicant pools. Given that labor supply is substantially lower in suburban areas than in the city (as a ratio of job openings to job seekers), however, it is not clear why suburban employers would be more selective than those in the city.

17. Ellwood, "The Spatial Mismatch Hypothesis," 149.

18. Harry J. Holzer, *What Employers Want: Job Prospects for Less-Educated Workers* (New York: Russell Sage Foundation, 1996), 55, 59.

19. Christopher Jencks and Susan E. Mayer, "Residential Segregation, Job Proximity, and Black Job Opportunities," in *Inner-City Poverty in the United States*, ed. Laurence Lynn Jr. and Michael G. H. McGeary (Washington, DC: National Academy Press, 1990), 187–222.

20. See Fernandez and Su, "Space and the Study of Labor Markets," for a review.

21. In a sample restricted to suburban employers, the coefficient for the interaction term between race and criminal background in a logistic regression predicting callbacks is—1.14 with a standard error of 0.59, $p = .055$.

22. Once again, however, it is important to acknowledge that the sample sizes are quite small in these comparisons, and therefore the stability of these estimates is

difficult to confirm. The sample sizes in figure 6.3 are 4, 13, 21, and 38; those in figure 6.4 are 5, 9, 4, and 19.

23. Note there is some slippage here between industry and occupation. The current coding scheme takes into account the fact that, within industries, some employers use different screening procedures for different job types. In the present sample, roughly 75 percent of restaurant jobs were waitstaff positions (with the remainder being positions for busboys, dishwashers, or cooks). The general results reported here hold true for this more specific job category, though the statistical power declines.

24. In a logistic regression predicting callbacks, the coefficient for the main effect of race is $-.87$ ($p < .01$), with the coefficient of the interaction between race and restaurant occupation reaching -1.34 ($p < .05$). These coefficients are from a model including main effects for race, criminal record, and restaurant occupation, with interactions between race and restaurant and race and criminal record (the latter interaction is not significant). Note once again that the sample sizes used for these comparisons are small: In figure 6.6, the sample sizes are 16, 35, 9, and 16; those for figure 6.7 are 9, 25, 1, and 3, respectively.

25. Gary S. Becker, *The Economics of Discrimination* (Chicago: University of Chicago Press, 1957). David Neumark," Sex Discrimination in Restaurant Hiring: An Audit Study," *Quarterly Journal of Economics* 111, no. 3 (1996): 915–41, conducted an audit study of restaurant employers in Philadelphia that found strong evidence of gender discrimination in hiring outcomes (race was not included as a variable in this study). Women were preferred to similarly qualified men in inexpensive restaurants, but in high-priced restaurants, male applicants were strongly favored. Neumark discusses the role of customer preferences in shaping the variable hiring practices across restaurant classes. See also Harry J. Holzer and Keith Ihlanfeldt, "Customer Discrimination and Employment Outcomes for Minority Workers," *Quarterly Journal of Economics* 113, no. 3 (1998): 835–67.

26. Roger Waldinger and Michael Lichter, *How the Other Half Works: Immigration and the Social Organization of Labor* (California: University of California Press, 2003), table 17.

Chapter 7

1. I am grateful to Harry Holzer, Michael Stoll, and Steven Raphael for allowing me to replicate many of the items from their survey in this study. See appendices 7A-C for additional details on the survey and sample.

2. This chapter focuses specifically on variation in the criminal record effect. The problems of capturing racial bias on a telephone survey prevent us from drawing much from these interviews on questions about race.

3. Devah Pager and Lincoln Quillian, "Walking the Talk: What Employers Say versus What They Do," *American Sociological Review* 70, no. 3 (2005): 355–80.

4. Jenni Gainsborough and Marc Mauer, "Diminishing Returns: Crime and Incarceration in the 1990s," policy report from the Sentencing Project, 2000; Bureau of Justice Statistics, 2002, "State Prison Admissions, 1999: Offense, by Admission Type."

5. Comparisons of the race effects with those from studies in other cities were presented in chapter 5 (see note 18).

6. A similar pattern can be found in a comparison of the responses to an identical question included in the employer survey of the Multi-City Study of Urban Inequality, administered between June 1992 and May 1994 in Atlanta, Boston, Detroit, and Los Angeles. Harry J. Holzer, *What Employers Want: Job Prospects for Less-Educated Workers* (New York: Russell Sage Foundation, 1996).

7. Bureau of Labor Statistics, 2002, *Local Area Unemployment Statistics*, Online Public Data Query (available from http://www.bls.gov/data).

8. Harry J. Holzer and Michael Stoll, *Employers and Welfare Recipients: The Effects of Welfare Reform in the Workplace* (San Francisco: Public Policy Institute of California, 2001).

9. By 2002 the Equal Employment Opportunity Commission of Wisconsin had record of fifty-one separate cases that had been brought up under charges of discrimination against individuals with criminal records; the earliest recorded case was in 1981.

10. It is also possible that the legal climate in Wisconsin places greater pressure on survey respondents to provide socially desirable responses. Employers in Milwaukee may hold similar opinions about ex-offenders to employers in other cities but be less likely to express their aversion to these applicants in survey questionnaires. Yet there is additional evidence to suggest that the greater openness expressed by Milwaukee employers to applicants with criminal records goes beyond mere rhetoric. Nearly half of the Milwaukee employers surveyed (48 percent) had hired one or more applicants with criminal records in the past year. By sharp contrast, only 23 percent of a recent sample of Los Angeles employers reported having hired one or more applicants with criminal records over the past year. Michael Stoll, Harry Holzer, and Raphael Steven, unpublished codebook for the Los Angeles worker study, 2002. Presumably, the reporting of actual hiring experiences is less subject to the pressures of social desirability than are attitude questions. If these self-reports are accurate, Milwaukee employers are indeed more open to and experienced with hiring applicants with criminal records.

11. These items were phrased in wording identical to the criminal record question above.

12. Surprisingly, there was virtually no difference in employer responses based on whether Chad was presented as black or white. The striking discrepancy between these findings and the results of the audit study cast doubt on the ability of surveys—even those using experimental designs to avoid direct racial comparisons—to generate accurate measures of racial bias. See Pager and Quillian, "Walking the Talk."

13. At the same time, it is important to note that changes in question wording can themselves produce significant variation in response patterns, without any corresponding change in underlying beliefs. In this case, the increasing receptivity to Chad could be more a function of the additional words associated with his description than the specific content of that description.

14. In observing the testers' experiences, employers' reactions appeared to follow a two-stage process. Upon initial review, the simple fact of the conviction drew significant attention, and for some this information was sufficient to rule out the applicant. For those willing to consider an applicant with a criminal record, the details of the conviction then became more relevant.

15. Bureau of Justice Statistics, 2002, "Recidivism of Prisoners Released in 1994."

16. Among state and federal prisoners who had used drugs in the month before the offense, roughly 1 in 7 had been treated for drug abuse since admission; just over one-quarter had enrolled in other drug abuse programs. See Bureau of Justice Statistics, 1999, "Substance Abuse and Treatment, State and Federal Prisoners, 1997."

17. Joan Petersilia, "Parole and Prisoner Reentry in the United States," in *Prisons: Crime and Justice: A Review of Research*, ed. Michael Tonry and Joan Petersilia (Chicago: University of Chicago, 1999), 497–529; Christopher Uggen, "Work as a Turning Point in

the Life Course of Criminals: A Duration Model of Age, Employment, and Recidivism," *American Sociological Review* 65, no. 4 (2000): 529–46. Note, however, that several studies using administrative data to examine the employment trajectories of ex-offenders find increases in rates of employment immediately following release from prison but steady declines thereafter. Becky Pettit and Christopher Lyons, "The Consequences of Incarceration on Employment and Earnings: Evidence from Washington State," working paper, University of Washington, 2002; Rosa Cho and Robert LaLonde, "The Impact of Incarceration in State Prison on the Employment Prospects of Women," working paper, University of Chicago, Harris School of Public Policy, 2005. These results have been interpreted as the short-term effect of parole surveillance (or a reflection of conditions of release), suggesting that attention to continuing employment postrelease may also be an important priority.

18. William Julius Wilson, *When Work Disappears: The World of the New Urban Poor* (New York: Vintage Books, 1996), 130–32.

19. Tian Zheng, Matthew J. Salganik, and Andrew Gelman, "How Many People Do You Know in Prison?: Using Overdispersion in Court Data to Estimate Social Structure in Networks," *Journal of the American Statistical Association* 101, no. 474 (2006): 409–23. Other demographic predictors include gender, age, education, employment status, income, and marital status.

20. This estimate is based on the exponentiated coefficient from a logistic regression ($\exp(1.41)$). Results are reported in Table 7B.1. Unfortunately, no comparable question was asked concerning attitudes about black applicants, as it is extremely difficult to obtain reliable direct information about race from survey questions.

21. Michael Stoll, Steven Raphael, and Harry J. Holzer, "Why Are Black Employers More Likely to Hire African Americans Than White Employers?" JCPR working paper #228, 2001.

22. Likewise, Jensen and Giegold report findings from employer interviews suggesting that the motivation level of ex-offenders "tends to be somewhat higher than the average found in the non-offender work force." W. Jensen and W. C. Giegold, "Finding Jobs for Ex-Offenders: A Study of Employers' Attitudes," *American Business Law Journal* 14 (1976): 195–225, at 198. Jolson reports even more favorable findings from a study of employers' ratings of employees according to ten criteria. Ex-offender employees were rated as superior to nonoffender employees on seven of the ten dimensions (ability to learn, quantity of work, quality of work, industry, cooperativeness, acceptability, and integrity). They were rated as marginally superior on availability and initiative, and inferior on longevity. Marvin A. Jolson, "Are Ex-Offenders Successful Employees?" *California Management Review* 17 (1975):67. For a review of related studies, see also Neal Miller, "Employer-Barriers to the Employment of Persons with Records of Arrest or Conviction: A Review and Analysis" (Washington, DC: U.S. Department of Labor, AS-PER, 1979, report no. PUR-79-3204-A), 16–17.

23. In fact, despite sensationalized coverage, claims based on an employee's criminal background remain a small minority of all negligent hiring cases. An analysis of negligent hiring claims filed in New York State finds that only 6 percent of cases (10 of 169) involved offenders with criminal backgrounds. Of these, plaintiffs prevailed only half the time. See Debbie Mukamal, "Negligent Hiring Case Law in New York," research memo prepared for the Legal Action Center, 2003.

24. Monica Scales, "Employer Catch-22: The Paradox between Employer Liability for Employee Criminal Acts and the Prohibition against Ex-Convict Discrimination," *George Mason Law Review* 11, no. 2 (2002): 419–40, at 424.

25. Court rulings in negligent hiring lawsuits have been highly inconsistent, varying widely over time and across jurisdiction. In some cases employers have been held
liable for failing to conduct a background check on a violent employee with a criminal
history. In others, the courts demonstrate a reluctance to deter employers from hiring
ex-offenders. For example, in 1983 the Minnesota Supreme Court asserted, "Were we
to hold that an employer can never hire a person with a criminal record at the risk of
later being held liable for the employee's assault, it would offend our civilized concept
that society must make a reasonable effort to rehabilitate those who have erred so they
can be assimilated into the community." See Jennifer Leavitt, "Walking a Tightrope:
Balancing Competing Public Interests in the Employment of Criminal Offenders," *Connecticut Law Review* 34 (2001):1301–2, esp. nn. 151–52, 162; see also David L. Gregory,
"Reducing the Risk of Negligence in Hiring," *Employee Relations Law Journal* 14, no. 1
(1988): 31–40.

26. David Wessell, "Racial Discrimination Is Still at Work," *Wall Street Journal*,
September 4, 2003; and David Wessell, "Fear of Bias Suits May Be Affecting Hiring
Decisions," *Wall Street Journal*, September 11, 2003. The text of readers' comments was
supplied in personal communication with David Wessell.

27. See also William Julius Wilson, *When Work Disappears: The World of the New Urban
Poor* (New York: Vintage Books, 1996), 127–28.

28. John Donahue III, "Advocacy versus Analysis in Assessing Employment Discrimination Law," *Stanford Law Review* 44 (1992):1583–1615.

29. Laura Beth Nielsen and Robert L. Nelson, "Scaling the Pyramid: A Sociolegal
Model of Employment Discrimination Litigation," in *Handbook of Employment Discrimination Research*, ed. Laura Beth Nielsen and Robert L. Nelson (Dordrecht, Netherlands:
Springer), 3–34. See also Barbara A. Curran, *The Legal Needs of the Public: The Final Report
of a National Survey* (Chicago: American Bar Association, 1977), 108, who finds that respondents are least likely to take *any* action in response to experiences of job discrimination compared to twenty-eight other legal problems. Richard E. Miller and Austin
Sarat, "Grievances, Claims, and Disputes: Assessing the Adversary Culture," *Law and
Society Review* 15, no. 3/4 (1980–81): 525–66. John J. Donahue III and Peter Siegelman,
"The Changing Nature of Employment Discrimination Litigation," *Stanford Law Review*
43, no. 5 (1991): 983–1033, n. 78, find that the probability of filing a lawsuit for claims
of employment discrimination was far lower than for any other type of perceived injury, with fewer than 4 percent of those involved in a dispute over discrimination in
housing, employment, or education actually making formal claims.

30. Richard E. Miller and Austin Sarat, "Grievances, Claims, and Disputes: Assessing
the Adversary Culture," *Law and Society Review* 15, no. 3/4 (1980–81): 525–66; Donahue
and Siegelman, "The Changing Nature of Employment Discrimination Litigation"; see
also Carroll Seron and Frank Munger, "Law and Inequality: Race, Gender . . . and, of
Course, Class," *Annual Review of Sociology* 22 (1996):187–212, for a review.

31. Laura Beth Nielsen and Aaron Beim, "Media Misrepresentation: Title VII, Print
Media, and Public Perceptions of Discrimination Litigation," *Stanford Law and Policy
Review* 15 (2004): 101–30.

32. John J. Donahue III and James Heckman, "Continuous versus Episodic Change:
The Effect of Federal Civil Rights Policy on the Economic Status of Blacks," *Journal of
Economic Literature* 29 (1991): 1603–43.

33. According to Donahue and Siegelman, "The Changing Nature of Employment
Discrimination Litigation," 1024, "Antidiscrimination laws may actually provide
employers a (small) net disincentive to hire . . . minorities." See also Richard Posner,

"The Efficiency and Efficacy of Title VII," *University of Pennsylvania Law Review* 136 (1987): 513–21.

34. See Donahue and Heckman, "Continuous versus Episodic Change."

35. RAND, *Controlling Cocaine: Supply versus Demand Programs*, ed. C. Peter Rydell and Susan S. Everingham RAND publications MR-331-ONDCP/A/DPRC, 1994; Jeremy Travis, Amy Solomon, and Michelle Waul, *From Prison to Home: The Dimensions and Consequences of Prisoner Reentry* (Washington, DC: Urban Institute Press, 2001).

36. Joan Petersilia, "Parole and Prisoner Reentry in the United States," in *Prisons: Crime and Justice: A Review of Research*, ed. Michael Tonry and Joan Petersilia (Chicago: University of Chicago, 1999), 497–529.

37. In cases where more than one person was responsible for hiring decisions, interviewers attempted to identify the individual most directly involved in the screening of entry-level workers. Once this person was identified, s/he served as the target respondent until a completion or refusal was secured. If the initial target was unavailable or unwilling to participate, attempts were made to contact alternative personnel (involved in hiring decisions) within the company.

38. The first version of this survey was developed for the Multi-City Study of Urban Inequality Employer Survey. See Harry J. Holzer, *What Employers Want: Job Prospects for Less-Educated Workers* (New York: Russell Sage Foundation, 1996). Holzer and his colleagues later modified the initial instrument to focus more closely on applicants with criminal records. The instrument used for the present study was further modified to reflect the priorities of this research project (see below).

39. Robert M. Groves and Lars E. Lyberg, "An overview of nonresponse issues in telephone surveys," in *Telephone Survey Methodology*, ed. Robert M. Groves (New York: Wiley, 1998), 191–212.

40. Response rates for surveys of top management and organizational representatives typically lag behind those of employees or of the general population. Yehuda Baruch, "Response Rate in Academic Studies: A Comparative Analysis," *Human Relations* 52 (1999): 421–38. Likewise, businesses have increasingly resisted participating in surveys, given the proliferation of market research firms as well as academics seeking employer participation for the growing number of studies involving businesses. Todd D. Remington, "Telemarketing and Declining Survey Response Rates," *Journal of Advertising Research* 32 (1992): 6–7.

41. There is also quite a bit of research investigating the effects of low response rates on survey outcomes. Keeter et al., for example, administered two identical questionnaires to national household samples using different levels of effort, the first resulting in a response rate of 36 percent, the second, 60.6 percent. Comparisons across 91 demographic, behavioral, attitudinal, and knowledge items found an average difference of 2 percent in the distribution of responses. Scott Keeter, Carolyn Miller, Andrew Kohut, Robert M. Groves, and Stanley Presser, "Consequences of Reducing Nonresponse in National Telephone Survey," *Public Opinion Quarterly* 64 (2000): 125–48. Likewise, Curtin et al. compared responses to the Survey of Consumer Attitudes using a full sample to responses when difficult-to-reach or difficult-to-convert respondents were excluded (thus simulating the sample population had less effort been used to reach these respondents). These authors report virtually no differences in cross-sectional estimates of "consumer sentiment," even when systematic differences in the demographics of each sample were observed. Richard Curtin, Stanley Presser, and Eleanor Singer, "The Effects of Response Rate Changes on the Index of Consumer Sentiment," *Public Opinion Quarterly* 64 (2000): 413–28. It seems, therefore, that fairly valid estimates can be

achieved even with suboptimal response rates. According to Curtin et al., there are diminishing returns to increasing response rates, with large gains in external validity achieved by increasing response rates from 20 to 40 percent while smaller gains are registered by moving from 40 to 60 percent. Curtin, Presser, and Singer, "The Effects of Response Rate Changes on the Index of Consumer Sentiment," 414.

Chapter 8

1. Ronald Mincy, *Nurturing Young Black Males* (Washington, DC: Urban Institute Press, 1994); Jeremy Travis, Amy Solomon, and Michelle Waul, *From Prison to Home: The Dimensions and Consequences of Prisoner Reentry* (Washington, DC: Urban Institute Press, 2001); Christian Parenti, *Lockdown America: Police and Prisons in the Age of Crisis* (New York: Verso, 1999); John Hagan, "The Social Embeddedness of Crime and Unemployment," *Criminology* 31, no. 4 (1993): 465–91; T. M. Hammett, *Health-Related Issues in Prisoner Reentry to the Community* (Washington, DC: Urban Institute, 2000).

2. Elijah Anderson, *Streetwise: Race, Class, and Change in an Urban Community* (Chicago: University of Chicago Press, 1990), chap. 7.

3. Robert Merton, "The Self-Fulfilling Prophecy," *Antioch Review* 8 (1948): 193–210.

4. From Bruce Link and Jo Phelan, "Conceptualizing Stigma," *Annual Review of Sociology* 27 (2001): 363–85, at 374. This quote was drawn from a study on the stigma of mental illness; the psychic reactions described, however, apply more broadly to other forms of stigma as well.

5. Jennifer Crocker, R. Luhtanen, B. Blaine, and S. Broadnax, "Collective Self-Esteem and Psychological Well-Being among White, Black, and Asian College Students," *Personality and Social Psychology Bulletin* 20 (1994): 502–13; Frantz Fanon, *Black Skins, White Masks* (New York: Grove, 1967); Glenn C. Loury, *The Anatomy of Racial Inequality* (Cambridge, MA: Harvard University Press, 2002). Whether or not the individuals themselves internalize negative attributions, a rational cost-benefit analysis of job search behavior indicates that the returns are lower for members of stigmatized groups. While some may become motivated to overcome these barriers through an effort of escalated intensity, many will likely to resign themselves to failure. See Jennifer Crocker and Brenda Major, "Social Stigma and Self-Esteem: The Self-Protective Properties of Stigma," *Psychological Review* 96 (1989): 608–30.

6. Elijah Anderson, *Code of the Streets: Decency, Violence, and the Moral Life of the Inner City* (New York: W. W. Norton, 1999) 244; see also David Harding, "Jean Valjean's Dilemma: The Management of Ex-Convict Identity in the Search for Employment," *Deviant Behavior* 24 (2003): 571–95.

7. Over time blacks, and young black men in particular, have become increasingly likely to drop out of the labor market altogether when faced with the prospect of long-term unemployment or marginal employment opportunities. Between 1979 and 1999, for example, the proportion of young black men with no more than a high school education who were working or looking for work declined from 82 percent to 68 percent. Harry J. Holzer, Paul Offner, and Elaine Sorensen, "What Explains the Continuing Decline in Labor Force Activity among Young Black Men?" *Labor History* 46, no. 1 (2005): 37–55, n. 3. For a discussion of the "discouraged worker" in the contemporary labor market, see also Donald R. Williams, "Young Discouraged Workers: Racial Differences Explored," *Monthly Labor Review* 7 (1984): 36–39.

8. Harry J. Holzer, *What Employers Want: Job Prospects for Less-Educated Workers* (New York: Russell Sage Foundation, 1996), 58–60.

9. See Mitchell Duneier, *Sidewalk* (New York: Farrar, Straus and Giroux, 1999), 377 n8, for a discussion of how the timing of opportunity can, in itself, have serious consequences for the emergence of deviance.

10. Of course, at least in the case of ex-offenders, it is not difficult to imagine why an employer would be reluctant to consider such an applicant; in many cases s/he may be right. But for those ex-offenders who actually do want to come clean, or for the increasing numbers in prison who were nothing more than petty criminals to begin with, the strong stigma of their past can severely limit the opportunities for legitimate employment. As we see in the audit study, even the most articulate and well-qualified "ex-offenders" have tremendous difficulty finding work.

11. Glenn Loury provides an elegant discussion of "the logic of self-confirming stereotypes" in which he articulates a vicious cycle initiated by statistical discrimination, whereby prior negative expectations lead to the emergence of real differences in job-relevant attributes, with the perceived link between the stigma (race and/or criminal record) and productivity ultimately becoming realized. Loury, *The Anatomy of Racial Inequality*, 26–33. Cass Sunstein discusses similar themes in his article, "Why Markets Don't Stop Discrimination." He further argues that the psychological dissonance between norms of meritocracy and the reality of inequality operate not only upon the victims of discrimination, through internalization and reduced investments. According to Sunstein, "the beneficiaries of the status quo tend to do the same, concluding that the fate of victims is deserved, or is something for which victims are responsible, or is part of an intractable, given, or natural order. . . . The reduction of cognitive dissonance thus operates as a significant obstacle to the recognition that discrimination is a problem, or even that it exists." Cass R. Sunstein, "Why Markets Don't Stop Discrimination," *Social Philosophy and Policy* 8, no. 2 (1991): 22–37, at 32.

12. John Yinger, *Closed Doors, Opportunities Lost* (New York: Russell Sage Foundation, 1995); Ian Ayres and Peter Siegelman, "Race and Gender Discrimination in Bargaining for a New Car," *American Economic Review* 85, no. 3 (1995): 304–21; Stanley Ridley, James A. Bayton, and Janice Hamilton Outtz, "Taxi Service in the District of Columbia: Is It Influenced by Patrons' Race and Destination?" (Washington, DC: Washington Lawyers' Committee for Civil Rights under the Law, 1989; mimeograph); Douglas A. Wissoker, Wendy Zimmerman, and George C. Galster, *Testing for Discrimination in Home Insurance* (Washington, DC: Urban Institute Press, 1997); Margery Turner and Felicity Skidmore, eds., *Mortgage Lending Discrimination: A Review of Existing Evidence* (Washington, DC: Urban Institute Press, 1999); Harry Cross, Genevieve Kenney, Jane Mell, and Wendy Zimmerman, *Employer Hiring Practices: Differential Treatment of Hispanic and Anglo Job Seekers* (Washington, DC: Urban Institute Press, 1990); Margery Turner, Michael Fix, and Raymond Struyk, *Opportunities Denied, Opportunities Diminished: Racial Discrimination in Hiring* (Washington, DC: Urban Institute Press, 1991); Marc Bendick Jr., Charles Jackson, and Victor Reinoso, "Measuring Employment Discrimination through Controlled Experiments," *Review of Black Political Economy* 23 (1994): 25–48.

13. Likewise, Douglas Massey and Nancy Denton provide compelling illustration of the ways in which small and subtle acts of discrimination against individuals can have a broader cumulative impact associated with community-level segregation and the concentration of poverty. Douglas Massey and Nancy A. Denton, *American Apartheid: Segregation and the Making of the Underclass* (Cambridge, MA: Harvard University Press, 1993), 182–83.

14. Jeff Manza and Christopher Uggen, *Locked Out: Felon Disenfranchisement and American Democracy* (New York: Oxford University Press, 2006); Bruce Western and Sara

McLanahan, "Fathers behind Bars: The Impact of Incarceration on Family Forma-
tion," *Contemporary Perspectives in Family Research* 2 (2001): 309–24; John Hagan and
Ronit Dinovitzer, "Collateral Consequences of Imprisonment for Children, Commu-
nities, and Prisoners," in *Prisons*, ed. M. Tonry and J. Petersilia (Chicago: University of
Chicago Press, 1999), 121–62; Jeremy Travis, Amy Solomon, and Michelle Waul, *From
Prison to Home: The Dimensions and Consequences of Prisoner Reentry* (Washington, DC: Urban
Institute Press, 2001); Dina Rose and Todd Clear, "Incarceration, Social Capital, and
Crime: Implications for Social Disorganization Theory," *Criminology* 36, no. 3 (1998):
441–79.

15. This shift in public opinion has been partly offset by the increased concerns
over security prompted by the attacks on the World Trade Center on September 11,
2001. Despite this powerful incident—which has, at the very least, increased the uses
of criminal background checks by employers—the American public appears open to a
more progressive approach to dealing with the problems of common street crime.

16. Hart Associates, "Changing Public Attitudes toward the Criminal Justice
System," poll conducted for the Open Society Institute, 2002.

17. Of those polled, 35 percent believed drug use should be treated as a
crime, and 10 percent indicated that it should be treated as both. Gallup Poll,
cited in Bureau of Justice Statistics, 2001, *Sourcebook of Criminal Justice Statistics*;
http://www.albany.edu/sourcebook/pdf/sb2001/sb2001-section2.pdf.

18. Hart Associates, "Changing Public Attitudes toward the Criminal Justice System."

19. Jon Wool and Don Stemen, "Changing Fortunes or Changing Attitudes? Sentencing and Corrections Reforms in 2003" (New York: Vera Institute of Justice, 2004).

20. Alfred Blumstein and Allen J. Beck, "Population Growth in U.S. Prisons, 1980-
1996," in *Prisons*, ed. Michael Tonry and Joan Petersilia (Chicago: University of Chicago
Press, 1999), 17–61.

21. Michael L. Prendergast, M. Douglas Anglin, and Jean Wellisch, "Treatment
for Drug-Abusing Offenders under Community Supervision," *Federal Probation* 59
(1995): 66–75; Joan Petersilia, "Parole and Prisoner Reentry in the United States,"
in *Prisons: Crime and Justice: A Review of Research*, ed. Michael Tonry and Joan Petersilia
(Chicago: University of Chicago, 1999), 497–529; Gerald Gaes, Timothy J. Flanagan,
Laurence L. Motiuk, and Lynn Stewart, "Adult Correctional Treatment," in *Prisons*, ed.
Michael Tonry and Joan Petersilia (Chicago: University of Chicago Press, 1999), 361–
426.

22. In 2003 there were a total of 1,183 drug courts operating in more than half
the states in the United States. C. W. Huddleston, K. Freeman-Wilson, and D. L. Boone,
*Painting the Picture: A National Report Card on Drug Courts and Other Problem-Solving Court
Programs in the United States* (Alexandria, VA: National Drug Court Institute, and Bureau
of Justice Assistance, 2004).

23. The Government Accountability Office conducted a systematic review of twenty-
seven evaluations of thirty-nine adult drug courts. Evaluations were selected on the
basis of methodological soundness, each including a control group generated through
random assignment or carefully matched to participants (using propensity scores,
risk assessments, or demographic characteristics) to strengthen causal inference. Ten
of the thirteen drug courts reporting rearrest data found significant reductions in
recidivism, ranging from 10 to 30 percentage points below nonparticipant controls.
Estimates of cost savings range from $1,000 to $15,000 per participant. Government
Accountability Office, "Adult Drug Courts: Evidence Indicates Recidivism Reductions

and Mixed Results for Other Outcomes," Report to Congressional Committees, GAO-05-219, 2005; see also S. Belenko, *Research on Drug Courts: A Critical Review: 2001 Update* (New York: National Center on Addiction and Substance Abuse at Columbia University, 2001).

24. According to economist Richard Freeman, "Given annual direct expenditures of [several tens of thousands of dollars] per prisoner, the costs of the criminal justice system, the loss of potentially productive citizens, as well as costs of crime to victims, my reading of the evidence is that virtually any program—be it schooling, crime prevention, or rehabilitation—that has even marginal success in making crime less attractive and legitimate work more rewarding for disadvantaged youths is likely to have a sizeable social payoff." Richard B. Freeman, "Crime and the Employment of Disadvantaged Youths" (National Bureau of Economic Research, 1991), 220.

25. See Jeremy Travis, Amy Solomon, and Michelle Waul, *From Prison to Home: The Dimensions and Consequences of Prisoner Reentry* (Washington, DC: Urban Institute Press, 2001) 172–76; Joan Petersilia, "Parole and Prisoner Reentry in the United States," in *Prisons: Crime and Justice: A Review of Research*, ed. Michael Tonry and Joan Petersilia (Chicago: University of Chicago, 1999), 497–529.

26. One year after release, 48 percent of RIO's high-risk clients had been rearrested compared with 57 percent of otherwise similar nonparticipants; 23 percent had returned to prison compared to 38 percent of the control group. Peter Fin, "Program Focus: Texas' Project Rio (Re-Integration of Offenders)," report prepared for the National Institute of Justice, the National Institute of Corrections, and the Office of Correctional Education, 1998.

27. For a review of existing studies using experimental designs, see Shawn D. Bushway and Peter Reuter, "Labor Markets and Crime Risk Factors," in *Preventing Crime: What Works, What Doesn't, What's Promising—A report to the United States Congress* (Washington: National Institute of Justice, 1997), chap. 6, which finds only mixed evidence for the effects of employment interventions on the outcomes of ex-offenders, while more recent reviews find larger and more consistent program effects. For example, David Wilson and colleagues present a meta-analysis of studies examining the impact of programs designed to promote employment among ex-offenders. This analysis concludes that, across the range of studies, program participation was associated with a roughly twofold increase in employment. David B. Wilson, Catherine Gallagher, and Doris L. MacKenzie, "A Meta-Analysis of Corrections-Based Education, Vocation, and Work Programs for Adult Offenders," *Journal of Research in Crime and Delinquency* 37 (2000): 360. An evaluation of the Center for Employment Opportunities, the largest employment intermediary serving ex-offenders in New York, is currently underway (by MDRC); this evaluation uses random assignment into program participation to control for selection effects (e.g., those who sign up for services may be more capable/motivated to begin with).

28. The Federal Bonding Program offers zero-deductible coverage. Employers are also eligible to receive a Work Opportunity Tax Credit for hiring ex-offenders, compensating up to 35 percent of the first $6,000 of an individual's wages for those who remain employed for at least 180 days. Wage subsidies are often underutilized by employers because of the burdens of paperwork required to take advantage of them. Here again, intermediaries could play a valuable role in facilitating the employment of ex-offenders by taking responsibility for the bureaucratic side of federal bonding or WOTC registration.

29. There is precedent for establishing caps on punitive damages, as in the cases of environmental pollution, aircraft disasters, medical malpractice, and others. See

Dermot Sullivan, "Employee Violence, Negligent Hiring, and Criminal Records Checks: New York's Need to Reevaluate Its Priorities to Promote Public Safety," *St. John's Law Review* 72 (1998): 581–605.

30. In fact, public opinion favors restricted access to criminal history information by employers. While most Americans believe that employers should have access to criminal records in some cases, the majority believe that rights of access should depend on whether the position involves sensitive work, such as handling money, dealing with children, or serving as security guards. Bureau of Justice Statistics, 2001, "Public Attitudes toward Uses of Criminal History Information," 32.

31. In fact, the laws that made court records public documents were framed well before anyone could have anticipated the widespread diffusion of this information made possible today through computerized database and Internet technology. Originally, court records were kept as paper files, with interested individuals requiring in-person requests at the local court house. This logistical inconvenience kept the use of the information to a minimum. Today, by contrast, the criminal records of individuals throughout the country can be readily accessed through automated systems and over the Internet, contributing to the use of criminal justice information in ways never intended by the original constitutional provision. By 2002, forty states reported that more than 75 percent of their criminal history records were automated, and twenty-five states allowed access to criminal records on the Internet. See Joan Petersilia, *When Prisoners Come Home: Parole and Prisoner Reentry* (New York: Oxford University Press, 2003), 107–12; Legal Action Center, "After Prison: Roadblocks to Reentry—A Report on State Legal Barriers Facing People with Criminal Records," ed. Paul Samuels and Debbie Mukamal (New York: Legal Action Center, 2004).

32. Even in the United States, the government imposes significant restrictions on access to patient information (Privacy Rule, HIPAA), as well as student records (Family Educational Rights and Privacy Act, or FERPA), with the rationale that such information could be used against individuals who have experienced health problems or irregular schooling experiences.

33. Again, one reason employers seek criminal history information on new employees is to protect themselves against potential negligent hiring lawsuits, in the event that the employee engages in harmful or destructive behavior. There is no indication that negligent hiring suits are more common in closed-record states than in states with no restrictions on access to criminal record information. In fact, one might expect that state regulations on access to criminal background information would free employers from the responsibility of deciding which prospective employees may or may not be at risk. See Sullivan, "Employee Violence, Negligent Hiring, and Criminal Records Checks."

34. In 2006, the city of San Francisco passed legislation that imposed substantial restrictions on the use of criminal background information in the screening of applicants for city jobs. Applicants will not be asked to submit criminal background information until the final stages of the hiring process, and employers will be held to fair hiring standards in evaluating whether a criminal conviction, once revealed, represents a reasonable basis for dismissal. Boston, Chicago, Minneapolis, and St. Paul have likewise taken steps to encourage the employment of ex-offenders within city employment. According to Mayor Richard M. Daley of Chicago, "Implementing this new policy won't be easy, but it's the right thing to do. . . . We cannot ask private employers to consider hiring former prisoners unless the City practices what it preaches." See Nicole Maharaj, "Task Force Calls Mayors to Action on Second Chance

Act" (2006), http://www.mayors.org/USCM/us_mayor_newspaper/documents/06_19_06/
secondchance.asp.

35. Larry Greenfeld, *Examining Recidivism* (Washington, DC: Bureau of Justice Statistics, NCJ 96501, 1985); Joan Petersilia, *When Prisoners Come Home: Parole and Prisoner Reentry* (New York: Oxford University Press, 2003), 215–20. Megan Kurlychek and colleagues
estimate that five years after arrest, ex-offenders in their midtwenties are just over 1
percent more likely to commit a crime than otherwise similar nonoffenders. Megan
C. Kurlychek, Robert Brame, and Shawn D. Bushway, "Scarlet Letters and Recidivism:
Does an Old Criminal Record Predict Future Offending?" *Crime and Public Policy* 5, no. 3
(2006): 483–504.

36. §605 15 U.S.C. §1681c.

37. Margaret Colgate Love, "Starting Over with a Clean Slate: In Praise of a Forgot-
ten Section of the Model Penal Code," *Fordham Urban Law Journal* 30 (2003): 1705–41;
Aidan R. Gough, "The Expungement of Adjudication Records of Juvenile and Adult
Offenders," *Washington University Law Quarterly* 147 (1966): 148.

38. Cited in Love, "Starting Over with a Clean Slate," 1714.

39. Legal Action Center, "After Prison: Roadblocks to Reentry—A Report on State
Legal Barriers Facing People with Criminal Records," ed. Paul Samuels and Debbie
Mukamal (New York: Legal Action Center, 2004)

40. Margaret Colgate Love, *Relief from the Collateral Consequences of a Criminal Conviction:
A State-by-State Resource Guide* (Washington, DC: Sentencing Project, 2005). A number
of states have also introduced "certificates of rehabilitation" or "certificates of relief
from disabilities" which indicate that an individual has remained crime free for a
specified amount of time. While these certificates have tangible benefits in terms of
renewed access to licensed occupations, it is unclear whether private employers will be
influenced by these certificates in considering an applicant's suitability.

41. Shawn D. Bushway, "Labor Market Effects of Permitting Employer Access to
Criminal History Records," *Journal of Contemporary Criminal Justice* 20 (2004): 276–91;
Harry J. Holzer, Steven Raphael, and Michael Stoll, "Perceived Criminality, Criminal
Background Checks, and the Racial Hiring Practices of Employers," *Journal of Law and
Economics* 49, no. 2 (2006): 451–80. The audit data provide only limited support for
this hypothesis: Employers who conduct official background checks (identified by
survey self-reports) were roughly 3 percent more likely to hire black nonoffenders than
were employers who do not do checks. Furthermore, only 15 percent of employers
reported conducting background checks at the initial stages of selection. A great deal
of informal screening thus takes place before more objective background checks are
administered.

42. Christopher Uggen, Jeff Manza, and Melissa Thompson, "Citizenship and Reintegration: The Socioeconomic, Familial, and Civic Lives of Criminal Offenders," *Annals of
the American Academy of Social and Political Science* 605 (2006): 281–310.

43. Conviction status underestimates the full impact of the criminal justice system on the rap sheets of young black men. An overwhelming number of arrests that
never lead to conviction are nevertheless reported by many criminal record databases,
often without information on the case's final disposition. Bureau of Justice Statistics,
"Survey of State Criminal History Information Systems, 2001" (Washington, DC: U.S.
Department of Justice, 2003).

44. See press release at http://www.eeoc.gov/press/12-5-97.html (last accessed
8/15/06).

45. Testimony of House Speaker Newt Gingrich before the House Sub-committee on Employer-Employee Relations on "The Future Direction of the Equal Employment Opportunity Commission," March 3, 1998, http://www.house.gov/ed_workforce/hearings/105th/eer/eeoc3398/gingrich.htm.

46. See Suzanne Ageton and Delbert S. Elliott, "The Effect of Legal Processing on Delinquent Orientation," *Social Problems* 22 (1974): 87–100; Anthony Harris, "Imprisonment and the Expected Value of Criminal Choice: A Specification and Test of Aspects of the Labeling Perspective," *American Sociological Review* 40 (1975): 71–87.

References

Ageton, Suzanne, and Delbert S. Elliott. 1974. "The effect of legal processing on delinquent orientation." *Social Problems* 22:87–100.

Aigner, Dennis J., and Glen G. Cain. 1977. "Statistical theories of discrimination in labor market." *Industrial and Labor Relations Review* 30:175–87.

Allen, Francis. 1981. *The decline of the rehabilitative ideal: Penal policy and social purpose.* New Haven: Yale University Press.

Allport, Gordon. 1954. *The nature of prejudice.* New York: Doubleday Anchor Books.

Altonji, Joseph G., and Charles R. Pierret. 2001. "Employer learning and statistical discrimination." *Quarterly Journal of Economics* 116:313–350.

American Friends Service Committee. 1971. *Struggle for justice.* New York: Hill and Wang.

Anderson, Elijah. 1990. *Streetwise: Race, class, and change in an urban community.* Chicago: University of Chicago Press.

———. 1999. *Code of the streets: Decency, violence, and the moral life of the inner city.* New York: W. W. Norton.

Arrow, Kenneth J. 1998. "What has economics to say about racial discrimination?" *Journal of Economic Perspectives* 12, no. 2: 91–100.

Austin, James. 1986. "Using Early Release to Relieve Prison Crowding: A Dilemma in Public Policy." *Crime and Delinquency* 32:404–502.

Austin, James, and Robert Lawson. 1998. "Assessment of California parole violations and recommended intermediate programs and policies." San Francisco: National Council on Crime and Delinquency.

Ayres, Ian, and Peter Siegelman. 1995. "Race and gender discrimination in bargaining for a new car." *American Economic Review* 85:304–321.

Banaji, M. R., C. Hardin, and A. J. Rothman. 1993. "Implicit stereotyping in person judgment." *Journal of Personality and Social Psychology* 65:272–281.

Barclay, Gordon, Cynthia Tavares, and Arsalaan Siddique. 2001. *International comparisons of criminal justice statistics, 1999*. London: Home Office of the United Kingdom.

Baruch, Yehuda. 1999. "Response rate in academic studies: A comparative analysis." *Human Relations* 52:421–438.

Becker, Gary S. 1957. *The economics of discrimination*. Chicago: University of Chicago Press.
———. 1975. *Human capital*. New York: Columbia University Press.

Becker, Howard. 1963. *Outsiders: Studies in the sociology of deviance*. New York: Free Press.

Beckett, Katherine. 1997. *Making crime pay: Law and order in contemporary American politics*. New York: Oxford University Press.

Beckett, Katherine, Kris Nyrop, Lori Pfingst, and Melissa Bowen. 2005. "Drug use, drug arrests, and the question of race: Lessons from Seattle." *Social Problems* 52:419–41.

Beckett, Katherine, and Theodore Sasson. 2000. *The politics of injustice: Crime and punishment in America*. Thousand Oaks, CA: Pine Forge Press.

Beckett, Katherine, and Bruce Western. 2001. "Governing social marginality: Welfare, incarceration, and the transformation of state policy." *Punishment and Society* 3:43–59.

Belenko, S. 2001. *Research on drug courts: A critical review: 2001 update*. New York: National Center on Addiction and Substance Abuse at Columbia University.

Bendick, Marc, Jr., Lauren Brown, and Kennington Wall. 1999. "No foot in the door: An experimental study of employment discrimination." *Journal of Aging and Social Policy* 10:5–23.

Bendick, Marc, Jr., Charles Jackson, and Victor Reinoso. 1994. "Measuring employment discrimination through controlled experiments." *Review of Black Political Economy* 23:25–48.

Bendick, Marc, Jr., Charles Jackson, Victor Reinoso, and Laura Hodges. 1991. "Discrimination against Latino job applicants: A controlled experiment." *Human Resource Management* 30:469–484.

Bennett, William J., John J. DiIulio Jr., and John P. Walters. 1996. *Body count: Moral poverty and how to win America's war against crime and drugs*. New York: Simon and Schuster.

Berman, Greg, and John Feinblatt. 2001. "Problem-solving courts: A brief primer." *Law and Policy* 23:125–140.

Bertrand, Marianne, and Sendhil Mullainathan. 2004. "Are Emily and Greg more employable than Lakisha and Jamal? A field experiment on labor market discrimination." *American Economic Review* 94:991–1013.

Blumstein, Alfred. 1982. "On the racial disproportionality of United States prison populations." *Journal of Criminal Law and Criminology* 73:1259–1281.
———. 1993. "Racial disproportionality revisited." *University of Colorado Law Review* 64:743–760.
———. 1995. "Youth violence, guns, and the illicit drug industry." *Journal of Criminal Law and Criminology* 86:10–86.

Blumstein, Alfred, and Allen J. Beck. 1999. "Population growth in U.S. prisons, 1980-1996." Pp. 17–61 in *Prisons*, edited by Michael Tonry and Joan Petersilia. Chicago: University of Chicago Press.

Blumstein, Alfred, and Richard Rosenfeld. 1998. "Explaining recent trends in U.S. homicide rates." *Journal of Criminal Law and Criminology* 88:1175–1217.

Blumstein, Alfred, and Joel Wallman (eds.). 2000. *The crime drop in America*. New York: Cambridge University Press.

Bobo, Lawrence. 2001. "Racial Attitudes and Relations at the Close of the Twentieth Century." Pp. 262–299 in *America Becoming: Racial Trends and Their Consequences*, edited by N. Smelser, W. J. Wilson, and F. Mitchell. Washington, DC: National Academy Press.

Bodenhausen, Galen. 1988. "Stereotypic biases in social decision making and memory: Testing process models of stereotype use." *Journal of Personality and Social Psychology* 55:726–737.

Bodenhausen, Galen, and M. Lichtenstein. 1987. "Social stereotypes and information processing strategies: The impact of task complexity." *Journal of Personality and Social Psychology* 52:871–880.

Boggs, Roderic, Joseph Sellers, and Marc Bendick, Jr., "Use of Testing in Civil Rights Enforcement." Pp. 345–376 in *Clear and convincing evidence: Measurement of discrimination in America*, edited by Michael Fix and Raymond J. Struyk (Washington, DC: Urban Institute Press, 1993).

Boshier, R., and Derek Johnson. 1974. "Does conviction affect employment opportunities?" *British Journal of Criminology* 14:264–268.

Bound, John, and Richard B. Freeman. 1992. "What went wrong? The erosion of relative earnings and employment among young black men in the 1980s." *Quarterly Journal of Economics* 107:201–32.

Bradburn, N. M. 1983. "Response effects." Pp. 289–318 in *Handbook of Survey Research*, edited by P. Rossi, J. Wright, and A. Anderson. New York: Academic Press.

Brand, R. Curtis, Jr., and William L. Claiborn. 1976. "Two studies of comparative stigma: Employer attitudes and practices toward rehabilitated convicts, mental and tuberculosis patients." *Community Mental Health Journal* 12:168–175.

Buikhuisen, W., and F. P. H. Dijksterhuis. 1971. "Delinquency and stigmatisation." *British Journal of Criminology* 11:185–187.

Bureau of Justice Statistics. 1993. "Sentencing in the federal courts: Does race matter?: Transition to sentencing guidelines, 1986-90." Washington, DC: U.S. Department of Justice, NCJ 145328.

———. 1994. "Comparing federal and state prison inmates, 1991." Washington, DC: U.S. Department of Justice.

———. 1995. "Prisoners in 1994." Washington, DC: U.S. Department of Justice.

———. 1997. "Lifetime likelihood of going to state or federal prison." Edited by Thomas P. Bonczar and Allen J. Beck. Washington, DC: U.S. Department of Justice.

———. 1997. "Prisoners in 1996." Washington, DC: U.S. Department of Justice, NCJ 164619.

———. 1997. "Substance abuse and treatment, state and federal prisoners, 1997." Washington, DC: U.S. Department of Justice.

———. 1999. "Correctional populations in the United States, 1996." Washington, DC: U.S. Department of Justice.

———. 1999. "Truth in sentencing in state prisons." Washington, DC: U.S. Department of Justice.

———. 1999. "Women offenders: Special report." Edited by L. A. Greenfeld and T. L. Snell. Washington, DC: U.S. Department of Justice.

———. 2000. "Correctional Populations in the United States, 1997." Washington, DC: U.S. Department of Justice, NCJ 177613.

————. 2000. "Incarcerated parents and their children." Washington, DC: U.S. Department of Justice.

————. 2000. "Key facts at a glance: Number of persons in custody of state correctional authorities by most serious offense 1980-99." Washington, DC: U.S. Department of Justice.

————. 2000. "Probation and parole in the United States, 2000." Washington, DC: U.S. Department of Justice.

————. 2000. *Sourcebook of criminal justice statistics.* Washington, DC: U.S. Department of Justice.

————. 2001. "Criminal victimization 2000: Changes 1999-2000, with trends 1993-2000." Washington, DC: U.S. Department of Justice.

————. 2001. "Prisoners in 2000." Edited by Allen J. Beck and Paige M. Harrison. Washington, DC: U.S. Department of Justice.

————. 2001. "Public attitudes toward uses of criminal history information." Washington, DC: U.S. Department of Justice, NCJ 187663.

————. 2001. "Trends in state parole, 1990-2000." Washington, DC: U.S. Department of Justice, NCJ 184735.

————. 2001. "Use and management of criminal history record information: A comprehensive report, 2001 update." Washington, DC: U.S. Department of Justice, NCJ 187670.

————. 2002. "Prison and jail inmates at midyear 2001." Edited by Allen J. Beck, Jennifer C. Karberg, and Paige M. Harrison. Washington, DC: U.S. Department of Justice.

————. 2002. "Recidivism of prisoners released in 1994." Edited by Patrick Langan and David Levin. Washington, DC: U.S. Department of Justice.

————. 2002. "State prison admissions, 1999: Offense, by admission type." Edited by Timothy Hughes. Washington, DC: U.S. Department of Justice, National Corrections Reporting Program.

————. 2003. "Compendium of state privacy and security legislation: 2002 overview." Washington, DC: U.S. Department of Justice, NCJ 200030.

————. 2003. *Education and correctional populations.* Washington, DC: U.S. Department of Justice, NCJ 195670.

————. 2003. "The nation's two crime measures." Washington, DC: U.S. Department of Justice, NCJ 122705.

————. 2003. "Prisoners in 2002." Washington, DC: U.S. Department of Justice. NCJ 200248.

————. 2003. *Sourcebook of criminal justice statistics*, 31st edition. Washington, DC: U.S. Department of Justice.

————. 2003. "Survey of state criminal history information systems, 2001." Washington, DC: U.S. Department of Justice, NCJ 200343.

————. 2004. "Felony sentences in state courts, 2002." Washington, DC: U.S. Department of Justice, NCJ 206916.

————. 2004. "Justice expenditure and employment in the United States, 2001." Washington, DC: U.S. Department of Justice, NCJ 202792.

————. 2004. "Key facts at a glance: Correctional Populations." Washington, DC: U.S. Department of Justice.

————. 2004. "Prison and jail inmates at midyear 2004." Washington, DC: U.S. Department of Justice.

————. 2005. "Probation and parole in the United States, 2004." Washington, DC: U.S. Department of Justice.

———. 2005. "Contacts between police and the public: Findings from the 2002 national survey." Washington, DC: U.S. Department of Justice, NCJ 207845.

———. 2005. "Homicide trends in the U.S.: Regional trends." Washington, DC: U.S. Department of Justice.

———. 2006. "Homicide trends in the U.S.: Trends by race." Washington, DC: U.S. Department of Justice.

———. 2006. "Prison and jail inmates at midyear 2005." Washington, DC: U.S. Department of Justice, NCJ 213133.

Bureau of Labor Statistics. 2002. "Local area unemployment statistics." Online Public Data Query. http://www.bls.gov/data.

———. 2003. "Occupational employment." *Occupational Outlook Quarterly* winter: 1–22.

Bushway, Shawn D. 2004. "Labor market effects of permitting employer access to criminal history records." *Journal of Contemporary Criminal Justice* 20:276–291.

———. 1998. "The impact of an arrest on the job stability of young white American men." *Journal of Research in Crime and Delinquency* 35:454–479.

Bushway, Shawn, Shauna Briggs, Faye Taxman, Mischelle Van Brakle, and Meridith Thanner. Forthcoming. "Private providers of criminal history records: Do you get what you pay for?" In *The impact of incarceration on labor market outcomes*, edited by Shawn Bushway, Michael Stoll, and David Weiman. New York: Russell Sage Foundation Press.

Bushway, Shawn D., and Peter Reuter. 1997. "Labor markets and crime risk factors." Chapter 6 in *Preventing crime: What works, what doesn't, what's promising*. A report to the United States Congress, prepared for the National Institute of Justice.

Bussey, Jenny, and John Trasviña. 2003. *Racial preferences: The treatment of white and African American job applicants by temporary employment agencies in California*. Berkeley, CA: Discrimination Research Center of the Impact Fund. Available at http://drcenter.org/studies/temp_applicants_03.pdf.

Butler, Richard, and James Heckman. 1977. "The government's impact on the labor market status of black Americans: A critical review." Pp. 235–281 in *Equal rights and industrial relations*, edited by Farrell Bloch and Leonard J. Hausman. Madison, WI: Industrial Relations Research Association.

Cahalan, Margaret Werner. 1986. *Historical corrections statistics in the United States, 1850-1984*: U.S. Department of Justice, Bureau of Justice Statistics. NCJ-102529.

California Department of Corrections. 1997. *Preventing parolee failure program: An evaluation*. Sacramento: California Department of Corrections.

Cancio, A. Silvia, T. David Evans, and David J. Maume. 1996. "Reconsidering the declining significance of race: Racial differences in early career wages." *American Sociological Review* 61:541–556.

Caplow, T., and J. Simon. 1999. "Understanding prison policy and population trends." Pp. 63–120 in *Prisons*, edited by Michael Tonry and Joan Petersilia. Chicago: University of Chicago Press.

Carneiro, Pedro, James J. Heckman, and Dimitriy V. Masterov. 2005. "Labor market discrimination and racial differences in premarket factors." *Journal of Law and Economics* 48 (2005): 1–39.

Castilla, Emilio. 2005. "Gender, race, and meritocracy in organizational careers." Paper presented at Culture and Inequality Workshop. Princeton University.

Caulkins, J. P., and D. McCaffrey. 1993. *Drug sellers in the household population*. Santa Monica: RAND Corp.

Cawley, John, Karen Conneely, James Heckman, and Edward Vytlacil. 1997. "Cognitive ability, wages, and meritocracy." Chap. 9 in *Intelligence, Genes, and Success: Scientists Respond to the Bell Curve*, edited by Bernie Devlin, Stephen Fienberg, Daniel Resnick, and Kathryn Roeder. New York: Springer Verlag.

Center on Wisconsin Strategy (COWS). 1996. *Milwaukee area regional economic analysis.* Center on Wisconsin Strategy, University of Wisconsin-Madison.

Chandra, Amitabh. 2000. "Labor-market dropouts and the racial wage gap: 1940-1990." *American Economic Review* 90:333–338.

Cho, Rosa, and Robert LaLonde. 2005. "The impact of incarceration in state prison on the employment prospects of women." Working paper, Harris School of Public Policy, University of Chicago.

Clear, Todd, Dina Rose, and J. A. Ryder. 2001. "Incarceration and the community: The impact of removing and returning offenders." *Crime and Delinquency* 47:335–351.

Cohen, Dov, and Richard E. Nisbett. 1997. "Field experiments examining the culture of honor: The role of institutions in perpetuating norms about violence." *Personality and Social Psychology Bulletin* 23:1188–1199.

Cohen, Jacqueline, and Jose Canela-Cacho. 1994. "Incapacitation and violent crime." Pp. 296–338 in *Understanding and preventing violence*, edited by Albert Reiss and Jeffrey Roth. Washington, DC: National Academy of Sciences.

Cole, David. 1995. "The paradox of race and crime: A comment on Randall Kennedy's 'politics of distinction.'" *Georgetown Law Journal* 83:2547–2571.

Collins, Randall. 1979. *The credential society: An historical sociology of education and stratification.* New York: Academic Press.

Collins, Sharon. 1989. "The marginalization of black executives." *Social Problems* 36:317–331.

Conley, Dalton. 1999. *Being black, living in the red: Race, wealth, and social policy in America.* Berkeley: University of California Press.

Connerly, Ward. 2000. *Creating equal: My fight against racial preferences.* San Francisco: Encounter Books.

Correll, Joshua, Bernd Wittenbrink, and Charles M. Judd. 2002. "The police officer's dilemma: Using ethnicity to disambiguate potentially threatening individuals." *Journal of Personality and Social Psychology* 83:1314–1329.

Cox, Brenda G., David A. Binder, B. Nanjamma Chinnappa, Anders Christianson, Michael J. Colledge, and Phillip S. Knott. 1995. *Business survey methods.* New York: John Wiley.

Crocker, Jennifer, R. Luhtanen, B. Blaine, and S. Broadnax. 1994. "Collective self-esteem and psychological well-being among white, black, and Asian college students." *Personality and Social Psychology Bulletin* 20:502–513.

Crocker, Jennifer, and Brenda Major. 1989. "Social stigma and self-esteem: The self-protective properties of stigma." *Psychological Review* 96:608–630.

Crocker, Jennifer, Brenda Major, and Claude Steele. 1998. "Social stigma." Pp. 504–553 in *Handbook of social psychology*, edited by D. Gilbert, S. Fiske, and G. Lindzey. Boston: McGraw Hill.

Cross, Harry, Genevieve Kenney, Jane Mell, and Wendy Zimmerman. 1989. *Differential treatment of Hispanic and Anglo job seekers: Hiring practices in two cities.* Washington, DC: Urban Institute Press.

———. 1990. *Employer hiring practices: Differential treatment of Hispanic and Anglo job seekers.* Washington, DC: Urban Institute Press.

Cullen, Francis T. 2005. "The twelve people who saved rehabilitation: How the science of criminology made a difference." *Criminology* 43:1–42.

Cullen, Francis T., and Paul Gendreau. 2000. "Assessing correctional rehabilitation: Policy, practice, and prospects." *Criminal Justice* 3:109–142.

Culp, Jerome, and Bruce Dunson. 1986. "Brothers of a different color: A preliminary look at employer treatment of white and black youth." Pp. 233–260 in *The black employment crisis*, edited by Richard B. Freeman and Harry J. Holzer.

Curran, Barbara A. 1977. *The legal needs of the public: The final report of a national survey.* Chicago: American Bar Association.

Curtin, Richard, Stanley Pressor, and Eleanor Singer. 2000. "The effects of response rate changes on the index of consumer sentiment." *Public Opinion Quarterly* 64:413–428.

Dale, Mitchell. 1976. "Barriers to the rehabilitation of ex-offenders." *Crime and Delinquency* 22:322–337.

Darley, J. M., and P. H. Gross. 1983. "A hypothesis-confirming bias in labeling effects." *Journal of Personality and Social Psychology* 44:20–33.

Devine, Patricia. 1989. "Stereotypes and prejudice: Their automatic and controlled components." *Journal of Personality and Social Psychology* 56:5–18.

Devine, P. G., and A. J. Elliot. 1995. "Are racial stereotypes really fading? The Princeton trilogy revisited." *Personality and Social Psychology Bulletin* 21:1139–1150.

Dickey, Walter. 1988. *Community corrections in 1987-1988.* Madison: Wisconsin Division of Corrections.

DiIulio, John, and Anne Morrison Piehl. 1991. "Does prison pay? The stormy national debate over the cost effectiveness of imprisonment." *Brookings Review* 9:28–35.

Dipboye, R. L. 1982. "Self-fulfilling prophecies in the selection-recruitment interview." *Academy of Management Review* 7:579–586.

Dixon, Travis L., and Daniel Linz. 2000. "Overrepresentation and underrepresentation of African Americans and Latinos as lawbreakers on television news." *Journal of Communication* 50:131–154.

Donahue, John J., III. 1992. "Advocacy versus analysis in assessing employment discrimination law." *Stanford Law Review* 44:1583–1615.

Donahue, John J., III, and James Heckman. 1991. "Continuous versus episodic change: The effect of federal civil rights policy on the economic status of blacks." *Journal of Economic Literature* 29:1603–1643.

Donahue, John J., III, and Peter Siegelman. 1991. "The changing nature of employment discrimination litigation." *Stanford Law Review* 43:983–1033.

Donahue, John J., III, and Peter Siegelman. 2005. "The evolution of employment discrimination law in the 1990s: A preliminary empirical investigation." Pp. 261–285 in *Handbook of employment discrimination research*, edited by L. B. Nielsen and R. L. Nelson. Dordrecht, Netherlands: Springer.

Dovidio, John F. 2001. "On the nature of contemporary prejudice: The third wave." *Journal of Social Issues* 57:829–849.

Dovidio, John F., and Samuel L. Gaertner. 2000. "Aversive racism and selection decisions." *Psychological Science* 11:315–319.

Downing, David. 1982. "Employer biases toward the hiring and placement of male ex-offenders." Ph.D. dissertation, Southern Illinois University.

D'Souza, Dinesh. 1995. *The end of racism: Principles for a multiracial society.* New York: Free Press.

Duncan, Birt L. 1976. "Differential social perception and attribution of intergroup violence: Testing the lower limits of stereotyping of blacks." *Journal of Personality and Social Psychology* 34:590–598.

Duneier, Mitchell. 1999. *Sidewalk*. New York: Farrar, Straus and Giroux.

Dyson, Michael Eric. 2005. *Is Bill Cosby right?: Or has the black middle class lost its mind?* New York: Basic Civitas Books.

Eberhardt, Jennifer L., Phillip Atiba Goff, Valerie J. Purdie, and Paul G. Davies. 2004. "Seeing black: Race, crime, and visual processing." *Journal of Personality and Social Psychology* 87:876–893.

Edin, Kathryn, Timothy Nelson, and Rochelle Parnal. 2003. "Fatherhood and incarceration as potential turning points in the criminal careers of unskilled men." Pp. 46–75 in *Imprisoning America: the social effects of mass incarceration*, edited by Mary Pattillo, David Weiman, and Bruce Western. New York: Russell Sage.

Ellwood, David. 1986. "The spatial mismatch hypothesis: Are there teenage jobs missing in the ghetto?" Pp. 147–185 in *The black youth employment crisis*, edited by Richard B. Freeman and Harry J. Holzer. Chicago: University of Chicago Press.

Entman, Robert M. 1990. "Modern racism and the images of blacks in local television news." *Critical Studies in Mass Communication* 7:332–345.

Entman, Robert M., and Andrew Rojecki. 2000. *The black image in the white mind: Media and race in America*. Chicago: University of Chicago Press.

Fagan, Jeffrey, Franklin E. Zimring, and June Kim. 1998. "Declining homicide in New York City: A tale of two trends." *Journal of Criminal Law and Criminology* 88:1277–1306.

Fairlie, Robert W., and William A. Sundstrom. 1997. "The racial unemployment gap in long-run perspective." *American Economic Review* 87:306–310.

Fanon, Frantz. 1967. *Black skins, white masks*. New York: Grove.

Farkas, George. 2003. "Cognitive skills and noncognitive traits and behaviors in stratification processes." *Annual Review of Sociology* 29:541–562.

Farkas, George, and Kevin Vicknair. 1996. "Appropriate tests of racial wage discrimination require controls for cognitive skill: comment on Cancio, Evans, and Maume." *American Sociological Review* 61:557–560.

Farley, Reynolds. 1996. "The new American reality: Who we are, how we got here, and where we are going." New York: Russell Sage Foundation.

Farmer, Amy, and Dek Terrell. 2001. "Crime versus justice: Is there a trade-off?" *Journal of Law and Economics* 44:345–366.

Farrington, David P., and Brandon C. Welsh. 2005. "Randomized Experiments in Criminology: What Have We Learned in the Last Two Decades?" *Journal of Experimental Criminology* 1:9–38.

Feagin, Joe R., and Melvin P. Sikes. 1994. *Living with racism: The black middle-class experience*. Boston: Beacon Press.

Federal Bureau of Investigation. 1991. "Crime in the United States." *Uniform Crime Reports, 1990.*

Fenton-O'Creevy, M. 1996. "Employees involvement and the middle manager." DBA diss., London Business School.

Fernandez, Roberto. 2006. "Race, spatial mismatch, and job accessibility: Evidence from a plant relocation." Working paper, MIT Sloan School of Management.

Fernandez, Roberto, and Celina Su. 2004. "Space and the study of labor markets." *Annual Review of Sociology* 30:545–569.

Festen, Marcia, and Sunny Fischer. 2002. *Navigating reentry: The experiences and perceptions of ex-offenders seeking employment.* Chicago: Urban League.

Fin, Peter. 1998. "Program Focus: Texas' Project RIO (Re-Integration of Offenders)." Report prepared for the National Institute of Justice, the National Institute of Corrections, and the Office of Correctional Education.

Finn, R. H., and P. A. Fontaine. 1985. "The association between selected characteristics and perceived employability of offenders." *Criminal Justice and Behavior* 12:353–365.

Fiske, Susan. 1998. "Stereotyping, prejudice, and discrimination." Pp. 357–411 in *The handbook of social psychology,* edited by Daniel Gilbert, Susan Fiske, and Gardner Lindzey. Boston: McGraw Hill.

Fiske, Susan, and S. L. Neuberg. 1990. "A continuum model of impression formation: From category-based to individuating processes: Influence of information and motivation on attention and interpretation." Pp. 1–74 in *Advances in experimental psychology,* edited by M. P. Zanna. New York: Academic Press.

Fix, Michael, George C. Galster, and Raymond Struyck. 1993. "An overview of auditing for discrimination." Pp. 1–68 in *Clear and convincing evidence: Measurement of discrimination in America,* edited by Michael Fix and Raymond J. Struyk (Washington, DC: Urban Institute Press).

Fix, Michael, and Raymond J. Struyk (eds.). 1993. *Clear and convincing evidence: Measurement of discrimination in America.* Washington, DC: Urban Institute Press.

Fix, Michael, and Margery Austin Turner (eds.). 1993. *A national report card on discrimination in America: The role of testing.* Washington, DC: Urban Institute.

Freeman, Richard B. 1987. "The relation of criminal activity to black youth employment." *Review of Black Political Economy* 16:99–107.

———. 1991. "Crime and the employment of disadvantaged youths." Cambridge, MA: National Bureau of Economic Research.

———. 1992. "On the economic analysis of labor market institutions and institutional change." Cambridge, MA: Harvard Institute of Economic Research.

———. 1994. "Crime and the job market." Cambridge, MA: National Bureau of Economic Research.

———. 2003. "Can we close the revolving door?: Recidivism vs. employment of ex-offenders in the U.S." Paper presented at Urban Institute Reentry Roundtable.

Freeman, Richard B., and Harry J. Holzer (eds.). 1986. *The black youth employment crisis.* Chicago: University of Chicago Press, for National Bureau of Economic Research.

Freeman, Richard B., and William M. Rodgers III. 1999. "Area economic conditions and the labor market outcomes of young men in the 1990s expansion." Cambridge, MA: National Bureau of Economic Research.

Fryer, Ronald G., Jr., and Steven D. Levitt. 2004. "The causes and consequences of distinctively black names." *Quarterly Journal of Economics* 119: 767–805.

Gaes, Gerald, Timothy J. Flanagan, Laurence L. Motiuk, and Lynn Stewart. 1999. "Adult correctional treatment." Pp. 361–426 in *Prisons,* edited by Michael Tonry and Joan Petersilia. Chicago: University of Chicago Press.

Gainsborough, Jenni, and Marc Mauer. 2000. "Diminishing returns: Crime and incarceration in the 1990s." Policy report from the Sentencing Project.

Gallup Organization. 1997. "The Gallup Poll social audit on black/white relations in the United States." Princeton, NJ: Gallup Organization.

Gans, Herbert J. 1969. "Culture and class in the study of poverty: An approach to anti-poverty research." Pp. 201–228 in *On understanding poverty: perspectives from the social sciences*, edited by D. P. Moynihan. New York: Basic Books.

———. 1995. *The war against the poor: The underclass and antipoverty policy*. New York: Basic Books.

Garfinkel, Harold. 1956. "Conditions of successful degradation ceremonies." *American Journal of Sociology* 61:420–424.

Garland, David. 1990. *Punishment in modern society: A study in social theory*. Chicago: University of Chicago Press.

———. 2001. *The culture of control: Crime and social order in contemporary society*. Chicago: University of Chicago Press.

Gfroerer, Joseph, and Marc Brodsky. 1992. "The incidence of illicit drug use in the United States, 1962-1989." *British Journal of Addiction* 87:1345–1351.

Gilbert, Daniel T., and Gregory Hixon. 1991. "The trouble with thinking: Activation and application of stereotypic beliefs." *Journal of Personality and Social Psychology* 60:509–517.

Gilliam, Franklin D., and Shanto Iyengar. 2000. "Prime suspects: The influence of local television news on the viewing public." *American Journal of Political Science* 44:560–573.

Gilliam, Franklin D., Jr., Shanto Iyengar, Adam Simon, and Oliver Wright. 1996. "Crime in black and white: The violent, scary world of local news." *Harvard International Journal of Press/Politics* 1:6–23.

Glueck, Sheldon, and Eleanor Glueck. 1950. *Unraveling juvenile delinquency*. New York: Commonwealth Fund.

Goffman, Irving. 1963. *Stigma: Notes on the management of a spoiled identity*. New York: Prentice Hall.

Gonnerman, Jennifer. 2004. *Life on the outside: The prison odyssey of Elaine Bartlett*. New York: Picador.

Gooden, Susan T. 1999. "The hidden third party: Welfare recipients' experiences with employers." *Journal of Public Management and Social Policy* 5:69–83.

Gottschalk, Marie. 2006. *The prison and the gallows: The politics of mass incarceration in America*. New York: Cambridge University Press.

Gough, Aidan R. 1966. "The expungement of adjudication records of juvenile and adult offenders." *Washington University Law Quarterly* 147:148.

Gould, John. 2002. "Zone defense." *Washington Monthly*, June, 33.

Government Accountability Office. 2005. "Adult drug courts: Evidence indicates recidivism reductions and mixed results for other outcomes." Report to Congressional Committees, GAO-05-219.

Graber, D. A. 1980. *Crime news and the public*. New York: Praeger.

Graham, Sandra, and Brian S. Lowery. 2004. "Priming unconscious racial stereotypes about adolescent offenders." *Law and Human Behavior* 28:483–504.

Greenfeld, Larry. 1985. *Examining Recidivism*. Washington, DC: Bureau of Justice Statistics, NCJ 96501.

Gregory, David L. 1988. "Reducing the risk of negligence in hiring." *Employee Relations Law Journal* 14:31–40.

Grodsky, Eric, and Devah Pager. 2001. "The structure of disadvantage: Individual and occupational determinants of black-white wage gap." *American Sociological Review* 66:542–567.

Grogger, Jeffrey. 1992. "Arrests, persistent youth joblessness, and black/white employment differentials." *Review of Economics and Statistics* 74:100–106.

———. 1995. "The effect of arrests on the employment and earnings of young men." *Quarterly Journal of Economics* 110:51–72.

Groves, Robert M., and Lars E. Lyberg. 1988. "An overview of nonresponse issues in telephone surveys." Pp. 191–212 in *Telephone survey methodology*, edited by Robert M. Groves. New York: Wiley.

Hagan, John. 1993. "The social embeddedness of crime and unemployment." *Criminology* 31:465–491.

Hagan, John, and Ronit Dinovitzer. 1999. "Collateral consequences of imprisonment for children, communities, and prisoners." Pp. 121–162 in *Prisons*, edited by M. Tonry and J. Petersilia. Chicago: University of Chicago Press.

Hakken, Jon. 1979. *Discrimination against Chicanos in the Dallas rental housing market: An experimental extension of the housing market practices survey*. Washington, DC: U.S. Department of Housing and Urban Development.

Hammett, T. M. 2000. *Health-related issues in prisoner reentry to the community*. Washington, DC: Urban Institute.

Harding, David. 2003. "Jean Valjean's dilemma: The management of ex-convict identity in the search for employment." *Deviant Behavior* 24:571–595.

Harris, Anthony. 1975. "Imprisonment and the expected value of criminal choice: A specification and test of aspects of the labeling perspective." *American Sociological Review* 40:71–87.

Harris, David. 1994. "Factors for reasonable suspicion: When black and poor means stopped and frisked." *Indiana Law Journal* 69:659–693.

Harrison, Roderick J., and Claudette E. Bennett. 1995. "Racial and ethnic diversity." Pp. 141–210 in *State of the union: America in the 1990s, social trends*, edited by R. Farley. New York: Russell Sage Foundation.

Hart Associates. 2002. Changing public attitudes toward the criminal justice system. Poll conducted for the Open Society Institute.

Hauser, Robert M. 2004. "Progress in schooling: A review." Pp. 271–318 in *Social inequality*, edited by Katherine Neckerman. New York: Russell Sage Foundation.

Heckman, James J. 1998. "Detecting discrimination." *Journal of Economic Perspectives* 12, no. 2: 101–116.

Heckman, James, and Peter Siegelman. 1993. "The Urban Institute audit studies: Their methods and findings." Pp. 187–258 in *Clear and convincing evidence: Measurement of discrimination in America*, edited by Michael Fix and Raymond J. Struyk. Washington, DC: Urban Institute Press.

Henson, Kevin D. 1996. *Just a temp*. Philadelphia: Temple University Press.

Hirsch, Barry T., and Edward J. Schumacher. 1992. "Labor earnings, discrimination and the racial composition of jobs." *Journal of Human Resources* 27:602–628.

Holzer, Harry J. 1987. "Informal job search and black youth unemployment." *American Economic Review* 77:446–452.

———. 1988. "Search methods used by unemployment youth." *Journal of Labor Economics* 6:1–20.

———. 1991. "The spatial mismatch hypothesis: What has the evidence shown?" *Urban Studies* 28:105–122.

———. 1996. *What employers want: Job prospects for less-educated workers*. New York: Russell Sage Foundation.

Holzer, Harry J., and Keith Ihlanfeldt. 1998. "Customer discrimination and employment outcomes for minority workers." *Quarterly Journal of Economics* 113:835–867.

Holzer, Harry J., Paul Offner, and Elaine Sorensen. 2005. "What explains the continuing decline in labor force activity among young black men?" *Labor History* 46:37–55.

Holzer, Harry J., Steven Raphael, and Michael Stoll. 2003. "Employer demand for ex-offenders: recent evidence from Los Angeles." Working paper, Urban Institute.
———. 2006. "Perceived criminality, criminal background checks, and the racial hiring practices of employers." *Journal of Law and Economics* 49:451–480.

Holzer, Harry J., and Michael Stoll. 2001. *Employers and welfare recipients: The effects of welfare reform in the workplace.* San Francisco: Public Policy Institute of California.

Holzer, Harry J., Michael Stoll, and Steven Raphael. 2002. Survey of Los Angeles employers (analysis of unpublished data).

Horn, Martin F. 2000. "Rethinking sentencing." *Corrections Management Quarterly* 5:34–40.

Hoynes, Hilary W. 2000. "The employment, earnings, and income of less skilled workers over the business cycle." Pp. 23–71 in *Finding jobs: Work and welfare reform*, edited by David Card and Rebecca M. Blank. New York: Russell Sage Foundation.

Huddleston, C. W., K. Freeman-Wilson, and D. L. Boone. 2004. *Painting the picture: A national report card on drug courts and other problem-solving court programs in the United States.* Alexandria, VA: National Drug Court Institute, and Bureau of Justice Assistance.

Husley, Lonnie Freeman. 1990. "Attitudes of employers with respect to hiring released prisoners." Ph.D. dissertation, Mankato State University.

Iguchi, M. Y., J. A. London, N. G. Forge, L. Hickman, T. Fain, and K. Riehman. 2002. "Elements of well-being affected by criminalizing the drug user." *Public Health Report* 117:146–50.

Ihlanfeldt, Keith R., and David L. Sjoquist. 1998. "The spatial mismatch hypothesis: A review of recent studies and their implications for welfare reform." *Housing Policy Debate* 9:849–892.

Irwin, J., and J. Austin. 1994. *It's about time: America's imprisonment binge.* 3rd ed. Belmont, CA: Wadsworth.

Jacobs, D., and R. E. Helms. 1996. "Towards a political model of incarceration." *American Journal of Sociology* 102:323–357.

Jacobs, James. 1983. *New Perspectives on Prisons and Imprisonment.* Ithaca: Cornell University Press.

Jacobson, Michael. 2005. *Downsizing prisons: How to reduce crime and end mass incarceration.* New York: New York University Press.

Jencks, Christopher. 1991. "Is the American underclass growing?" Pp. 28–100 in *The urban underclass*, edited by C. Jencks and P. E. Peterson. Washington, DC: Brookings Institution.

Jencks, Christopher, and Susan E. Mayer. 1990. "Residential segregation, job proximity, and black job opportunities." Pp. 187–222 in *Inner-city poverty in the United States*, edited by Laurence Lynn Jr. and Michael G. H. McGeary. Washington, DC: National Academy Press.

Jencks, Christopher, and Meredith Phillips (eds.). 1998. *The black-white test score gap.* Washington, DC: Brookings Institution Press.

Jensen, W., and W. C. Giegold. 1976. "Finding jobs for ex-offenders: A study of employers' attitudes." *American Business Law Journal* 14:195–225.

Johnson, James D., Mike S. Adams, William Hall, and Leslie Ashburn. 1997. "Race, media, and violence: Differential racial effects of exposure to violent news stories." *Basic and Applied Social Psychology* 19:81–90.

Johnson, William, and Derek Neal. 1998. "Basic skills and the black-white earnings gap." Pp. 480–497 in *The black-white test score gap*, edited by Christopher Jencks and Meredith Phillips. Washington, DC: Brookings Institution Press.

Jolson, Marvin A. 1975. "Are ex-offenders successful employees?" *California Management Review* 17:65–73.

Kain, John. F. 1992. "The spatial mismatch hypothesis: Three decades later." *Housing Policy Debate* 2:371–460.

Katz, Michael B. 1989. *The undeserving poor: From the war on poverty to the war on welfare.* New York: Pantheon Books.

Keeter, Scott, Carolyn Miller, Andrew Kohut, Robert M. Groves, and Stanley Presser. 2000. "Consequences of reducing nonresponse in national telephone survey." *Public Opinion Quarterly* 64:125–148.

Kennedy, Randall. 1994. "The state, criminal law, and racial discrimination: A comment." *Harvard Law Review* 107:1255–1278.

Kesteren, John van, Pat Mayhew, and Paul Nieuwbeerta. 2000. "Criminal victimisation in 17 industrialized countries, 1999." The Hague: Dutch Ministry of Justice.

Kling, Jeffrey. 2006. "Incarceration length, employment, and earnings." *American Economic Review* 96:863–876.

Klite, P., R. A. Bardwell, and J. Salzman. 1997. "Local TV news: Getting away with murder." *Harvard International Journal of Press/Politics* 2:102–112.

Kurki, Leena. 1997. "International crime survey: American rates about average." *Overcrowded Times* 8:1–7.

Kurlychek, Megan C., Robert Brame, and Shawn D. Bushway. 2006. "Scarlet letters and recidivism: Does an old criminal record predict future offending?" *Crime and Public Policy* 5:483–504.

Kutner, Bernard, Carol Wilkins, and Penny Rechtman Yarrow. 1952. "Verbal attitudes and overt behavior involving racial prejudice." *Journal of Abnormal Social Psychology* 47:649–52.

Kuziemko, Ilyana, and Steven Levitt. 2004. "An empirical analysis of imprisoning drug offenders." *Journal of Public Economics* 88:2043–2066.

Lacy, Karyn R. 2004. "Black spaces, black places: Strategic assimilation and identity construction in middle-class suburbia." *Ethnic and Racial Studies* 27:908–930.

Lahey, Joanna. 2005. "Age, women, and hiring: An experimental study." NBER Working Paper 11435.

LaPiere, Richard T. 1934. "Attitudes vs. actions." *Social Forces* 13:230–237.

Lawrence, Sarah, and Jeremy Travis. 2004. "The new landscape of imprisonment: Mapping America's prison expansion." Washington, DC: Urban Institute.

Leavitt, Jennifer. 2001. "Walking a tightrope: Balancing competing public interests in the employment of criminal offenders." *Connecticut Law Review* 34:1281–1315.

Legal Action Center. 2004. "After prison: Roadblocks to reentry. A report on state legal barriers facing people with criminal records." Edited by Paul Samuels and Debbie Mukamal. New York: Legal Action Center.

Levine, Marc, and Sandra Callaghan. 1998. *The economic state of Milwaukee*: University of Wisconsin-Milwaukee, Center for Economic Development.

Levitt, Steven D. 1996. "The effect of prison population size on crime rates: Evidence from prison overcrowding litigation." *Quarterly Journal of Economics* 111:319–51.

———. 2004. "Understanding why crime fell in the 1990s: Four factors that explain the decline and six that do not." *Journal of Economic Perspectives* 18, no. 1: 163–190.

Link, Bruce G., and J. C. Phelan. 2001. "Conceptualizing stigma." *Annual Review of Sociology* 27:363–385.

Lipschultz, J. H., and M. L. Hilt. 2002. *Crime and local television news: Dramatic, breaking, and live from the scene.* Mahwah, NJ: Lawrence Erlbaum Associates.

Lodder, LeAnn, Scott McFarland, and Diana White. 2003. *Racial preferences and suburban employment opportunities.* Chicago: Legal Assistance Foundation of Metropolitan Chicago.

Loury, Glenn C. 2002. *The anatomy of racial inequality.* Cambridge, MA: Harvard University Press.

Love, Margaret Colgate. 2003. "Starting over with a clean slate: In praise of a forgotten section of the model penal code." *Fordham Urban Law Journal* 30:1705–1741.

———. 2005. *Relief from the collateral consequences of a criminal conviction: A state-by-state resource guide.* Washington, DC: Sentencing Project.

Ludwig, Jack. "A Gallup poll social audit: The state of black/white relations in the U.S." *Polling Report* 17:1–8.

Lye, Linda. 1998. "Title VII's tangled tale: The erosion and confusion of disparate impact and the business necessity defense." *Berkeley Journal of Employment and Labor Law* 19:315–361.

Lynch, James P., and William Sabol. 2000. "Prison use and social control." Pp. 7–44 in *Criminal justice 2000: Policies, processes, and decisions of the criminal justice system*, edited by Julie Horney. Washington, DC: U.S. Department of Justice.

Lynch, Mona. 1999. "Waste managers? New penology, crime fighting, and the parole agent identity." *Law and Society Review* 32:839–869.

Maharaj, Nicole. 2006. "Task Force Calls Mayors to Action on Second Chance Act." http://www.mayors.org/USCM/us_mayor_newspaper/documents/06_19_06/secondchance.asp.

Manza, Jeff, and Chris Uggen. 2006. *Locked out: Felon disenfranchisement and American democracy.* New York: Oxford University Press.

Mare, Robert D. 1995. "Changes in educational attainment and school enrollment." Pp. 155–213 in *State of the union: America in the 1990s, economic trends*, edited by R. Farley. New. York: Russell Sage Foundation.

Mare, Robert D., and Christopher Winship. 1984. "The paradox of lessening racial inequality and joblessness among black youth: Enrollment, enlistment and employment, 1964-1981." *American Sociological Review* 49:39–55.

Martinson, Robert. 1974. "What works? Questions and answers about prison reform." *Public Interest* 35:22–54.

———. 1979. "New views: A note of caution regarding sentencing reform." *Hofstra Law Review* 7:242–258.

Massey, Douglas, and Nancy A. Denton. 1993. *American apartheid: Segregation and the making of the underclass.* Cambridge, MA: Harvard University Press.

Massey, Douglas, and Garvey Lundy. 2001. "Use of black English and racial discrimination in urban housing markets: New methods and findings." *Urban Affairs Review* 36:452–469.

Mauer, Marc. 1999. *Race to incarcerate*. New York: New Press.

———. 2001. "The causes and consequences of prison growth in the United States." Pp. 4–14 in *Mass imprisonment: Social causes and consequences*, edited by David Garland. London: Sage Publications.

May, Bruce E. 1995. "The character component of occupational licensing laws: A continuing barrier to the ex-felon's employment opportunities." *North Dakota Law Review* 71:187.

Mayer, William G. 1993. "Poll trends: Trends in media usage." *Public Opinion Quarterly* 57:593–611.

McAneny, L. C. (ed.) 1995. "Gallup Poll on Crime." *Gallup Poll Monthly* 352, no. 3: 1–10.

McGuire, J. 1995. *What works? Reducing reoffending*. New York: Wiley.

Merton, Robert. 1948. "The self-fulfilling prophecy." *Antioch Review* 8:193–210.

Milgram, Stanley. 1974. *Obedience to authority: An experimental view*. New York: Harper and Row.

Miller, Neal. 1979. "Employer-barriers to the employment of persons with records of arrest or conviction: A review and analysis." Washington, DC: U.S. Department of Labor, ASPER.

Miller, Richard E., and Austin Sarat. 1980-81. "Grievances, claims, and disputes: Assessing the adversary culture." *Law and Society Review* 15:525–566.

Mincy, Ronald. 1994. *Nurturing young black males*. Washington, DC: Urban Institute Press.

Moore, Joan. 1996. "Bearing the burden: How incarceration weakens inner-city communities." *Journal of the Oklahoma Criminal Justice Research Consortium* 3 (August): 43–54.

Moss, Philip, and Chris Tilly. 2001. *Stories employers tell: Race, skill, and hiring in America*. New York: Russell Sage Foundation.

Mukamal, Debbie. 2003. "Negligent hiring case law in New York." Research memo prepared for the Legal Action Center.

Murnane, Richard, John Willett, and Frank Levy. 1995. "The growing importance of cognitive skills in wage determination." *Review of Economics and Statistics* 77: 251–266.

Murray, Charles. 1984. *Losing ground: American social policy, 1950-1980*. New York: Basic Books.

Nagin, Daniel. 1998. "Criminal deterrence research at the outset of the twenty-first century." *Crime and Justice* 23:1–42.

Nagin, Daniel, and Joel Waldfogel. 1998. "The effect of conviction on income through the life cycle." *International Review of Law and Economics* 18:25–40.

National Advisory Commission on Criminal Justice Standards and Goals. 1973. *Corrections*. Washington, DC: U.S. Government Printing Office.

National Research Council (NRC). 2004. "Measuring racial discrimination. Panel on methods for assessing discrimination." Edited by Rebecca M. Blank, Marilyn Dabady, and Constance F. Citro. Washington, DC: Committee on National Statistics, Division of Behavior and Social Sciences and Education, National Academies Press.

Neal, Derek, and William Johnson. 1996. "The role of premarket factors in black-white wage differences." *Journal of Political Economy* 104:869–895.

Needels, Karen E. 1996. "Go directly to jail and do not collect? A long-term study of recidivism, employment, and earning patterns among prison releases." *Journal of Crime and Delinquency* 33:471–496.

Nelson, Marta, Perry Deess, and Charlotte Allen. 1999. *The first month out: Post-incarceration experiences in New York City*. New York: Vera Institute of Justice.

Neumark, David. 1996. "Sex discrimination in restaurant hiring: An audit study." *Quarterly Journal of Economics* 111:915–941.

———. 1999. "Wage differentials by race and sex: The roles of taste discrimination and labor market information." *Industrial Relations* 38:414–445.

Newman, Katherine. 1999. *No shame in my game: The working poor in the inner city*. New York: Random House.

Nielsen, Laura Beth, and Aaron Beim. 2004. "Media misrepresentation: Title VII, print media, and public perceptions of discrimination litigation." *Stanford Law and Policy Review* 15:101–30.

Nielsen, Laura Beth, and Robert L. Nelson. 2005. "Scaling the pyramid: A sociolegal model of employment discrimination litigation." Pp. 3–34 in *Handbook of employment discrimination research*, edited by L. B. Nielsen and R. L. Nelson. Dordrecht., Netherlands: Springer.

Nolan, James. 2001. *Reinventing justice: The American drug court movement*. Princeton, NJ: Princeton University Press.

Nunes, Ana, and Brad Seligman. 2000. *A study of the treatment of female and male applicants by San Francisco Bay area auto service shops*. Berkeley, CA: Discrimination Research Center of the Impact Fund.

Olivares, Kathleen M., Velmer S. Burton Jr., and Francis Cullen. 1996. "The collateral consequences of a felony conviction: A national study of state legal codes 10 years later." *Federal Probation* 60:10–17.

Oliver, Mary Beth. 1994. "Portrayals of crime, race, and aggression in 'reality-based' police shows: A content analysis." *Journal of Broadcasting and Electronic Media* 38:179–192.

O'Neill, June. 1990. "The role of human capital in earnings differences between white and black men." *Journal of Economic Perspectives* 4, no. 4: 25–45.

Pager, Devah. 2001. "Criminal careers: The consequences of incarceration for occupational attainment." Paper presented at American Sociological Association Annual Meeting, Anaheim.

———. 2002. "The consequences of incarceration for employment outcomes." Paper presented at American Sociological Association Annual Meetings, Chicago.

———. 2003. "The mark of a criminal record." *American Journal of Sociology* 108:937–975.

Pager, Devah, and Jeremy Freese. 2006. "Who deserves a helping hand? Attitudes about government assistance for the unemployed by race, cause of unemployment, and worker history." Paper presented at Annual Meetings of the American Sociological Association, Montreal.

Pager, Devah, and Lincoln Quillian. 2005. "Walking the talk: What employers say versus what they do." *American Sociological Review* 70:355–380.

Pager, Devah, and Bruce Western. 2006. "Discrimination in low wage labor markets." Working paper, Princeton University, Department of Sociology.

Palmer, Ted. 1975. "Martinson revisited." *Journal of Research in Crime and Delinquency* 12:133–152.

Palys, Theodore S. 1976. "An assessment of legal and cultural stigma regarding unskilled workers." *Canadian Journal of Criminology and Corrections* 18:247–257.

Parcel, Toby L., and Charles W. Mueller. 1983. *Ascription and labor markets: Race and sex differences in earnings.* New York: Academic Press.

Parenti, Christian. 1999. *Lockdown America: Police and prisons in the age of crisis.* New York: Verso.

Pawasarat, John, and Lois M. Quinn. 2000. Survey of job openings in the Milwaukee metropolitan area: week of May 15, 2000. Employment and Training Institute, University Outreach, University of Wisconsin-Milwaukee.

Payne, B. Keith. 2001. "Prejudice and perception: The role of automatic and controlled processes in misperceiving a weapon." *Journal of Personality and Social Psychology* 81:181–192.

Petersilia, Joan. 1999. "Parole and prisoner reentry in the United States." Pp. 497–529 in *Prisons*, edited by Michael Tonry and Joan Petersilia. Chicago: University of Chicago Press.

———. 2002. "Community corrections." Pp. 483–508 in *Crime: Public policies for crime control*, edited by James Q. Wilson and Joan Petersilia. Oakland, CA: Institute for Contemporary Studies Press.

———. 2003. *When prisoners come home: Parole and prisoner reentry.* New York: Oxford University Press.

Pettit, Becky, and Christopher Lyons. 2002. "The consequences of incarceration on employment and earnings: Evidence from Washington State." Working paper, University of Washington, Department of Sociology.

Pettit, Becky, and Bruce Western. 2004. "Mass imprisonment and the life course: Race and class inequality in U.S. incarceration." *American Sociological Review* 69:151–69.

Phillips, Kevin. 1969. *The Emerging Republican Majority.* New Rochelle, NY: Arlington House.

Piehl, Anne Morrison, and John J. DiIulio Jr. 1995. "'Does prison pay?' revisited: Returning to the crime scene." *Brookings Review* 13:21–25.

Posner, Richard. 1987. "The efficiency and efficacy of Title VII." *University of Pennsylvania Law Review* 136:513–521.

Prendergast, Michael L., M. Douglas Anglin, and Jean Wellisch. 1995. "Treatment for drug-abusing offenders under community supervision." *Federal Probation* 59:66–75.

President's Commission on Law Enforcement and Administration of Justice. 1967. *The problem of crime in a free society.* Washington, DC: U.S. Government Printing Office.

Purnell, Thomas, William Idsardi, and John Baugh. 1999. "Perceptual and phonetic experiments on American English dialect identification." *Journal of Language and Social Psychology* 18:10–30.

Quillian, Lincoln, and Devah Pager. 2001. "Black neighbors, higher crime? The role of racial stereotypes in evaluations of neighborhood crime." *American Journal of Sociology* 107:717–767.

RAND. 1994. *Controlling cocaine: supply versus demand programs.* Los Angeles: RAND.

Raphael, Steven, and David F. Weiman. 2005. "The impact of local labor market conditions on the likelihood that parolees are returned to custody." Working paper, University of California-Berkeley.

Reiman, Jeffrey. 1979, 2004. *The rich get richer and the poor ger prison: Ideology class, and criminal justice.* Boston: Allyn and Bacon.

Reiss, Albert J., Jr., and Jeffrey A. Roth (eds.). 1993. *Understanding and preventing violence.* Washington, DC: National Academy of Sciences.

Reitz, Kevin. 1998. "Sentencing." Pp. 542–62 in *The handbook of crime and punishment*, edited by Michael Tonry. New York: Oxford University Press.

Remington, Todd D. 1992. "Telemarketing and declining survey response rates." *Journal of Advertising Research* 32:6–7.

Reskin, Barbara. 1998. *The realities of affirmative action in employment*. Washington, DC: American Sociological Association.

Riach, Peter, and Judith Rich. 1991-1992. "Measuring discrimination by direct experimentation methods: Seeking gunsmoke." *Journal of Post-Keynesian Economics* 14:143–150.

———. 2002. "Field experiments of discrimination in the market place." *Economic Journal* 112:480–518.

Ridley, Stanley, James A. Bayton, and Janice Hamilton Outtz. 1989. "Taxi service in the District of Columbia: Is it influenced by patrons' race and destination?" (mimeograph). Washington, DC: Washington Lawyers' Committee for Civil Rights under the Law.

Romer, Daniel, Kathleen H. Jamieson, and Nicole J. deCouteau. 1998. "The treatment of persons of color in local television news: Ethnic blame discourse or realistic group conflict?" *Communication Research* 25:286–305.

Rose, Dina, and Todd Clear. 1998. "Incarceration, social capital, and crime: Implications for social disorganization theory." *Criminology* 36:441–479.

Rosenfeld, R. 2000. "Patterns in adult homicide, 1980–1995." Pp. 130–163 in *The crime drop in America*, edited by Alfred Blumstein and Joel Wallman. New York: Cambridge University Press.

Rothbart, M., M. Evans, and S. Fulero. 1979. "Recall for confirming events: Memory processes and the maintenance of social stereotyping." *Journal of Experimental Social Psychology* 15:343–355.

Rothman, David. 1971. *The discovery of the asylum: Social order and disorder in the republic*. Boston: Little, Brown, and Co.

Sabol, William J., Katherine Rosich, Kamala Mallik Kane, David P. Kirk, and Glenn Dubin. 2002. "The influences of truth-in-sentencing reforms on changes in states' sentencing practices and prison populations." Research Report, Urban Institute.

Saenger, Gerhart, and Emily Gilbert. 1950. "Customer reactions to the integration of negro sales personnel." *International Journal of Opinion and Attitude Research* 4:57–76.

Sagar, H. A., and J. W. Schofield. 1980. "Racial and behavioral cues in black and white children's perceptions of ambiguously aggressive acts." *Journal of Personality and Social Psychology* 39:590–598.

Sampson, Robert. 1987. "Urban black violence: The effect of male joblessness and family disruption." *American Journal of Sociology* 93:348–382.

Sampson, Robert, and John H. Laub. 1993. *Crime in the making: Pathways and turning points through life*. Cambridge, MA: Harvard University Press.

———. 2005. "A life-course view of the development of crime." *Annals of the American Academy of Political and Social Science* 602:12–45.

Sampson, Robert, and Janet Lauritsen. 1997. "Racial and ethnic disparities in crime and criminal justice in the United States." *Crime and Justice: Ethnicity, Crime and Immigration: Comparative and Cross-National Perspectives* 21:311–374.

Saxonhouse, Elena. 2004. "Unequal protection: Comparing former felons' challenges to disenfranchisement and employment discrimination." *Stanford Law Review* 56:1597–1639.

Scales, Monica. 2002. "Employer catch-22: The paradox between employer liability for employee criminal acts and the prohibition against ex-convict discrimination." *George Mason Law Review* 11:419–440.

Schichor, David. 1997. "Three strikes as a public policy: The convergence of the new penology and the McDonaldization of punishment." *Crime and Delinquency* 43:470–492.

Schuman, Howard, Charlottee Steeh, Lawrence Bobo, and Maria Krysan. 1997. *Racial attitudes in America: Trends and interpretations*. Cambridge, MA: Harvard University Press.

Schwartz, Richard, and Jerome Skolnick. 1962. "Two studies of legal stigma." *Social Problems* 10:133–142.

SEARCH. 2005. "Report of the national task force on the commercial sale of criminal justice record information." National Consortium for Justice Information and Statistics.

Seron, Carroll, and Frank Munger. 1996. "Law and inequality: Race, gender . . . and, of course, class." *Annual Review of Sociology* 22:187–212.

Shapiro, Isaac, and Robert Greenstein. 2005. "Cuts to low-income programs may far exceed the contribution of these programs to deficit's return." Washington, DC: Center on Budget and Policy Priorities.

Sheley, Joseph F., and Cindy D. Ashkins. 1981. "Crime, crime news, and crime views." *Public Opinion Quarterly* 45:492–506.

Shover, Neil. 1996. *Great pretenders: Pursuits and careers of persistent thieves*. Boulder, CO: Westview.

Simon, Jonathan. 1993. *Poor discipline: Parole and the social control of the underclass, 1890-1990*. Chicago: University of Chicago Press.

Smith, Tom W. 1991. *Ethnic images*. General Social Survey technical report 19. Chicago: National Opinion Research Center, University of Chicago.

Sneiderman, Paul M., and Thomas Piazza. 1993. *The scar of race*. Cambridge, MA: Harvard University Press.

Spelman, W. 2000. "The limited importance of prison expansion." Pp. 97–129 in *The crime drop in America*, edited by Alfred Blumstein and Joel Wallman. New York: Cambridge University Press.

Steinberg, Stephen. 1995. *Turning back: The retreat from racial justice in American thought and policy*. Boston: Beacon Press.

Stoll, Michael, Steven Raphael, and Harry J. Holzer. 2001. "Why are black employers more likely to hire African Americans than white employers?" JCPR Working Paper #228.

Strauss, David A. 1991. "The law and economics of racial discrimination in employment: The case for numerical standards." *Georgetown Law Review* 79:1619.

Sullivan, Dermot. 1998. "Employee violence, negligent hiring, and criminal records checks: New York's need to reevaluate its priorities to promote public safety." *St. John's Law Review* 72:581–605.

Sullivan, Mercer L. 1989. *"Getting paid": Youth crime and work in the inner city*. Ithaca, NY: Cornell University Press.

Sunstein, Cass R. 1991. "Why markets don't stop discrimination." *Social Philosophy and Policy* 8:22–37.

Taggart, W. A., and R. G. Winn. 1993. "Imprisonment in the American states." *Social Science Quarterly* 74:736–749.

Tomaskovic-Devey, Donald, and Sheryl Skaggs. 1999. "An establishment-level test of the statistical discrimination hypothesis." *Work and Occupations* 26:420–443.

Tomaskovic-Devey, Donald, Melvin Thomas, and Kecia Johnson. 2005. "Race and the accumulation of human capital across the career: A theoretical model and fixed-effects application." *American Journal of Sociology* 111:58–89.

Tonry, Michael. 1995. *Malign neglect: Race, crime, and punishment in America*. New York: Oxford University Press.

Travis, Jeremy. 2005. *But they all come back: Facing the challenges of prisoner reentry*. Washington, DC: Urban Institute Press.

Travis, Jeremy, Amy Solomon, and Michelle Waul. 2001. *From prison to home: The dimensions and consequences of prisoner reentry*. Washington, DC: Urban Institute Press.

Trope, Yaacov, and Erik P. Thomson. 1997. "Looking for truth in all the wrong places? Asymmetric search of individuating information about stereotyped group members." *Journal of Personality and Social Psychology* 73:229–241.

Turner, Margery, Michael Fix, and Raymond Struyk. 1991. *Opportunities denied, opportunities diminished: Racial discrimination in hiring*. Washington, DC: Urban Institute Press.

Turner, Margery, and Felicity Skidmore (eds.). 1999. *Mortgage lending discrimination: A review of existing evidence*. Washington, DC: Urban Institute Press.

Uggen, Chris. 2000. "Work as a turning point in the life course of criminals: A duration model of age, employment, and recidivism." *American Sociological Review* 65:529–546.

Uggen, Christopher, Jeff Manza, and Melissa Thompson. 2006. "Citizenship and Reintegration: The Socioeconomic, Familial, and Civic Lives of Criminal Offenders." *Annals of the American Academy of Social and Political Science* 605:281–310.

Uniform Crime Reports. 1993. *Age-specific arrest rates and race-specific arrest rates for selected offenses, 1965-1992*. Washington, DC: U.S. Department of Justice.

———. 2003. *Age-specific arrest rates and race-specific arrest rates for selected offenses, 1993-2001*. Washington, DC: U.S. Department of Justice.

U.S. Census Bureau. 2002. "2001 supplementary survey profile: Milwaukee-Waukesha, WI PMSA." Washington, DC: U.S. Census Bureau.

U.S. Department of Health and Human Services. 1998. *Prevalence of substance use among racial and ethnic subgroups in the United States, 1991-1993*. Washington, DC: Substance Abuse and Mental Health Services Administration.

———. 1999. *National household survey on drug abuse: Population estimates 1998*. Washington, DC: Substance Abuse and Mental Health Services Administration.

———. 1999. *Summary of findings from the 1998 national household survey on drug use*. Washington, DC: Substance Abuse and Mental Health Services Administration.

U.S. Department of Justice. 1992. *The case for more incarceration*. Washington, DC: U.S. Government Printing Office.

———. 1994. *An analysis of non-violent drug offenders with minimal criminal histories*. Washington, DC: U.S. Department of Justice.

U.S. Department of Justice, Federal Bureau of Investigation, Criminal Justice Information Services (CJIS) Division. 1993. *Age-specific arrest rates and race-specific arrest rates for selected offenses, 1965-1992*. Uniform Crime Reports.

Virag, Thomas, Brenda Cox, and J. Valley Rachel. 1990. "National household survey on drug use 1988." Triangle Park, NC: National Institute on Drug Abuse, Research Triangle Institute.

Wacquant, Loic. 2001. "Deadly symbiosis: When ghetto and prison meet the mesh." *Punishment and Society* 3, no. 1: 95–134.

Waldfogel, J. 1994. "Does conviction have a persistent effect on income and employment?" *International Review of Law and Economics* 14:103–119.

Waldinger, Roger. 1999. *Still the promised city? African-Americans and new immigrants in postindustrial New York.* Cambridge, MA: Harvard University Press.

Waldinger, Roger, and Michael Lichter. 2003. *How the other half works: Immigration and the social organization of labor.* Berkeley: University of California Press.

Weber, Max. 1968. *Economy and society: An outline of interpretive sociology.* New York: Bedminster Press.

West, Cornel. 1993. *Race matters.* Boston: Beacon Press.

Western, Bruce. 2002. "The impact of incarceration on earning." *American Sociological Review* 67:526–546.

———. 2006. *Punishment and inequality in America.* New York: Russell Sage Foundation.

Western, Bruce, and Katherine Beckett. 1999. "How unregulated is the U.S. labor market? The penal system as a labor market institution." *American Journal of Sociology* 104:1030–1060.

Western, Bruce, Jeffrey R. Kling, and David F. Weiman. 2001. "The labor market consequences of incarceration." *Crime and Delinquency* 47:410–427.

Western, Bruce, and Sara McLanahan. 2001. "Fathers behind bars: The impact of incarceration on family formation." *Contemporary Perspectives in Family Research* 2:309–324.

Western, Bruce, and Becky Pettit. 2000. "Incarceration and racial inequality in men's employment." *Industrial and Labor Relations Review* 54:3–16.

———. 2005. "Black-white wage inequality, employment rates, and incarceration." *American Journal of Sociology* 111:553–578.

Wienk, Ronald E., Clifford E. Reid, John C. Simonson, and Frederick J. Eggers. 1979. *Measuring discrimination in American housing markets: The housing market practices survey.* Washington, DC: U.S. Department of Housing and Urban Development.

Williams, Donald R. 1984. "Young discouraged workers: racial differences explored." *Monthly Labor Review* 7:36–39.

Wilson, David B., Catherine Gallagher, and Doris L. MacKenzie. 2000. "A meta-analysis of corrections-based education, vocation, and work programs for adult offenders." *Journal of Research in Crime and Delinquency* 37:347–368.

Wilson, James Q. 1985. *Thinking about crime.* Rev. ed. New York: Vintage.

Wilson, William Julius. 1978. *The declining significance of race: Blacks and changing American institutions.* Chicago: University of Chicago Press.

———. 1987. *The truly disadvantaged: The inner city, the underclass, and public policy.* Chicago: University of Chicago Press.

———. 1996. *When work disappears: The world of the new urban poor.* New York: Vintage Books.

Winant, Howard. 2006. "The Dark Side of the Force: One Hundred Years of the Sociology of Race." Pp. 432–662 in *Sociology of America: The ASA Centennial History, edited by* Craig Calhoun. Chicago: University of Chicago Press.

Wissoker, Douglas A., Wendy Zimmerman, and George C. Galster. 1997. *Testing for discrimination in home insurance.* Washington, DC: Urban Institute Press.

Wool, Jon, and Don Stemen. 2004. "Changing fortunes or changing attitudes? Sentencing and corrections reforms in 2003." New York: Vera Institute of Justice.

Word, C. O., M. P. Zanna, and J. Cooper. 1974. "The nonverbal mediation of self-fulfilling prophecies in interracial interactions." *Journal of Experimental Social Psychology* 10:109–120.

Wright, Erik Olin. 1973. *The politics of punishment: A critical analysis of prisons in America.* New York: Harper and Row.

Wyle, Clem. 1946. "The employment of released offenders." *Probation* 25:9–20.

Yinger, John. 1995. *Closed doors, opportunities lost.* New York: Russell Sage Foundation.

Young, Alford. 2003. *The minds of marginalized black men: Making sense of mobility, opportunity, and future life chances.* Princeton, NJ: Princeton University Press.

Zedlewski, Edwin. 1987. *Making confinement decisions: The economics of deincarceration.* Washington, DC: U.S. Department of Justice.

Zheng, Tian, Matthew J. Salganik, and Andrew Gelman. 2006. "How many people do you know in prison?: Using overdispersion in court data to estimate social structure in networks." *Journal of the American Statistical Association* 101:409–423.

Index

Page numbers followed by f indicate figures; page numbers followed by t refer to tables.

Made in the USA
San Bernardino, CA
31 August 2014